Leith's All-Party Cookbook

Leith's All-Party Cookbook

by Prudence Leith

Studio Vista London

For my mother

who can't cook for toffee, but gives marvellous parties anyway

Acknowledgements are due to the following for permission to reproduce illustrations: The Walker Art Gallery, Liverpool, page 26; The Bodleian Library, Oxford (MS Douce 211), page 27 (top); Marshall Cavendish Ltd, *Bible Today*, page 27 (bottom); Bibliothèque de l'Arsenal, Paris, page 66 (top); Kungliga Biblioteket, Stockholm, page 66 (bottom); Guildhall Library and Art Gallery, London, page 67; Reay Tannahill, *The Fine Art of Food* (Folio Society, London, 1968), page 104 (top) and page 154; Roger-Viollet, Paris, page 101; Rayne Kruger, page 114; Service photo de la Réunion des Musées Nationaux, Paris, page 131; The British Museum, London, page 141; The Tate Gallery, London, page 143; Weidenfeld and Nicolson Ltd, *The Victorian Scene*, pages 144 and 165; Photographie Giraudon (reproduced by special permission of the Municipality of Bayeux), page 166 (bottom); Bibliothèque Nationale, Paris, page 166 (top); National Portrait Gallery, London, page 164; Radio Times Hulton Picture Library, page 176.

The illustrations on pages 46, 47 and 104 (bottom) are reproduced by permission of *Punch*; the illustration on page 113 is reproduced from MS CCC 161 with the permission of the President and Fellows of Corpus Christi College, Oxford; on page 142 by permission of the Trustees of the Wallace Collection, London; on page 153 by courtesy of the Trustees, the National Gallery, London.

The photographs reproduced on pages 25, 28, 45, 48, 65, 68, 102, 103, 132, 163, and those used on the cover, were specially taken for the book by John Turner.

The table accessories used for the cover photographs were lent by Messrs Heal & Son Ltd, Tottenham Court Road, London W1.

The line drawings are by Marie-Louise Luxemburg.

© Prudence Leith 1972

Designed by Ian Craig
Published in London by Studio Vista Publishers
Blue Star House, Highgate Hill, London N19

Set in 12 on 13 point Times New Roman

Printed by W & J Mackay Limited,
Chatham

ISBN 0 289.70185.6

Contents

Introduction I Forethoughts
  Planning 7
  The menu 8
  Keeping food fresh 8
  Cooking in quantity 8
  Short cuts 9
  Coffee 9
  Presentation (including garnishes) 9

Introduction II Cheese and Wine
  Cheese 12
  Wine 13
  Wine cups and cocktails 15
  Quantities 16

1 Cocktail Parties 17

2 Cheese and Wine Parties (and variations) 29

3 Dinner Parties 32
  Small dinner parties 33
  Large dinner parties 61
  Unusual dinner parties 72

4 Buffet Parties 75

5 After-Theatre Suppers 93

6 Dances and Balls 97

7 Children's Parties 107

8 Young Teenagers' Parties 116

9 Garden Parties 117

10 Breakfast Parties ('Brunch') 120

11 Lunch Parties 123

12 Tea Parties 133

13 Outdoor Parties   138
  Barbecues   138
  Clambakes   140
  Beach parties   145
  Picnics   148

14 Weddings, Christenings and Anniversaries   151
  Wedding receptions   151
  Christening parties   161
  Anniversary parties   161

15 Annual Feasts   169
  Hallowe'en parties   169
  Thanksgiving Day   171
  Christmas dinner and tea   171
  New Year's Eve parties   181
  Twelfth Night parties   182

Check lists   184

Index   191

Note

Quantities are given in Imperial, American and metric measures. In order to arrive at easily manageable amounts it is not always possible to calculate an exact equivalent, but the measures given have been tested and found successful.

Oven settings

Gas Mark	Electricity F	Electricity C	Definition
$\frac{1}{4}$	240	105	Very low
$\frac{1}{2}$	265	120	
1	290	135	Low
2	310	150	
3	335	165	
4	355	180	Moderate
5	380	195	
6	400	210	Hot
7	425	225	
8	445	230	Very hot
9	470	245	

Introduction I · Forethoughts

Planning

I have been catering for parties one way and another for ten years, and quite often I know that the woman I am working for is an excellent cook, and a capable organizer. Yet she is calling for professional help, not because she lacks the time or ability to cope with her party herself, but because she is *frightened*. She finds it quite nerve-racking enough deciding what to wear and whom to ask without having to worry about the food and drink as well. But often after the party she confesses that she told her guests she did all the food herself—either out of guilt that she did not, or because the praise she got seemed wasted on a caterer! There is nothing like the glow of smug pride when someone says the food is divine and will not believe you did it all yourself. *And it is very easy.* I cannot emphasize enough that even the most inexperienced cook can cook beautifully for twenty people if she chooses her menu right. Besides, the party will cost less than half a caterer's bill for the same thing.

'Keep it simple' seems such an appalling cliché that I hesitate to pound it home again, but it really is the answer to catering at home. No one wants—or can eat—twenty different kinds of canapé at a cocktail party, so a choice of four or five is enough.

The other well-worn maxim is: plan ahead. I always write a programme, almost a diary, of what is to be done several days ahead, what the day before, and what on the day. I am against *any* last-minute rush in the kitchen when the guests are in the drawing-room. Not only does it lead to the hostess feeling left out while everyone else is downing martinis, but the knowledge that there are still things to do hangs over her like a grey weight all afternoon, and makes welcoming guests a nervy business.

One word about nerves: the most sophisticated hostess feels jumpy before her guests arrive. I think one answer to is ask a couple that you know well to come ahead of the others, so that you can legitimately have a steadying drink, and because talking to friends dispels anxiety.

Obviously the first essential in planning ahead is to decide what sort of party you are giving. (The following chapters on various kinds of parties will, I hope, be a help.) Then, having decided on how many guests are practicable, go carefully, pen and paper in hand, through the whole procedure—*arrival, drinks, food, departure.* Imagine the guests arriving (as an extreme example, if it is a wedding for three hundred you should tell the police, get the automobile society to put up signs, borrow the neighbours' field for a car park!) The first thing they think of is shedding their coats and perhaps finding the lavatory; so you should allocate a bedroom for coats (and hire a few coat-rails if it is a large party in winter), make sure that the lavatory is stocked with tissues etc., and that the light over the dressing table or bathroom mirror works. Then they want a drink. Go carefully through the bar check list (page 184), decide about ordering, and about chilling the drink, serving it, clearing the glasses. Next you will be feeding them: choose the menu, making shopping lists and a programme for how you are going to get it all cooked. Make mental, if not actual, notes about who will be bringing in the food, who serving the wine. Make lists of the china, silver, glasses and linen you may need to borrow or hire if you have not enough. And so on, right up till the guests leave (cab telephone number?)—by which time it will not matter profoundly if you have given up the count-down schedule. Whatever that schedule is to be, some aspects common to most parties merit attention. Here they are, in no particular order.

The menu

When choosing a menu, some simple guide-lines are important. The first is to make sure the meal is balanced. If there is fruit in the starter, the dessert should not contain fruit. Cream should not appear in more than two courses at most. If the main course is fish, the first course should not contain fish or seafood. If the main course is hearty, say Osso Buco (page 53), a light starter and dessert are essential. If there is brandy in the duck dish, it is foolish to put Cointreau in the fruit salad; and so on. The menus in this book need not be followed slavishly. The recipes for large parties are given in small cookable quantities so that they can be used for smaller numbers as well.

Keeping food fresh

As far as I am concerned, the best thing since the telephone is polythene wrap (Saran-wrap in America, Handi-wrap in England), in which food can be wrapped and still remain visible: no nasty discoveries, when cleaning out the refrigerator, of little packages of foil that have been lurking behind the milk bottles for a month. It is also the party-giver's best friend, as dishes, especially those with mayonnaise which forms a skin, salads that wilt or sandwiches that harden, can be covered with the film and will stay beautifully fresh for hours—like the wrapped grapes and cheeses in a supermarket.

Cooking in quantity

It is dangerous to cook hot dishes for fifty people all at once. Large amounts of food take a long time to cool, and while warm in the middle and cold on the outside, almost perfect breeding conditions for bacteria exist. In as little as six hours the day's work may be lost. I did exactly this years ago when cooking a chicken casserole for a party: it was to be delivered by 8 p.m. so I started early and got it all made by 10 a.m.—and all bad by 4 p.m. I had left the huge amount of stew, with the lid on (further slowing up the cooling), sitting in the warm kitchen all day. With half an hour till the stores closed, and no one to help, I had a very nasty time dashing from shop to shop buying up all the chickens they had, and cooking as though demented, and all the time weeping with terror.

Food, then, should cool as quickly as possible, so doubling the quantities in a recipe is about as far as one should go. Chicken is notorious for spoiling, so anything with chicken stock in it should be treated with care.

Another good reason for repeating the recipe four times rather than in one large amount, is that most gravies and sauces require browning of the meat or vegetables at the beginning. This is the most important part of the process. It produces that brown, gritty residue sticking to the bottom of the pan, and when the stock or liquid is added, and the pan well scraped, this is what gives the sauce its colour and flavour. I cannot over-emphasize the importance of browning well when the recipe calls for it. Tasteless stews are produced by cheating on the job.

Reheating should also be done in small quantities. Bulk heating leads to over-cooking, too much stirring, and the danger of burning the bottom.

Most cold dishes can be prepared in bulk, but it is important not to skimp the amounts. For example, when the recipe for eight says 'one tablespoon of chopped herbs', this should be four tablespoons when the recipe is quadrupled, not 'Oh, one looks enough'.

Short cuts

When I left the Cordon Bleu School I was full of their rigorous attention to detail, their concern that everything should be home-made, and nothing skimmed lightly over—everything thorough and perfect. I then became rather confident and took short cuts and cheated happily, until I realized that the food did not taste half so good, and I had to return to the rules. Fish boiled in salted water just does not taste as good as fish cooked in a carefully prepared *court-bouillon*. This does not mean that no cheating is permissible. I am a great believer in using the best of 'convenience foods', and buying ready-made dishes where time is short. I have included a menu that could consist largely of bought dishes (page 89). But using the local delicatessen is expensive, though not, of course, as expensive as calling in caterers, or going to an hotel or restaurant.

Coffee

Katharine Whitehorn in a London *Observer* feature, *Sluts' Handbook*, suggested the perfect way to use instant coffee and still defeat the coffee-snob. All you do is burn a few coffee beans under the grill until the aroma of roasting coffee has permeated the whole house, then serve instant coffee with bravado. I am not entirely with Miss Whitehorn, because I think that after a good dinner real coffee finishes off the proceedings very happily, but when it comes to large parties I am with her all the way—or rather I would go further, and forget about roasting the beans. Real coffee made in large quantities is a risk; it can boil, and therefore taste bitter, or be lukewarm by the time everyone is served. A good teaspoonful of instant coffee in the cup, topped up with boiling water, is perfectly acceptable and easy to manage. I generally spoon the coffee into the cups, set (without their saucers) on the kitchen table, pour in the water, and then put the cups on to the saucers ready waiting on the tray(s). This avoids splashing into the saucers and having to rinse and dry them while the coffee gets cold. Add two small sugar bowls to each large tray of cups, and two jugs of cream, so that more than one guest can help himself at a time as the tray is carried round.

Presentation

I remember a fine and serious restaurant where every dish in the set meal was perfect, yet the over-all impression was one of bland dreariness: oeufs en cocotte with cream to start; blanquette of veal, cauliflower in white sauce, and salsify for the main course; and cheesecake to finish—the whole menu white, and all creamy. What is more, it was served on white plates. If the blanquette had been plain rare roast beef, and the cheesecake had been topped with tangerines or grapes, it would have been a beautifully balanced, good-looking meal.

As important as colour is the question of quantity. I have a horror of large portions, clumsy helpings of food piled on my plate. And although I do not want dainty morsels, if I am to enjoy the dessert, and perhaps a savoury, to be over-helped to the main course and vegetables tends to take away my appetite. Even when ravenous, I would rather eat two helpings than be daunted by a mountain.

Garnishing is a dreadful word, reminiscent of radishes made into roses and boars' heads carved out of lard. Too often elaborate decoration is really a disguise to fool one into believing that the cooking has been as painstaking as the dressing-up. But of course if the first impression of a dish is a sorry mess, it will have to taste sublime for the eater to get over his prejudices and appreciate its worth. So garnishing, whether one likes the word or not, can be a great help, provided—and this is the first rule—that it is appropriate: watercress leaves floating on a creamy watercress soup, orange slices round a duck dish containing orange juice, hazelnuts on a hazelnut meringue cake, and so on. It is affectation to decorate a salad with great sprigs of parsley—no one is going to eat the parsley, and it would be far more appropriate to use a small sprig of watercress, or chop the parsley and toss it in the salad—which brings me to chopped parsley. Everyone knows that a handful of chopped parsley does wonders for the appearance of almost any dish—but again it should be *relevant* and used with some restraint. One often finds every dish—first course, soup, main course and all the vegetables—sprinkled with chopped parsley, and it is a relief not to find it on the dessert.

When decorating the salads and platters for a buffet, it is important not to use the same garnishes for all of them. Decide what goes well with each dish and resist the temptation to use up the rest of the black olives on a dish quite unsuited to olives.

Another good rule when garnishing is to decide before starting what the finished dish is to look like. Do not add garnishes haphazardly all over the place, or the result may look overdone and disordered rather than pleasing. For hors d'oeuvre (unless they are to be served in the compartmented platters which I myself dislike—all the compartments tend to be the wrong size, or too few) and for cocktail savouries, one of the most successful ways is simply to lay everything you have in neat rows, making sure that two red foods are not next to each other but spaced among the white, green or whatever (see page 25).

Other tricks are to surround the food with a ring of garnish, like the fillet of beef with aspic (page 83) and the egg mousse surrounded by cucumber (page 56); and to lattice the top with thin strips of anchovy, pimento, ham or pastry (see illustration, page 132).

For hot dishes the garnish, if any, must be simple and quick to do. A bunch of watercress, or a handful of chopped herbs, or a few pieces of orange, walnut, tomato—whatever is suitable—tossed on the top is the most that is ever needed.

Paper frills can be had rather expensively from stationers and butchers for putting on the ends of cutlets. I find them a little affected, but they are useful if the guest wants to hold his lamb cutlet or chicken drumstick in his fingers, and are a good way of disguising the fact that the bones of the crown roast (page 84) are a bit charred. Ham frills (home-made or bought) are not only pretty, but a great help to the frustrated carver who finally grabs the bone in one hand and carves with the other. To make a ham frill (see drawing), cut a piece of greaseproof (waxed) paper about two foot long and six inches wide. Fold it in half lengthwise. With scissors, snip the folded side in two-inch straight cuts parallel with the end of the paper, which, when opened flat, should now contain cuts across the width like a railway grid; then fold it lengthwise again, but this time the opposite way from the first fold, and do not press down. Using a pin to secure the end, wrap the paper round the ham bone.

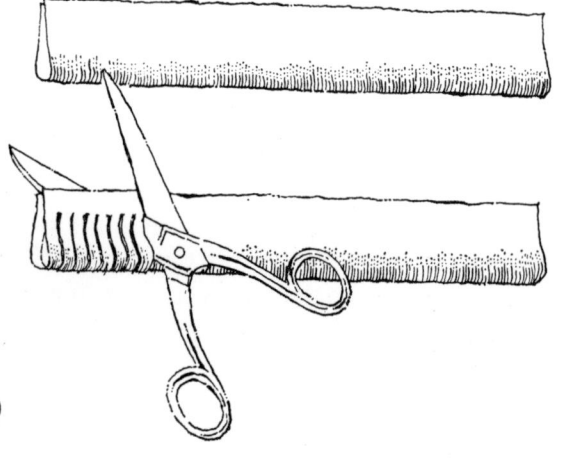
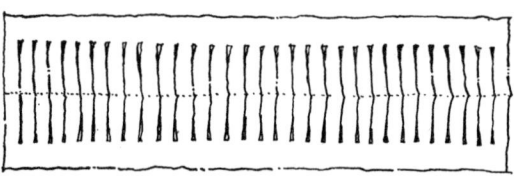
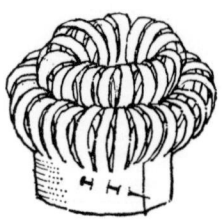

Aspic, if it is a good brand such as Maggi's (unless you are a dedicated and skilled cook you will not be making your own!), is very pleasant in small amounts but it should never be thick and clumsy. If the top of a mousse is to be glazed with it, the decoration must be set in aspic in the bottom of the mould or dish, so that when the mousse is turned out the decoration will be on top (see egg mousse with aspic, page 132). Aspic can also be painted on cold dishes, especially fish like trout or salmon, to give them a shine and keep them looking fresh. It is not necessary, as all dishes can be made to look delicious without it, but for a special occasion it makes them look formal, grand and glossy. The aspic is allowed to cool to the point of setting before being painted on to the food—two or three coats are necessary if some decoration such as tarragon leaves or thin slices of cucumber are being set under it. Chopped aspic is much simpler, and often as effective—see, for example, the fillet of beef on page 132. Aspic can be used only for cold dishes.

Cress of the mustard-and-cress variety is ideal for scattering (neither so thickly as to obscure the food beneath, nor too meanly) on platters of sandwiches, whether open or ordinary. It is also useful as a garnish for salads or cold dishes, when little bunches are often prettier than scattered handfuls. Most cooks will say cress should be washed in a sieve before use, but as this makes it wet and limp I suggest washing the leaves in their box by holding them under the tap, then leaving them, still growing until needed.

Watercress is seldom inappropriate, either to cold or to hot dishes, but it should not be too heavily used. As with parsley, one is inclined to get too much of it. Take a few sprigs, wash them, and break off the stalks. Now plant the bunch of leaves into the side of the food, so that you have a little bouquet of cress at either end of the dish, or perhaps a thin row all down one side, as when covering the gutted side of a salmon (page 132).

Radishes are excellent for giving colour to pale dishes. They look good tossed into a green salad, or used to garnish cocktail savouries (see page 25). Thinly sliced into rings they make useful decorations for cold food—especially egg dishes such as the egg mousse on page 56. It is possible to make roses out of them by peeling back the skin into 'petals', but the radishes wilt more quickly if this is done to them, and to me it smacks more of artifice than art.

Olives, both black and green and preferably stoned (there is a good cheap cherry-and-olive-stoner on the market), are useful if the dish has associations with the Mediterranean—such as salad niçoise (page 76). Black olives look good among the cocktail canapés (page 25) or with a tray of *crudités* (raw washed sticks of celery, green pepper, cucumber, sprigs of raw cauliflower, fresh radishes, raw mushrooms, raw asparagus: generally served with a 'dip' such as garlicky mayonnaise).

Lemons. I prefer fish dishes to be garnished with *quarters* of lemon rather than thin slices. After all, the lemon segment can be squeezed, but getting the juice out of a slice involves mashing it laboriously with a fork. (The stringy centre of the lemon segment should be cut away, otherwise it may deflect the juice into your eye instead of onto the food.) It is tempting to use occasional lemon slices purely for decoration as they do look pretty and professional. A row of alternate slices of lemon and cucumber down the middle of a pink scotch salmon enhances its pale freshness (page 132).

Fried bread croûtons of any shape (fried slowly in butter until crisp right through and evenly brown) are useful for many dishes besides soup. I think they are particularly delicious with a casserole containing a good rich sauce. Triangular ones placed round a dish of coq au vin (page 69) lift it from the stew class into the festive.

Introduction II ·
Cheese and Wine

Cheese

The refrigerator is fine for storing cheeses if they are well wrapped and not kept in the coldest part. After all, cheese is transported, kept and sold refrigerated long before even the retailer on the corner gets it. But for the best flavour, *bouquet* and texture, it should be allowed to 'breathe' or become *chambré*, like wine, before it is eaten. A beautiful Brie will lose all its assets—the seductive oozing, delicate smell, and lingering creamy taste— if served cold.

Cheese has other affinities with wine. Cheese snobs, like wine snobs, abound. People become impassioned in the defence of their favourite. Almost as much nonsense is talked about the selecting, storing, serving and consuming of cheese as of wine. But for most of us, it is a question of having a few ounces of perfect cheese for the family, or occasionally a few pounds for a party. Buy from a good delicatessen, or a supermarket where the turnover is quick and the manager pleasant. And do not be frightened to take back a piece of Brie smelling vaguely like ammonia or a solid, unappetising Camembert.

Rather than write a dissertation on the world's cheeses, I have simply listed my personal favourites, all of which I would serve at a large wine and cheese party. At a small one I would choose only two firm cheeses (say Cheddar and Double Gloucester or Edam) and two soft (say Dolce Latte or Gorgonzola, and Brie). After dinner I prefer to serve one cheese only, or two at most. Two-inch morsels of cheese on a tray are too reminiscent of the unappetising offerings of the 'international' hotel.

English cheeses

CHEDDAR The connoisseur's cheddar is English, sharp-flavoured with a dryness of taste, though the cheese is cool and moist. But I confess to enjoying the mild New Zealand 'mousetrap', or the fairly strong nutty Canadian.

DERBY A white flaky texture but not crumbly. Tangy taste and rich flavour.

CHESHIRE A hard, slightly salty cheese, similar to cheddar; usually yellow, sometimes red.

DOUBLE GLOUCESTER Rather strong orangey colour with very mild flavour, and crumbly texture.

STILTON Generally considered the Prince of Cheeses. At its best is both creamy and crumbly, the taste both sharp and mild. It should never be waxy, hard or yellowed. The colour should be ivory with blue veining. A half Stilton is a good cheese for a party, and is served with a spoon, the guests digging out the middle. The practice of pouring port into the hollow is good neither for the cheese nor for the port. Stilton can also be bought in small segments.

French cheeses

BRIE A creamy, almost runny, soft mild cheese with a distinctive flavour. It can be bought in wedges but because these are well wrapped, it is difficult to be sure of their condition.

Pieces bought from a whole flat Brie are perhaps better. If the curd in the middle is chalky it is under-ripe and if very yellow and hardened it has gone too far. It should not smell very strongly. Buy only a day at most before eating as it does not keep well and, if under-ripe when bought, it does not always ripen satisfactorily.

CAMEMBERT Pale yellow, smooth soft mild cheese at its best, but gets stronger as it ripens. It should not be served too smelly, though. The skin should be edible and slightly bitter, but not sticky and yellowed.

ROQUEFORT A good strong salty cheese, blue-veined, and both crumbly and creamy. Like Stilton, if it is yellowed or waxy it is too old.

The 'CHEVRE' or goat's cheeses vary from the dry, fine-textured, bullet-hard, to the soft, mild and creamy. They are worth looking for, but outside France are often difficult to find.

Italian cheeses

GORGONZOLA A firm white cheese with a creamy texture and blue veining, and a pungent strong taste.

DOLCE LATTE A much creamier and milder edition of Gorgonzola. An excellent buy, and not expensive.

Cream cheeses of the smooth, curd or cottage varieties are rather dreary on a cheese-board but useful in cooking, especially for sweet dishes like cheesecakes. Parmesan is not, in my opinion, for eating; but when fresh it is excellent for cooking. The grated dried stuff sold in drums (and too often thrown on to otherwise good soup) bears no relation to real Parmesan. Ordinary strong cheddar is better.

Wine

Once upon a time people just drank wine without talking endlessly about it. Then the pundits embarrassed the ordinary mortal with their talk of sprightly little wines with forward noses and skimpy bodies. And the unhappy man retreated, out of countenance, and plumped for wines he could pronounce—not daring to show his ignorance or experiment with unfamiliar names.

Now I think the whole thing is being absurdly reversed. The anti-snobbery, de-bunking league has gone too far, advocating indiscriminate glugging. Drinking anything you like with anything is all very well, but there is no point in drinking an expensive claret with a plateful of curry.

Some sort of guide for the real beginner is a help. Even if you really like sweet Sauternes with roast beef, it is unfair to assume that your guests will share your pre-dilections. After each menu I have made suggestions for suitable wines but you may have your own preferences. If, however, you do not, you should not be afraid to ask your wine-merchant's advice. Wine-merchants are mostly a lot less pompous and intimidating than some of their customers.

If wines are to be stored for longer than a few months, cellar conditions should be obtained. The temperature should not be higher than 68° fahrenheit nor lower than 55°, but above all it should not fluctuate more than a few degrees. Wine is pretty tolerant stuff, and will come to no harm in a damp cellar—in fact damp cellars are ideal—though the labels may well suffer. The bottles should be stored lying down to keep the inside of the cork in contact with the wine. If they are stood upright for long periods the corks may dry out, allowing too much air to get through and spoil the wine.

Red wines

The colder a wine the more is its flavour or sweetness repressed. Hence red wines are generally served at room temperature; there are a few exceptions, notably young Beaujolais which is often drunk chilled. But I would far rather a restaurant wine waiter served me a slightly chilly red wine, than one which has been hastily warmed up by being dumped in the vegetable water or stood on the stove. I have seen both these practices, and it is difficult to blame the wine waiter when the customer is rejecting his wine as not *chambré*. The best thing to be done, if you have forgotten to bring the wine out of the cold in time, is to pour a little of it—or all of it if you like—into the glasses, and encourage your guests to warm them in their hands. Another forgivable trick is to pour the wine into a decanter already warmed by having hot water run over the outside. This will just take the chill off the wine. The perfect answer is to serve a white wine or sherry while you eat the first course, and allow the red time to warm up.

The cork should be drawn in time to let the wine 'breathe' (i.e. take in air, which liberates taste and smell). The younger or cheaper the wine the longer this time should be—anything up to eight hours.

As a general rule, good cheap wine is young and hardy. Chianti, Spanish Rioja, and the *vin ordinaire* wines of France can stand a great deal of abuse. They do not need perfect cellar conditions, they do not mind travelling, they need not be decanted. And they should be drunk young.

Fine wines are everything that *vin ordinaire* is not. They are impossible to drink when young, being generally very harsh and full of tannin. They mature over the years in cask and bottle, and the better the vintage the longer this takes and the longer the wine will stay perfect. (Some really great years—1945 in Bordeaux, for instance—produced wines that have taken a quarter of a century or more to reach their best.) Being very expensive, they are worth treating well. Their delicacy makes them vulnerable to movement or changes in temperature. Be sure to get the wine you need at least a week before the party and stand the bottles upright (to allow the sediment to settle at the bottom) until you need them. Mature wines need little breathing: half an hour is quite enough (given longer, they may deteriorate). If there is sediment in the bottle it is worth decanting the wine or pouring it all out, without righting the bottle between glasses, and leaving the last inch of sediment and wine in the bottle. Constant tipping and righting of the bottle when pouring shakes the sediment into the wine, which then looks murky and tastes bitter. Red wines are generally served with the main meat dish or with cheese, though this is not obligatory.

White wines

White wines are usually served cooled, but they should not be over-chilled. Chilling dulls the taste and sweetness; champagne that is almost frozen might as well be soda water for all the flavour it has.

The average refrigerator can adequately chill one or two bottles in two hours; if you need to fill it with bottles allow six hours. But the best method is to put the bottles in ice and water for half an hour—for large quantities a tub or bucket is ideal.

Champagne can be drunk with anything—including breakfast. Other sparkling wines imitating champagne should be selected with care: they vary from the delicious to the disgusting. Champagne is less likely to spray the room if opened when chilled, and handled without shaking. Pushing the cork out with two thumbs is a bad practice; a high proportion of eye casualties are caused by flying champagne corks. Have a glass handy. Hold the bottle in a horizontal position, one hand round the bottom, the other firmly holding the cork which should be twisted out gently—some barmen swear the trick is to twist the bottle, not the cork. If the wine does spray, simply put your hand (or thumb if it is big enough) over the top.

The Riesling wines (and some of the finest are the German Mosels or Moselles) have an excellent balance of sweetness and acidity which makes them splendid for cocktail parties, aperitifs or just plain drinking at any time of the day or night. Loire wines have a crisp dryness which goes well with first courses or salads. The slightly more full-bodied white Burgundies are suitable for drinking with main courses, or right through the meal.

The really sweet white wines of Germany and Bordeaux can be the nectar of the gods, but at fairly god-like prices. They are best served with dessert, especially with fresh soft fruit such as raspberries.

Wine Cups and Cocktails

In order not to get too involved in this subject—books of recipes are innumerable—I am confining myself to the drinks mentioned elsewhere in this book.

Champagne cocktails
Put a cube of sugar in each glass, and add a good teaspoon of brandy. Some people add a dash of angostura bitters as well. Top up with well-chilled champagne. Imitation champagne is permissible, and often indistinguishable from the real thing.

Strawberry champagne cup
Soak strawberries in a mixture of orange juice, grated orange rind and sugar, and pour well-chilled champagne over them just before serving. Proportions of strawberries to champagne can vary from a few strawberries to flavour the champagne to a little champagne to flavour the strawberries.

A cheaper version is made by using half white wine and half bitter lemon, or a sparkling wine—even a pink one—instead. A dash of curaçao or brandy is good too.

Sangria
Mix red wine and soda water half-and-half (tonic water is sometimes used instead of soda). Add a good dash of brandy, slices of orange and lemon, and plenty of ice. Sweeten to taste. I generally dissolve the sugar in a little warm water and allow to cool before adding it, as sugar dissolves with extreme reluctance in cold liquids.

Black Velvet
Since this is a half-and-half mixture of champagne and stout (dark beer), opinions differ as to whether it should be served chilled like the former or at room temperature like the latter. Traditionally made with Guinness.

Teetotaller's tipple
2 tablespoons brown sugar
½ pint/¼ litre/10 fl. oz strong black tea (strained)
½ pint/¼ litre/10 fl. oz water
2 tablespoons lime juice cordial
8 oz bottle tonic water
Slices of orange and lemon
Mint leaves
A few pieces of finely-pared cucumber peel
Ice-cubes

While the tea is still hot add the sugar. Stir in the water, lime juice, slices of fruit and cucumber peel. Chill well. Chill the tonic water unopened, and just before serving add it to the rest of the ingredients with plenty of ice-cubes and a few mint leaves.

Quantities

Deciding how much drink to buy for a party is a tricky question that often perplexes the most experienced party-giver. But over the years I have reached the following conclusions which are by no means rigid but can be helpful.

The young and the very old do not drink much alcohol. But the young (especially teenagers expending energy on a dance floor) will drink about six soft drinks each. If only wine is served, either still or sparkling, allow half a bottle per head for a cocktail party or wedding, three-quarters for a dance or dinner. For an evening party when only beer and wine are served, assume that half the men will drink beer (but you know your friends better than I do) and they may drink six pints each. The other men and the women will probably average three-quarters of a bottle of wine.

Except at weekends, people tend to drink less at lunch, when the thought of work in the afternoon stops lunchtime drinks running on, than they do in the evening.

Drinking is very brisk at the beginning of a party—so do not panic, thinking, 'At this rate we'll be out of booze in an hour', because towards the end guests will probably be sipping slowly, or refusing drinks altogether.

Very few people drink only their special brand of aperitif like Campari or Punt-e-Mes, so do not worry if you feel that you cannot get embroiled in the endless aperitif list. If in doubt, offer sherry or wine.

The most difficult calculation is how much to order when mixed drinks are served—wine, whisky, the lot. Very roughly, I would expect about half the guests to drink hard liquor, and allow one bottle to every four people. Assume that the other half will drink wine, and allow half to three-quarters of a bottle each. Remember, though, that champagne is more popular than still wine, so that if the wine is not champagne, more hard liquor will be drunk. For a party for one hundred people, expected to stay three hours, I would order:

30 bottles champagne
7 bottles Scotch whisky
4 bottles gin
2 bottles vodka
1 bottle each of brandy and sherry
3 dozen 8 fl. oz bottles soda water
3 dozen 8 fl. oz bottles tonic water
1 dozen each of tomato juice, ginger ale and bitter lemon
(If champagne is not included, I would double the rest of the order.)

Many suppliers will provide the drinks on a sale-or-return basis (you pay for any bottles you open, and return the rest). This means that you can safely over-order, but they will advise you on how much to take if you are unsure. They will probably lend glasses free of charge too—for stand-up parties be sure to order at least two glasses per person, as people lose their glasses all the time.

1·Cocktail Parties

Most people say they hate cocktail parties, yet they continue to give and to go to them. For the ordeal—if ordeal it truly is—to be as painless as possible for the hostess, she must keep the guest-list within bounds. It is far pleasanter to have two parties on successive days, with, say, about forty people at each, than a big crush for eighty with everyone stuck fast, cheek by jowl and very hot. The simplest way to determine how many people can comfortably be fitted into a room is to allow at least three square feet per person. This assumes that everything is moved out except for a few small tables (for ashtrays, etc.) and possibly one large sofa that five or six people can perch on if the strain of standing finally fells them. Of course, if there is space for people *and* chairs (and dining chairs are often possible), so much the better—the room will look much more like home—but cocktail parties were invented to enable one to polish off the maximum number of friends at a go.

If the hosts are to cope with all the serving of drinks and food themselves, then let me say at once that it would be foolish to attempt hot food. The hostess will either forget the sausages in the oven, or get cross because she has turned into the maid-of-all work instead of the radiant entertainer. If, however, the budget allows of some help, the ideal ratio is one waiter or waitress to every twenty-five people. If the food is all cold, and a limited choice of drinks is served (say, champagne and orange juice), then one server can cope with thirty guests. But if there is a greater variety of drinks and some hot food, one server to twenty would be wiser. I am assuming that hired professional help is used: if you are making do with students, friends or family, resign yourself to less efficient, if more informal, service. Husbands and sons tend to talk to the guests and neglect their duties.

It is usual for a cocktail party invitation to state what time the guests are expected to leave as well as to arrive. This is a help not only to the hostess, who will anyway end up having to scramble eggs for a few obstinate stayers-on, but also to the guests who can plan their evening accordingly.

Use the party check list on page 184 to see that everything has been thought of, and at all costs organize matters so that a few hours are left for a lie-down or a slow bath before the guests come.

There are literally hundreds of delicious canapés that party-givers have thought up over the years, and it is very easy to invent your own. The important points are that the cocktail snack should be small enough to get into the mouth whole, not too messy to pick up, and should keep well without going soggy for at least six hours (to avoid any last minute preparation). Variety is not important. Four or five different kinds are enough, and if the choice is limited it cuts down on cost and time.

Allow eight bits per head if the party is to last for two hours, ten for three hours, and fourteen if you suspect that no one at all will go home to supper. If the party is at lunch-time some people will regard it as lunch, so it would be a good idea to include a few fairly hearty snacks (see Cocktail Lunch/Supper Party on page 22).

After years of experiment in my catering business we have found that the canapés described below are the most successful. They keep well, taste good, and look more home-made and fresh than aspic works-of-art produced commercially. Nearly all the preparation can be done the day before, and the platters of canapés can be completed, garnished (see page 9), and covered in polythene four hours before the guests arrive.

COCKTAIL PARTY FOR 30
(allowing eight pieces each)

Smoked salmon triangles

Asparagus rolls

Caviar eggs

Stuffed dates

Prawn Ritz

(Preparation on the day before follows recipes.)

For notes on garnishing, see pages 9–11.

Light wine, slightly chilled, is a good addition to the usual cocktail-party bar; Muscadet, Yugoslav Riesling or rosé. If champagne or champagne cocktails (page 15) are served instead of or as well as the usual short drinks, other wine is not necessary.

Smoked salmon triangles (makes 60)
15 slices of brown bread
Butter
Pepper
15 slices of smoked salmon

Butter the bread, sprinkle with pepper, and lay the smoked salmon slices carefully on the bread. Cut off the crusts, and cut the slices into four small triangles. (See page 25.)

Asparagus rolls (makes 30)
15 slices of very fresh brown bread
Butter
Pepper and salt
15 pieces of tinned asparagus

Drain the asparagus well on absorbent paper. It should be as dry as possible. Butter the bread, season, and cut off the crusts. Lay a piece of asparagus along the edge of a slice of bread and roll up. Trim the edges neatly and cut in half. If the slice of bread is very large it will have to be trimmed or the roll will be too thick. If the bread is not fresh enough to roll easily without cracking, the slices (with the crusts cut off) can be lightly rolled with a rolling pin before buttering: this makes them easier to roll up. If the rolls are inclined to unravel, lay them tightly packed in a box for a few hours (or overnight) in the refrigerator. (See page 25.)

Caviar eggs (makes 30)
10 hard boiled eggs
1 tablespoon sour cream
1 tablespoon mock caviar (Danish lump fish roe)
Pepper

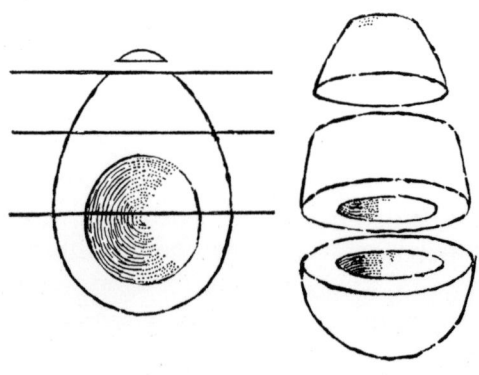

Trim the pointed end from each egg. Cut the eggs across in three (see drawing). Remove the yolks and mash or sieve them until smooth. Add enough sour cream to make a soft but not sloppy paste. Stir in the caviar and season with pepper. Fill the egg-white 'cups' with the mixture, using a forcing bag or spoon; and treating the slice of egg-white like a base, simply pipe a swirl of mixture onto it. Decorate the top of the egg with a little extra caviar. (See page 25.)
Large stuffed eggs, for which the eggs are split lengthwise, are unsuitable for cocktail parties, where the snacks should be small enough to eat in one mouthful.

Stuffed dates (makes 60)

60 dates (about 2 boxes)
¾ lb/350 grams/1½ cups cream cheese
4 oz/100 grams/½ cup nibbed almonds

Brown the almonds under the grill (broiler) and allow to cool. Cut the dates open lengthwise. Replace each stone with a teaspoon of cream cheese. Slightly close the dates, leaving the cheese showing. Dip the cheese into the nuts (page 25).

Prawn Ritz (makes 60)

60 Ritz crackers (about 1 packet) or
  small savoury biscuits
Butter
1 lb/450 grams/2 cups frozen peeled
  prawns
Paprika
4 tablespoons very thick mayonnaise
  (see next recipe)

Thaw the prawns. Butter the crackers well. Squeeze out any moisture from the prawns—they should be quite dry. Mix with the mayonnaise and spoon a blob on to each biscuit. Sprinkle with paprika. (See page 25.)

Mayonnaise

2 egg yolks
½ pint/¼ litre/10 fl. oz olive oil (or
  ¼ pint each olive and salad oil)
1 tablespoon of tarragon or wine
  vinegar
Squeeze of lemon
1 teaspoon French mustard
Salt and pepper

Put the yolks into a bowl with the mustard, and beat well with a wooden spoon. Add the oil, literally drop by drop, beating all the time. The mixture should be very thick by the time half the oil is added. Beat in the lemon juice. Resume pouring in the oil, going rather more confidently now, but alternating the dribbles of oil with small quantities of vinegar. If the mixture curdles, another egg yolk should be beaten in a separate bowl, and the curdled mixture beaten drop by drop into it. Add salt and pepper to taste.

On the day before

Smoked salmon triangles Make completely, pack into a plastic box, or wrap in foil or polythene, and keep in the refrigerator overnight.
Asparagus rolls Make the rolls, but do not cut in half. Leave overnight in the refrigerator, packed in a plastic box and well covered.
Caviar eggs Boil the eggs, shell them, cut them up and make yolk mixture. Keep this covered overnight in the refrigerator. Put whites into a bowl of water until next day.
Stuffed dates Stuff the dates but do not add the nuts. Brown the nuts ready for tomorrow. Store dates, covered, in refrigerator.
Prawn Ritz Make the prawn mixture, keep in refrigerator.
Garnishes Prepare the radishes, wash the cress. Keep in a plastic bag in refrigerator.

COCKTAIL PARTY FOR 60
with hot and cold snacks
(allowing eight pieces each)

Chicken livers wrapped in bacon

Curried prawn bouchées

Cocktail sausages

Smoked salmon wheels

Pâté on baked bread

Celery filled with cream cheese

(*Preparation on the day before follows recipes.*)

For notes on garnishing, see pages 9–11.

I suggest sparkling wine. Champagne (by itself or as an alternative to short drinks) is perfect but expensive. A dry sparkling hock or sparkling white Burgundy is cheaper and very good.

Chicken livers wrapped in bacon (makes 60)

2 lb/1 kilo chicken livers
60 small slices fatty bacon
(Wooden cocktail sticks)

Trim and discard the discoloured part from the livers. Roll each liver in a piece of bacon, and lay them side by side in a roasting pan, fairly tightly packed to prevent unravelling. Cook in a hot oven (425°F, gas mark 7) for about 15 minutes or until they are just beginning to go brown on top. Drain well. Stick a cocktail stick into each roll. They are now ready to serve, but if they are to be reheated, remove them from the roasting pan and keep in a cool place until needed. If the cocktail sticks are stuck in before reheating, make sure they are wood and not plastic. Reheat at 400°F, gas mark 6, for 10 minutes.

Curried prawn bouchées (makes 60)

60 bouchée cases, cooked. (Use either a packet of frozen cocktail vol-au-vent cases, or buy them ready-made from a baker's, or follow this recipe for homemade ones.)

2 lb/1 kilo puff pastry (recipe, page 83)
Beaten egg

Roll out the pastry to about the thickness of a penny. With a small round pastry cutter stamp it out in rounds. With slightly smaller cutter or the end of a large plain piping nozzle mark a circle in the centre of each round, but be careful not to stamp the pastry through. With the beaten egg brush only the top of the outer rings. Cook on a baking sheet (400°F, gas mark 6), until very brown and crisp—about 12 minutes. Cool.

For the filling
1 lb/450 grams frozen peeled prawns, thawed
1 oz/30 grams/2 tablespoons butter
1 oz/30 grams/1 heaped tablespoon flour
Half an onion, finely chopped
1 teaspoon mild curry powder
Up to ½ pint/¼ litre/10 fl. oz creamy milk
Salt and pepper

Melt the butter, add the onion and cook slowly until pale and transparent. Stir in the curry powder, fry for a further minute, and then stir in the flour. Add the prawns and their liquid and bring to the boil, stirring. It will get very thick. Stir in enough of the milk to make a soft but still thick paste. Season with salt and pepper. Fill the bouchées with the mixture. If they are to be reheated they should not be filled with hot mixture, as this tends to make the pastry soggy. Reheat for 10 minutes at 400°F, gas mark 6.

Cocktail sausages (makes 120)

60 chipolata or 120 cocktail sausages (4 lb/2 kilos)
(Cocktail sticks)

Chipolata sausages can be made into cocktail size by twisting each sausage into two. After twisting, cut them apart. Put them into a greased roasting pan and cook in a moderate to hot oven (400°F, gas mark 6) for 20 minutes or until beginning to brown. The roasting pan should be shaken at intervals to prevent the sausages sticking. They should be stirred around to prevent those on the edge getting browner than those in the middle. Drain well. Stick in the cocktail sticks.

Smoked salmon wheels (makes about 120)

1 very large square-edged loaf of brown bread
Butter, well softened
About 3 lb/1½ kilos of thinly sliced smoked salmon

Put the loaf of bread on a board and carefully cut off the top crust all along the length of the loaf. Butter the top of the bread, being careful not to crumble it. Now cut as thin a horizontal slice as you can. Again butter the loaf and cut off the next slice and so on through the loaf. You should end up with about 10 or 12 long slices. Cut off the crusts, and lay smoked salmon on all the slices. Now, starting at one end, roll them up carefully. Cut each roll into about 10 thin rounds.

Pâté on baked bread (makes about 60)

15 large slices of white bread
Butter
1 lb/½ kilo of smooth pâté (fish or meat) beaten until soft
Slices of black olive for decoration

With a small round cutter, cut four rounds out of each slice of bread. Bake in a cool oven until crisp and dry like rusks. When cool spread well with butter, and pipe a swirl of pâté onto each. Decorate with a slice of olive.

Celery filled with cream cheese (makes about 60)

10 sticks of celery
¾ lb/350 grams/1½ cups cream cheese
Chives, finely chopped
Pepper and salt

Wash and scrub the celery, and cut into two-inch lengths. If the sticks are very wide they should be split into two. Cream the cheese, and add the chives, pepper and salt. Using a fluted nozzle, pipe the cheese into the hollow of the celery sticks. It may be necessary to trim the underside of each celery stick to prevent it rolling over when on a plate.

On the day before

Chicken livers wrapped in bacon Prepare completely but take care not to overcook, as reheating will dry them out a little. Keep overnight in a cool place.

Curried prawn bouchées Make the pastry cases and keep them in an airtight container or polythene bag. Make the filling and keep it in a covered bowl in the refrigerator overnight.

Cocktail sausages Prepare completely but take care not to overcook. Keep overnight in a cool place.

Smoked salmon wheels Prepare completely, and pack them between layers of polythene in a plastic box. Keep well covered in refrigerator. Alternatively, the final slicing into wheels can be left till the day of the party.

Pâté on baked bread Make the baked bread rounds and store in a tin or plastic bag overnight. Make the pâté mixture and keep it in a cool place. Cut the olive slices ready for decoration.

Celery filled with cream cheese Cut the celery pieces, wash them, and keep in a polythene bag in the refrigerator overnight. Make the filling and keep in a cool place.

Garnishes Prepare the radishes and wash the cress. Put them in a plastic bag in the refrigerator.

COCKTAIL LUNCH/SUPPER PARTY FOR 40
(allowing nine pieces each)
plus fruit and cheese

Open smoked salmon sandwiches

French bread with pâté and cress

Miniature egg-and-chive
sandwiches

Stuffed curried eggs

Cucumber filled with blue cheese

Cheese profiteroles

Pumpernickel with salami

Potted shrimps on water biscuits

Fresh fruit

Cheese

Though the food is eaten in the fingers like cocktail canapés, this is really a buffet party meant to replace lunch or supper, especially if space is limited or finances do not stretch to the hiring of staff, plates or silver.

(*Preparation on the day before follows recipes.*)

For notes on garnishing, see page 9–11.

I would serve a young Beaujolais, or a North Italian wine from the Alto Adige—soft light wine somewhere between red and rosé. Of course no wine need be served, but as the food is substantial enough to replace lunch or supper, wine would be an excellent accompaniment.

Open smoked salmon sandwiches (makes 80)

40 large slices bread (about 2 large
  loaves), preferably rye
40 slices smoked salmon (about 2½ lb
  or 1¼ kilos)
Salted butter
Lemon juice
Black pepper

These are best made with very thinly sliced rye bread, and the best smoked salmon. However, perfectly good open sandwiches are made with ordinary brown bread and cheaper smoked salmon. Sprinkle a very little pepper and a few drops of lemon juice on the buttered bread before adding the salmon. Open sandwiches look best cut across diagonally to form large triangles.

French bread with pâté and cress (makes 40 canapés)

40 thin round slices of fresh French
  bread (about 3 short loaves)
Butter
About 1½ lb/¾ kilo pâté (e.g. chicken
  liver pâté, page 95.)
1 box mustard-and-cress

Butter the bread slices, spread thickly with the pâté, and scatter the snipped cress over them.

Miniature egg-and-chive sandwiches (makes 40)

20 large slices white bread
Butter
4 hard-boiled eggs
1 tablespoon chopped chives
1 large tablespoon thick mayonnaise
Salt and pepper
2 drops anchovy essence

Chop the eggs and mix with the chives, mayonnaise, and anchovy essence. Season with salt and pepper. Butter the bread and make sandwiches with the filling. After cutting away the crusts, quarter diagonally. When arranging the sandwiches, stand them in rows, pointed up so that the filling can be seen.

Stuffed curried eggs (makes 40)

20 hard-boiled eggs
1 teaspoon mild curry powder
½ oz/15 grams/1 tablespoon butter
1 large tablespoon thick mayonnaise

Split the eggs lengthwise and remove the yolks. Mash or sieve the yolks, stir in the mayonnaise. Melt the butter; add the curry, and fry for one minute. Mix this into the yolk mixture. Using a teaspoon or a piping bag and nozzle, fill the egg-white hollows with this mixture.

Cucumber filled with blue cheese (makes about 40)

2 cucumbers
1 lb/½ kilo cream cheese
¼ lb/100 grams blue cheese (Danish
   Blue, Dolce Latte or Stilton)
Salt and pepper

Beat the cheeses well together to get a soft smooth paste, adding a little milk if the mixture remains very hard. Season with salt and pepper. Cut the cucumber into rounds about ¾ inch thick. With a grapefruit knife or a teaspoon remove a little of the cucumber flesh from each round to form a slight hollow. Dry the rounds well with absorbent paper. Fill a teaspoon of cheese mixture into each hollow.

Thinner slices of cucumber, not scooped out at all, make a good base for creamy mixtures, but they should not be put together more than an hour in advance, or the salt in the mixture causes the cucumber to become wet and the filling is liable to slide off. Hollowing out the thicker slice prevents this, but is a little more trouble.

Cheese profiteroles (makes about 40)

Choux pastry for the profiteroles:
3 oz/80 grams/6 tablespoons butter
1½ gills/¼ litre/7½ fl. oz water
3 eggs, lightly beaten
3¾ oz/100 grams/¾ cup flour

For the cheese filling:
1 oz/30 grams/2 tablespoons butter
1 oz/30 grams/1 heaped tablespoon
   flour
½ pint/¼ litre/10 fl. oz milk
2 tablespoons cream
2 oz/60 grams/½ cup grated cheddar
   cheese
Salt, pepper, cayenne

The *profiteroles* are easy to make if the instructions and exact quantities are rigidly adhered to. Start by setting the oven at 400°F, gas mark 6. Put the butter and water together in a large saucepan. Bring slowly to the boil so that by the time the water boils the butter is completely melted. *Immediately* the mixture is really boiling fast, tip in all the flour and draw the pan off the heat. Working as fast as you can, beat the mixture hard with a wooden spoon: it will soon become thick and smooth and leave the sides of the pan. Stand the bottom of the saucepan in a basin or sink of cold water to speed up the cooling process. When it is cool, beat in the eggs a little at a time until the mixture is soft, shiny and smooth. If the eggs are large it may not be necessary to add all of them. The mixture should be of dropping consistency—not too runny. ('Dropping consistency' means that the mixture will fall off a spoon rather reluctantly and all in a blob. If it runs off it is too wet; if it will not fall off even when the spoon is slightly jerked, it is too thick.) Put small teaspoons of the mixture on a baking sheet, about 3 inches apart. Bake for about 20 minutes. The profiteroles should swell, and become fairly brown. If they are taken out when only slightly brown they will be rather soggy when cool. Cut off the top third of each profiterole and allow to cool. Spoon the filling into each base and replace the tops.

To make *the cheese filling*, melt the butter, take the pan off the heat and stir in the flour. Add the milk, beating out lumps as you go. Return the pan to the heat; boil, beating the mixture all the time. Add the cheese; when it has melted stir in the cream. Season with salt, pepper and a touch of cayenne. Set aside to cool.

Pumpernickel with salami (makes 40)

20 slices of pumpernickel bread
  (2–3 packets)
Butter
1 lb/½ kilo salami, skinned and thinly
  sliced
2 pickled cucumbers

Get the delicatessen to skin and slice the salami on their machine, as thinly as they can. Cut each slice of pumpernickel into two, or cut two rounds out of it with a pastry cutter. Butter, and cover with overlapping slices of salami. Decorate with thin slices of the pickled cucumber.

Potted shrimps on water biscuits (makes 40)

40 water biscuits (about 2 packets)
Butter
3 large pots of potted shrimps

Butter the biscuits, and on to each pile a spoonful of shrimps, pressing them enough to make them stick together.

Fresh fruit

Choose fruit that is easy to eat, like grapes and cherries. Also cut small segments of skinned melon, banana, apple and pear. Peel oranges and tangerines, and break into segments. Put them all into a bowl, sprinkle liberally with lemon juice, and almost bury with ice cubes. Set a pile of paper napkins by the side. This way the fruit is easy to eat (whole pears and oranges are seldom tackled at a party); the lemon juice keeps the apples, bananas and pears white; the ice makes the whole thing look marvellously fresh and Italian as well as chilling it. The fruit should not be prepared more than an hour beforehand. Forks or cocktail sticks would help guests who are loath to use their fingers.

Cheese

It should be the sort that can easily be eaten in the fingers, or readily added to cheese biscuits. Most hostesses over-estimate. One good piece of Cheshire and a small Edam, plus perhaps a pound of Brie, would be ample for this party. Fresh, very clean celery in a jug, a few radishes and peeled new carrots are good accompaniments.

On the day before

Open smoked salmon sandwiches Make completely and store overnight in polythene or plastic, well covered, in the refrigerator.

French bread with pâté and cress Make the canapés but do not scatter with cress. Store overnight in an airtight box or covered in polythene in the refrigerator.

Miniature egg-and-chive sandwiches Make completely, and store well wrapped overnight in the refrigerator.

Stuffed curried eggs Boil the eggs, make the filling and store both the whites and filling in a cool place overnight. Cooked egg whites keep their shape if kept in a bowl of water.

Cucumber filled with blue cheese Make the filling but do not cut the cucumber until you are ready to put the canapés together.

Cheese profiteroles Make completely, and store overnight in a polythene bag in the refrigerator. The pastry will be squashy and soft, but nonetheless delicious. If firmer pastry is wanted, the profiteroles should be kept chilled or frozen overnight, and the cheese mixture added only a few hours before the party.

Potted shrimps on water biscuits Take the shrimps out of the freezer to thaw, but do not make the canapés until a few hours before the party.

Garnishes Trim and wash the radishes and the cress. Prepare the celery and carrots for the cheese board. Put everything in a plastic bag in the refrigerator.

Lorenzo and Isabella by Millais

Ahasuerus and Esther with guests

Cornes pour cornes

2 · Cheese and Wine Parties (and Variations)

For young or unsophisticated guests a cheese and wine party—to which I would add beer or cider—is ideal.

If the wine is drinkable, the cheese good, and the bread hot, the evening can be a great success. Unhappily though, too often the wine is over-sweet or vinegary and the cheese sweaty. I have seen many a middle-aged gentleman leave a party because he could not bear being denied his usual whisky and asked to drink *bad* wine instead. But few people would object to good wine—by which I do not mean expensive wine. It would be foolish to spend a fortune on château-bottled clarets when the reason for not offering hard liquor or champagne is probably to limit the cost. Ask a reliable wine merchant, or a friend who knows about wine, what is good to buy. (See the section on wine, page 13.)

Inexpensive wine can be bought in gallon or half-gallon bottles, but it is a mistake to assume these are always cheaper than bottles. Very often there is no difference and most suppliers will allow some discount for purchases by the case (generally 12 bottles). Another snag to bulk buying is that it very often lands one with a gallon bottle, three quarters full, after the party—and once opened the wine will not keep long. A modern answer has been a plastic vacuum pack with a tap so that glassfuls can be drawn off without air entering the pack and spoiling the wine, but I find this depressingly efficient. Wine bottles about the place seem much more inviting.

Now for the cheese. Allow $\frac{1}{4}$ lb per person, not more—it is surprising how little gets eaten: being very filling, two slabs of bread and cheese are enough for anyone. Having decided how many pounds of cheese you will need, decide what kinds to buy. If you have twenty guests (and are therefore buying 5 lb of cheese), a choice of four would be reasonable: say 1 lb Brie, two large Boursin, 1 lb Double Gloucester or Cheshire, and a piece of Cheddar (always the most popular cheese). Lay them on a pastry board or a large tray, and between them put little piles of washed and trimmed radishes, celery sticks, small tomatoes, long slivers of cucumber, and perhaps black olives and slices of mild pickled cucumber. Surround the board with fresh vine leaves or, failing them, use crisp lettuce leaves, preferably of a variety that does not wilt easily (like Webb's Wonder, Cos or Scarolle). Everything can be laid out long before the arrival of the guests if it is all tightly covered in a sheet of polythene and kept in a cool place, but not refrigerated as this hardens and spoils soft cheese. Any runny cheese like Brie should perhaps be left in its wrapper to prevent oozing all over the board before the first guest has got to it. (See list of cheeses on pages 12 and 13).

A variety of bread looks attractive, but again beware of over-catering—having to throw away the staff of life or watch it slowly mould is most distressing.

For a small party, two types of bread—say french and dark rye—would be enough. For a big party I would have: french, rye, brown wholemeal, bread sticks, and assorted biscuits (crackers). Small brown and white rolls, perhaps with sesame or poppy seeds on

top, are easy to handle if space for slicing bread is limited. Buttering some of them in advance also eases serving.
General check-list, page 184.

Wine and pâté party

This is a variation on the simple wine and cheese party—where various pâtés are served instead of, or as well as, the cheeses. Make some of your own (see Chicken liver pâté, page 95, and the terrine, page 150) and buy some from a good delicatessen or grocer.

Dips and spreads

Savoury pastes are also delicious with wine, accompanied by plenty of bread, biscuits (crackers), and *crudités*. Here is a possible selection:—
Curried mayonnaise
Garlic cream
Avocado dip
Sardine pâté
Taramasalata
Caviar cream

Curried mayonnaise
See page 73.

Garlic cream
See page 73.

Avocado dip
2 avocados, mashed
1 clove garlic, crushed
1 tablespoon chopped chives
½ lb/250 grams/1 cup cream cheese
6 walnuts, chopped
2 slices fatty bacon

Grill the bacon until crisp and chop finely. Combine everything else, beat well, and add the bacon.

Sardine pâté
See page 118.

Taramasalata (serves 6–8)
2 slices of white bread with crusts cut off
1 large clove of garlic, crushed
8 oz/250 grams bottled smoked cod's roe *or* 1 lb/½ kilo fresh smoked roe
1 pint/½ litre/20 fl. oz olive oil
Ground black pepper
Juice of 1 lemon

Hold the bread slices under the tap to wet them well. Put them into a mixing bowl with the cod's roe and the crushed garlic (if fresh roe is used the skin should be discarded first). With a wooden spoon or electric whisk, beat very well. Now add the oil very slowly, almost drop by drop (as with mayonnaise, page 19) beating all the time. The idea is to form a smooth emulsion, and adding the oil too fast will result in a rather oily, curdled mixture. The amount of oil added is a matter of personal taste: the more oil you add, the paler and creamier the mixture becomes and the more delicate in flavour. Stop when you think the right balance of blandness and smoked-roe taste is achieved. Add lemon juice and black pepper to taste.

Taramasalata can also be served as a spread for cocktail snacks, or with toast or fresh rolls.

Caviar cream
2 small jars Danish lump fish roe
½ pint/¼ litre/10 fl. oz thick cream
Juice of one lemon
Salt
Black pepper

Whip the cream stiffly, stir in the lump fish roe and lemon juice. Season with salt and pepper.

3 · Dinner Parties

(See also next chapter on Buffet Parties)

An evening of good company, good wine and good food must be one of the oldest civilized pleasures. It is also perhaps one of the hardest to achieve. A blend of the right people, in the right frame of mind, with the right atmosphere—so much is fortuitous, a matter of luck, almost of alchemy. It is true that the vital elements in all this are the personality of the hostess, and what she provides to eat and drink, but even reliance on these can prove to be unfounded if she is overwrought and things go wrong—a guest is an hour late; the host runs out of sherry; the main course is overcooked. But take comfort: your friends are not in your house to test your gastronomic skill or to taste the sauce like competition judges. They are there simply to meet each other and to have an enjoyable evening. They *want* to enjoy themselves. No one is going to have his evening spoilt because you forgot the salad. With this knowledge firmly in mind, you need not be anxious. Relax, and let the alchemy work. Here are some ideas for helping it along.

Do not invite people because they invited you, unless you really *have* to. If someone wants to be your friend, and you do not want to be his, having him to dinner is not going to help you disengage. Next, if you have to invite people whom you find dull, do not mix them with those you find fascinating, who may find them as dreary as you do. Put your boring friends together. Surprisingly, this works: boring people do not often find each other so. And you will still have a good evening because you will be elated by the success of it. When it comes to people you like, just mix them up regardless. An eighteen-year-old student will not bore or be bored by an eighty-year-old diplomat. I think hostesses worry far too much about whether their guests will like each other. They probably will; and if they do not, their differences should make for stimulating discussion.

Having decided on the guests, plan the menu. I must stress that food never need be grand: even kings and queens must like steak and kidney pie and treacle tart. But it should be *soignée*—done with dedication. People are always pleased and impressed when it is plain that trouble has been taken for them; and this does not apply only to the food. It may be vanity, but somehow it is insulting to find the towels in the bathroom grubby and to be asked to help set the table. I do not know why—it should not be so, but it is. No-one minds informality, but it is upsetting to find yourself at children's supper when you were expecting to meet the social lions of the town. So tell your friends what is expected of them, whether it is supper or dinner, what you are wearing (so that they can follow suit); and then keep your promises.

Set the table in the morning (cover it with an old tablecloth to keep the dust off) and forget about it. Table-setting needs care. (See drawing.) Knives and forks should be neatly lined up, glasses sparkling, linen crisp. It is surprising what a difference care makes, even in this. Linen napkins are a satisfying extravagance, though for fairly informal parties soft paper napkins are fine. Flowers should be low enough not to obstruct the diners' view of each other, and the lighting arranged to show the food clearly, without harshly illuminating people's faces.

I do not think rules ever matter as much as care, and etiquette is just good common sense formalized into conventions.

At very grand occasions the hostess leads her male guest of honour into dinner, followed by the host with the female guest of honour. The rest follow, pairing themselves off, but not with their spouses. The perfectly-mannered male offers his arm to the lady of his choice, and in they sail. The rear is brought up by the odd men out (if any). Should there be odd women out they are shepherded in together, before the last couple. Seating depends on the shape of the table and the number of guests. Ideally the host presides over one end (furthest from the door to the kitchen), the hostess over the other, but the hostess often has to sit at the side in order to achieve the man-next-to-woman pattern round the table. The host has the lady guest of honour on his right, the hostess the male guest of honour on *her* right. Everyone else is placed according to rank down the table, starting at the top (the host's end): hence the expression 'below the salt' for the not-so-important. A complication is that no gentleman may sit next to his wife, though he may sit opposite her.

Today the usual practice is for the hostess to lead the way to the dining room, her guests following in a straggle and her husband bringing up the rear. Name cards are on the table, and the guests sort themselves out. Alternatively the hostess has memorized her seating plan, guided less by rank than by her own discretion. Except for her, the ladies sit down straight away, the gentlemen hovering until she is seated. If she is managing the party without help it is a good idea for her to have put the first course ready on the table. She then serves the rest of the dinner, with her husband perhaps following up with the sauce or vegetables and helping to clear away. Serving should be from the left of each guest, clearing from the right. If the hostess has many dishes to offer—vegetables and sauces etc.—she should go straight round the room, lady-gentleman-lady-gentleman, instead of trying to serve the ladies first. If waiters are used they must serve the chief lady guest first and then all the other ladies, the hostess, the chief male guest and the other men, ending with the host. The hostess should start eating as soon as everyone is served, or she may find her guests waiting for her while their food gets cold. If she is managing without help, the wine should be put on the table, and the guests told to help themselves—the host keeping a wary eye open and topping up the glasses. One wine (generally chosen to go with the main course) is considered enough for the whole meal today, though it *is* pleasing to be offered a dry white wine with the first course, claret or burgundy with the meat, and possibly even a sweet white wine with the pudding or dessert. (See page 13 on Wines.)

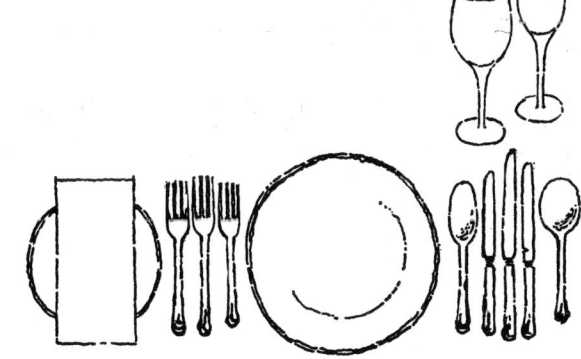

Small Dinner Parties

Recipes are on the pages indicated. Those for Menus A–C are for eight people and assume one hand to help in the kitchen and with serving; Menus D–J are for six people, and the hostess should comfortably manage on her own. (Menus H–J are inexpensive.)

Menu A, page 34

Seafood coquille

Filet de boeuf en croûte
Fennel baked in the oven
Petit pois à la française

Green fruit salad

Camembert fritters

Menu B, page 37

Blinis with sour cream and caviar

Carré of lamb
Mixed buttered beans
Baked tomatoes

Passion fruit syllabub

Chicken liver and bacon savoury

Menu C, page 40

Haddock soufflé with crab or lobster
    sauce

Roast partridge
Game chips (or chip baskets)
Red cabbage
Glazed carrots

Pineapple with kirsch

Dolce Latte and Double Gloucester
    cheeses

Menu D, page 43

Smoked trout mousse with smoked
    salmon

Filet de boeuf à la Bourguignonne
Creamed potatoes
Courgettes (zucchini) with tomatoes

Annabel's cheesecake

Menu E, page 49

Consommé caviar

Stuffed boned roast duck
Mange-tout peas in onion sauce
Orange and water cress salad

Athol brose

Menu F, page 51

Iced gaspacho

Poulet François I
Buttered rice
Green salad

Chocolate mousse

Menu G, page 52

Grape and mint ring

Osso buco
Buttered rice

Walnut and lemon meringue cake

Menu H, page 54

Tuna and flageolet salad

Sauté of kidneys Turbigo
Peas
Buttered rice

Latticed apple flan

Menu I, page 56

Egg mousse

Pigeon casserole with celery and walnuts
Buttered leaf spinach
Potatoes boulangère

Blackcurrant fool

Menu J, page 58

Grapefruit, prawn and almond cup

Curried beef
Fried rice
Side dishes

Apricot slice

DINNER FOR 8: MENU A

Seafood coquille

Filet de boeuf en croûte
Fennel baked in the oven
Petit pois à la française

Green fruit salad

Camembert fritters

(Preparation on the day before follows recipes.)

Serve a Loire wine (a Pouilly-fumé or a Sancerre) with the first course, and follow it with a really good Burgundy—a Chambertin, for example. Serve port with the Camembert fritters.

Seafood coquille (serves 8)

8 scallops, cleaned, or 1 lb/½ kilo
    frozen scallops
(8 scallop shells)
½ lb/230 grams cooked peeled prawns
1 quart/1 litre fresh mussels
½ lb/230 grams crabmeat, frozen or
    canned
½ pint/¼ litre/10 fl. oz white wine
1 onion, finely chopped
2 oz/50 grams/4 tablespoons butter
1 oz/30 grams/1 heaped tablespoon
    flour
½ lb/230 grams button mushrooms
½ pint/¼ litre/10 fl. oz milk
1 bayleaf
4 tablespoons finely chopped parsley
Pepper, salt
2 tablespoons cream

Thaw the scallops, prawns and crabmeat if frozen. Remove the hard piece of muscle from the scallops. Scrub the mussels, removing the 'beard' and discarding any that are broken or open. Put them in a large saucepan. Pour on the wine, put on the saucepan lid, and leave over moderate heat until all the mussels are opened (about 6 minutes).

Fry the chopped onion very gently in the butter until cooked and transparent. Slice the mushrooms and add them, and continue to cook for 4 minutes. Remove from the heat, stir in the flour, and add the crabmeat, the prawns, and the scallops, each with their liquid. Remove the mussels from their shells, discard the 'rubber band' round each, and put in with the other shellfish. Strain the liquid the mussels were cooked in and add it with the milk and the bayleaf. Bring slowly to the boil, stirring carefully all the time. Simmer very gently until the scallops are cooked —about ten minutes. Add salt and pepper to taste. Add the cream and parsley. If the sauce is now too thin, strain it and thicken it by adding a teaspoon of *beurre manié* (see below). Pour on to the seafood again and serve the mixture in the warmed scallop shells.

Beurre manié is a mixture of equal quantities of butter and flour worked together to form a paste. It is used for thickening liquids. Drop a small piece into the liquid, and whisk hard until it boils. 1 oz of *beurre manié* will thicken ½ pint liquid to the consistency of thin cream.

Filet de boeuf en croûte

See page 82

Fennel baked in the oven (serves 8)

3 lb/1½ kilos Florence fennel (the
    vegetable, not the herb)
Juice of two lemons
2 tablespoons chopped mint
2 tablespoons chopped parsley
2 oz/50 grams/4 tablespoons butter

Discard any discoloured outside leaves and quarter the heads of fennel neatly. Lay the pieces in a roasting pan or fireproof dish. Melt the butter, and add the chopped herbs and the lemon juice. Pour this over the fennel. Cover tightly with a lid, or foil, and bake in the oven until the fennel is quite tender (about ¾ hour at 350°F, gas mark 4).

Petits pois à la française (serves 8)

2 lb/1 kilo peas, shelled
    (use frozen peas if fresh are not
    available)
1 large mild onion, finely sliced
1 small lettuce, shredded
(*continued overleaf*)

Put everything together in a thick-bottomed saucepan. Cover tightly (a double sheet of greaseproof (waxed) paper put over the pan before the lid is pushed down makes a good seal). Cook on very gentle heat until the peas are tender

35

¼ pint/⅛ litre/5 fl. oz water
1 oz/30 grams/2 tablespoons butter
Salt, black pepper and sugar
Handful each of mint and parsley

—about 20 minutes (10 if frozen). Remove the herbs. The liquid may be thickened by the addition of *beurre manié* (see page 35) if preferred, but care should be taken not to mash the peas while stirring.

Green fruit salad (serves 8)
1 lb/½ kilo Chinese gooseberries
1 lb/½ kilo white grapes
1 green dessert apple
1 lb/½ kilo greengages
1 small ripe melon with green flesh
2 tablespoons kirsch

For the syrup:
8 oz/230 grams/1 cup granulated sugar
1 pint/¾ litre/20 fl. oz water
Pared rind of a lemon, and the juice
  of half of it

Put the sugar and water on together to boil and add the lemon rind. Boil until the syrup looks tacky and thick. Remove from heat and allow to cool. Do not peel the apple, but core it and cut into thin slivers. Put immediately into the syrup. Peel and slice the gooseberries, stone and quarter the greengages and halve and take the seeds out of the grapes. Using a melon baller make the melon flesh into balls, or simply cut into even-sized cubes. Put all this into the syrup and add the lemon juice and kirsch.

Camembert fritters (serves 8–10)
2 ripe Camembert cheeses
Beaten egg (about 2)
Fresh white breadcrumbs
Oil for frying
Sprigs of parsley

Chill the camembert in the refrigerator for an hour or so before cooking. Heat the oil in a deep-fat fryer until smoking hot. Test for heat by putting in a crumb: if it starts to sizzle immediately the fat is ready. Cut the chilled camembert into small wedges and roll each first in beaten egg, then in breadcrumbs. Fry until brown all over. Fried parsley is delicious with the fritters. The parsley sprigs should be quite dry. They are then deep fried in the fat with the fritters, and should go dark in colour and become crisp. The fritters are eaten with a fork.

On the day before
The seafood coquille can be prepared and cooked the day before. Reheat it in a saucepan before serving, taking care not to let it burn at the bottom. Alternatively heat it in the oven. Spoon into the coquille shells at the last minute.
Filet de boeuf en croûte Prepare the dish as far as brushing the pastry with egg wash, but do not return it to the oven. Cover it with a polythene sheet and keep in a cool place. Half an hour before serving, the polythene should be removed and the beef put into a preheated oven for its final cooking. If it is to be cooked at all in advance, keep it warm in a very cool oven (250°F, gas mark ½).
Fennel baked in the oven Prepare the fennel and leave it with the butter, lemon juice etc. in the ovenproof dish, but do not cook it until the next day. It can be baked at the same time as the fillet of beef, but it should go in ½ hour before, and be set on the bottom shelf.
Petits pois à la française Cook completely the day before. Reheat in oven or on top.
Green fruit salad can be prepared completely the day before, provided the fruit is well coated in syrup and kept refrigerated until needed.
Camembert fritters Assemble the ingredients, and put the cheese in the refrigerator to chill, but the fritters must be made at the last minute. The cheese can be chilled, cut, rolled in egg and crumbs and then refrigerated until needed, but there is a danger of ripe cheese running, even in the refrigerator, so unless the cheese is not very ripe—which would be a pity—this is not advisable.

DINNER FOR 8: MENU B

Blinis with sour cream and caviar

Carré of lamb
Mixed buttered beans
Baked tomatoes

Passion fruit syllabub

Chicken liver and bacon savoury

(Preparation on the day before follows recipes.)

Serve vodka or champagne with the blinis, and a good claret—say a 1961 Château Margaux—with the lamb.

Blinis with sour cream and caviar (serves 8–10)

½ lb/220 grams/1½ cups buckwheat flour
½ lb/220 grams/1½ cups plain flour
1½ oz/50 grams/1½ tablespoons fresh yeast (or half the quantity if using dried yeast)
1 dessertspoon sugar
1¼ pints/1 litre/25 fl. oz warm milk
3 eggs
Good pinch of salt
1 tablespoon melted butter
Lard for frying
Sour cream
Caviar (or lump fish roe)
Butter

Put the buckwheat flour into a warm dry mixing bowl. Cream the yeast with the sugar and add half the milk. Mix well. Pour the yeasty milk into the buckwheat flour and mix to a paste. Cover the bowl with a sheet of greased polythene or a cloth, and leave in a warm place to rise.
Sift the plain flour with the salt into another basin. Make a hollow (or 'well') in the centre and drop in two whole eggs and one egg yolk, reserving one egg white. Gradually mix to a batter, bringing in the flour, and adding the melted butter and the rest of the milk. Beat well. Now beat this batter into the yeasty one, cover with the greased polythene or cloth again and leave in a warm place for 2 hours. Just before cooking, whip the remaining egg white and fold it into the mixture. Grease a griddle iron or very heavy frying pan lightly with lard. Heat it gently over steady heat. When it is hot pour enough of the batter onto the griddle to make a blini the size of a saucer. When bubbles rise, turn it over and cook the other side to a gentle brown. Keep the blinis in a warm oven when they are cooked. Serve hot, buttered, with sour cream and caviar. The caviar is spread on and a dollop of sour cream added. Danish lump-fish roe (mock caviar) makes a good substitute for the real thing, and smoked salmon blinis are just as good. (Put a rolled slice of smoked salmon on each blini and serve with sour cream.)

Carré of lamb (serves 8–10)

Two pairs of best-ends of lamb, trimmed into racks
1 oz/30 grams/2 tablespoons butter
Sprig of rosemary
Salt, black pepper
½ oz/15 grams/1 level tablespoon flour
¾ pint/½ litre/15 fl. oz stock
1 bunch watercress
(Paper cutlet frills)

Set the oven at 400°F, gas mark 6. The best-ends should be trimmed so that each rack consists of six or seven bones. All the fat is removed and the bones are cut back and scraped clean. Lay the carrés in the roasting pan, skinned side up, so that the bones are not sticking up (they char easily if near the top). Dot with butter, crumble the rosemary over them and season with salt and pepper. Roast for an hour if fairly underdone lamb is wanted, for an hour and a half for well-done lamb. Baste two or three times during cooking.

Take the lamb out of the pan and put on a heated platter. Keep warm while making the gravy. Pour off the fat from the pan leaving the sediment and juice. Sprinkle in the flour, and stir well, using a metal spoon to scratch up all the brown bits from the bottom of the pan. Add the stock and bring to the boil, stirring. Taste and season with salt and pepper. Put the frills (if you have them) on the ends of the cutlet bones, and a bouquet of watercress at each end of the dish. Serve at once. Hand the gravy separately.

Mixed buttered beans (serves 8)

10 oz/300 grams/dried haricot beans
1½ oz/50 grams/3 tablespoons butter
1 onion, finely sliced
Pinch of thyme
Clove of garlic, crushed
Pepper and salt
½ lb/250 grams broad (Lima) beans, shelled
½ lb/250 grams french (green) beans, topped and tailed

Put the haricot beans in a bowl and cover with lukewarm water. Soak for 3–4 hours or overnight if more convenient. Drain them, put them in a large saucepan and cover with fresh warm water. Put on the lid, and bring to the boil as slowly as possible. This should take at least 45 minutes. Then simmer for one hour. Drain well. Spread the butter round a large casserole. Put in the haricot beans, crushed garlic, sliced onion, thyme, pepper and salt. Cover with fresh water and put on the lid or cover with foil. Bake in oven at 325°F, gas mark 3, for 3½ hours, checking occasionally that the dish has not become dry—it may be necessary to add a little more water. Now add the french and broad beans, mix in gently and continue cooking for a further hour. When the haricot beans are tender the dish is done.

Baked tomatoes (serves 8)

8 tomatoes
1 large onion, finely chopped
2 oz/50 grams/4 tablespoons butter
1 tablespoon chopped parsley
Salt and pepper

Cut the tomatoes in half and put them in a roasting pan or shallow ovenproof dish, cut sides up. Put a spoonful of chopped onion on each. Season with salt and pepper. Melt the butter and trickle it over the tomatoes. Bake in the oven, set at 400°F, gas mark 6, for 20 minutes or until soft but not collapsed. Scatter the parsley over them before serving.

Passion fruit syllabub (serves 8)

36 passion fruit (granadillas)—if unavailable use canned
½ pint/¼ litre/10 fl. oz thick cream
1 egg white
1 sherry glass sweet sherry
1 dessertspoon sugar

Scoop out the passion fruit flesh and add the sherry. Divide between eight glasses. Whip the cream until stiff. Whisk the egg white stiffly, stir in the sugar, and fold into the whipped cream. Put a large spoonful of cream into each glass. Chill before serving.

Chicken liver and bacon savoury (serves 8)

1 lb/450 grams chicken livers
8 large slices fatty bacon
8 large flat mushrooms
1 oz/30 grams/2 tablespoons butter
8 rounds white bread
Oil for frying
Salt and black pepper
1 dessertspoon chopped parsley

Trim the discoloured parts from the chicken livers. Remove the rind from the bacon and lay the slices on a board. If they are rather thin, spread them out sideways by pressing with the flat of a knife. Divide the livers between the bacon slices and roll them up. Put the rolls into a roasting pan, side by side and tightly packed to prevent the livers slipping out or the bacon unravelling during cooking. Cook in a hot oven (450°F, gas mark 8) until slightly browned (about 15 minutes).

Trim the stalks from the mushrooms. Lay the mushrooms side by side in another roasting pan, and dot with the butter. Add salt and pepper and put in the oven below the chicken liver rolls. They are done when the mushrooms are tender in the thickest part.

Using a round cutter, cut the middle out of each slice of bread. Heat ½ inch of oil in a frying pan and carefully fry the bread rounds on both sides until golden. Drain on absorbent paper.

To dish the savoury, put the fried bread on a heated platter, cover each piece with a cooked mushroom (dark side up) and place a bacon and liver roll on top. Mix the juices from the two roasting pans together, and pour over. Scatter over the parsley before serving.

On the day before

Blinis are best mixed on the day of eating, and fried at the last minute, but they are still delicious if made the day before and reheated in butter in a frying pan. The caviar and sour cream must be served at the last minute.

Carré of lamb, like all roasts, is best eaten straight from the oven. In order not to have to make the gravy at the last minute, the trimmings from the carrés can be roasted the day before and the gravy made from them. When the carrés are done the juices (but not the fat, which must be poured off) can be added to the made gravy.

Mixed buttered beans should be cooked the day before. Indeed the soaking could start two days before, though it is quite easy to do the dish in a day.

Baked tomatoes can be done in advance, but cooking them is as simple as reheating them, so put them in the oven with the lamb. Prepare them the day before and leave covered in polythene until needed.

Passion fruit syllabub Leave the scooped-out fruit and sherry mixture covered in the refrigerator. The cream can be whipped and added four or five hours before the party. Keep chilled until needed.

Chicken liver and bacon savoury Cook the bacon rolls, but undercook them slightly. Cook the mushrooms. Prepare the bread, but if you are cooking it in advance, it must be fried slowly until crisp right through. This is not as satisfactory as bread freshly fried and slightly soft in the middle. Put the savoury together as late as you conveniently can. The completed dish—without the dusting of chopped parsley—will stay quite happily in a warming cupboard for an hour or more.

DINNER FOR 8: MENU C

Haddock soufflé
    with crab or lobster sauce

Roast partridge
Game chips (or chip baskets)
Red cabbage
Glazed carrots

Pineapple with kirsch

Dolce Latte and Double
    Gloucester cheeses

(*Preparation on the day before follows the recipes.*)

Serve a white Burgundy, not too grand (a Chablis or a young Puligny Montrachet would be excellent), with the soufflé; and a Pomerol with the partridge.

Haddock soufflé (serves 8)

1 lb/½ kilo fresh haddock fillet
1 sliced onion
1 bayleaf
6 peppercorns
1 pint/¾ litre/20 fl. oz milk
1 oz/30 grams/2 tablespoons butter
    (plus ½ oz for greasing dishes)
1½ oz/45 grams/3 level tablespoons
    plain flour
2 oz/50 grams/4 heaped tablespoons
    fresh white breadcrumbs
Salt, pepper and paprika
1 teaspoon chopped fennel (the herb)
1 tablespoon chopped parsley
5 egg yolks
6 egg whites

Butter two 6-inch soufflé dishes. Set the oven at 350°F, gas mark 4. Skin the haddock fillets (but don't throw away the skins). Lay them in an ovenproof dish, pour over the milk, and put in the onion, bayleaf, and peppercorns. Cover with the fish skins, and poach in the oven until cooked (about ½ hour). Take out, but do not switch off oven. Strain off the liquid into a bowl or jug. Pour enough of the hot fish liquid onto the breadcrumbs to soak them (about ¼ pint). Melt the butter, add the flour and stir over gentle heat for one minute. Draw the pan off the heat, pour on the rest of the milk the fish was cooked in, and stir while gently bringing to the boil. You should now have a very thick white sauce. Flake the fish very finely or better still put it into an electric blender or pound in a mortar. Add it to the sauce with the fennel and parsley and the soaked breadcrumbs. Beat in the egg yolks. Season with salt, pepper and paprika. Whisk the egg whites till stiff but not dry-looking. (When the whisk is pulled up out of the egg whites a soft peak should stick up.) Using a large metal spoon, fold them into the fish mixture taking care not to over-stir. Turn the mixture into the soufflé dishes. With a knife cut through the mixture 2 or 3 times to release any over-large air pockets. Put in the middle of the oven to bake. They will take about 30 minutes, and should be served promptly—before they begin to sink.

If for any reason the soufflé cannot be served the minute it is cooked, leave it in the oven with the heat turned off. It should be all right for 10 minutes or so. Serve with Crab or Lobster Sauce (see following recipe). Any fish can be substituted for the haddock. Lobster or crab make delicious, though expensive, soufflés.

Crab or lobster sauce

About 1 lb/½ kilo fish heads, bones or
skin
½ pint/¼ litre/10 fl. oz water
A few slices of onion
Bunch of parsley
1 small can crab or lobster meat
1 oz/30 grams/2 tablespoons butter
1 dessertspoon flour
1 teaspoon paprika
¼ pint/⅛ litre/5 fl. oz milk
1 tablespoon sherry
1 tablespoon thick cream
Salt and pepper

Put the fish heads and/or the bones and skin into a saucepan with the water, onion slices and parsley. Cover and boil until the liquid is reduced by half. Strain, and mix the stock with the milk.
Break up the crab or lobster meat with a fork, removing any inedible membranes. Melt the butter in a saucepan and stir in the flour. Cook gently for half a minute. Add paprika and cook a few more seconds. Draw the pan off the heat, blend in the stock and milk, and return to the heat. Stir or whisk until the sauce boils. Heat the crab or lobster meat in a separate pan with the sherry and when hot add it to the sauce. Stir in the cream and season with salt and pepper. Serve with fish soufflé, or with poached or grilled fish.

Roast partridge (serves 8)

8 small partridges trussed with a piece
of fat bacon tied over each
Butter
¼ pint/⅛ litre/5 fl. oz red wine
Salt and pepper
Watercress

For the bread sauce
2 cups/200 grams breadcrumbs
¾ pint/½ litre/15 fl. oz milk
1 peeled onion stuck with three cloves
Salt and pepper
1 oz/30 grams/2 tablespoons butter

For the breadcrumbs
2 cups fresh white crumbs
3 oz/80 grams/6 tablespoons butter

For the game chips
1 lb/½ kilo large potatoes
Deep fat for frying

Set the oven at 400°F, gas mark 6. Put the birds in a large roasting pan and dot them with butter. Pour in the wine. When the oven is hot put them in and cook, basting once or twice, for 25–35 minutes—depending on whether the birds are to be slightly underdone or cooked through. Take them out and keep warm. Boil up the juices in the pan, adding salt and pepper, and pour over the birds.
To make the *bread sauce*, heat the milk and pour onto the crumbs. Sink the onion stuck with cloves into the mixture and leave to infuse for at least one hour. When needed, reheat, simmer for five minutes, remove the onion, and add salt and pepper to taste. Stir in the butter.
The *breadcrumbs* are simply fried in the butter until brown. Use a large heavy frying pan, and add more butter if necessary. They burn easily, so fry slowly, stirring frequently.
To make the *game chips*, peel and slice the potatoes in wafer-thin slices. Rinse them and dry them on a cloth. Fry in hot deep fat until crisp and pale brown. Drain on absorbent paper. (Alternatively, see below for Game Chip Baskets.)
Serve the partridges garnished with the watercress and the game chips. Serve the bread sauce in a sauceboat, and the breadcrumbs in a bowl with a teaspoon.

Game chip baskets filled with chestnuts (serves 8)

About 1½ lb/¾ kilo potatoes
Oil for deep frying
1 large can whole unsweetened chestnuts
Handful of raisins
Small bunch of white grapes, halved
  and with seeds removed
Coffee-cupful of pinenuts (optional)
1½ oz/45 grams/3 tablespoons butter

Dip a small wire strainer or sieve into the deep fat to get it well greased. Line it with overlapping raw game chips (preferably cut on a patterned cutter or mandolin so that they look slightly like woven straw). Using a small ladle or similar round-shaped object to prevent the chips floating away from the strainer as you cook them, deep-fry the 'basket' until golden and crisp. Drain well on absorbent paper and repeat until you have one basket for each person.

Melt the butter and add the drained chestnuts, raisins, grapes and pinenuts. Sauté until hot and beginning to brown. Just before serving, fill the baskets with this mixture.

(A gadget for making the baskets is available in shops selling to the catering trade, but the sieve-and-ladle works perfectly well.)

Red cabbage (serves 8)

1 red cabbage
2 onions, coarsely sliced
2 cooking apples, peeled and sliced
2 dessert apples, peeled and sliced
2 oz/50 grams/4 tablespoons butter
1 tablespoon brown sugar
1 tablespoon vinegar
Pinch of ground cloves
Salt, black pepper

Shred the cabbage and discard the hard stalks. Soak in warm water for an hour. Using a large pot, fry the sliced onion in the butter until it begins to soften. Add the drained but still wet cabbage, apples, sugar, vinegar, cloves and salt and pepper. Cover tightly and cook very slowly, turning over and stirring every half an hour. Cook for two hours, or until the whole mass is very soft and reduced. During the cooking it may be necessary to add a little water. Taste and add more salt, pepper or sugar if necessary.

Glazed carrots (serves 8)

2½ lb/1 kilo carrots
½ pint/¼ litre/10 fl. oz water
1 tablespoon butter
Small pinch salt
1 dessertspoon sugar
Ground black pepper
1 tablespoon chopped mint and parsley
  mixed

Peel the carrots and cut them into thin rounds or sticks. Put everything except the pepper and herbs into a saucepan, and cover with a well-fitting lid. Cook gently for 30 minutes or so, shaking the pan frequently towards the end of the cooking. The water should evaporate, leaving the carrots browning slightly in the remaining butter and sugar. Once the carrots are tender (until then it is important to simmer the saucepan only very slowly) the lid can be removed, and the heat turned up to hurry the evaporation of the water. But do not go away and leave them, as they brown and burn very quickly once the water has evaporated. Season with pepper and mix in the herbs. (These carrots, often called Carrottes Vichy—strictly, Vichy water should be used—are frequently served too salty. This is because the cook has automatically salted the water as much as for ordinary boiled carrots, forgetting that all the salt will be left with the carrots when the water has evaporated.)

Pineapple with kirsch (serves 8)

1 large pineapple
Kirsch
Caster (powdered) sugar

Cut the top and bottom off the pineapple so that you are left with a cylinder of fruit. With a sharp knife cut round inside the skin—working first from one end and then from the other—so that you can push the flesh out in one piece from the skin. Try not to pierce or tear the skin. Slice the pineapple very finely.

Stand the pineapple skin in a shallow bowl. Put the fruit back in it, sprinkling kirsch and sugar between the slices. Put back the top of the pineapple, and provide a fork for the guests to extract the slices, and a spoon for scooping up some of the kirsch-flavoured juice which will have run into the dish.

On the day before

Haddock soufflé Prepare the base (fish, breadcrumb and milk mixture) and butter the soufflé dishes. The whites must be whipped and added just before cooking. If, when you come to finish the soufflé, the base has become too solid, reheat it in a saucepan, adding perhaps a very little cream, but do not add much liquid.

Crab or lobster sauce Make completely.

Roast partridges Bard (i.e. tie the bacon over the breasts) and put ready in their roasting pan with the wine. They must be roasted just before serving.

Make the *bread sauce*, omitting the butter, which can be added when reheating.

Prepare the *game chips* and leave them soaking in water. They can be completed the day before, and reheated in the oven, but are not so good. If it is impossible to cook them just before serving, buy ordinary crisps (potato chips) in a packet and heat them in the oven.

Game chip baskets If making the baskets the day before, underfry them slightly. Make the filling. Just before serving re-fry the baskets, heat the chestnut and raisin mixture in a frying pan or in the oven, and fill them as you dish up.

Red cabbage Cook completely and when needed reheat with a little extra butter.

Glazed carrots Cook completely and reheat either in the oven or in a little more butter in the pan.

Pineapple with Kirsch The pineapple can be cut the day before, but if this is done, spoon the kirsch-flavoured liquid that will have run into the dish (which should be deep enough to contain it) back into the top of the pineapple before serving.

MENU D: DINNER FOR 6

Smoked trout mousse with
   smoked salmon

Filet de boeuf à la Bourguignonne
Creamed potatoes
Courgettes (zucchini) with
   tomatoes

Annabel's cheesecake

(*Preparation on the day before follows recipes.*)

Serve a Moselle with the smoked trout mousse; and a red Burgundy, say a Volnay, with the beef.

Smoked trout mousse with smoked salmon
See page 62.

Filet de boeuf à la Bourguignonne (serves 6)

3 lb/1½ kilos piece of fillet of beef
12 small button onions or shallots, peeled
½ lb/230 grams flat mushrooms
½ pint/¼ litre/10 fl. oz red wine
½ pint/¼ litre/10 fl. oz beef stock
Bouquet garni (a bayleaf, a bunch of parsley, a stick of celery and a sprig of thyme, all tied together with a piece of string)
1 tablespoon fat or oil
1 oz/30 grams/2 tablespoons butter
¾ oz/25 grams/1 level tablespoon flour
Salt, pepper

Cut the beef into thick steaks. Heat the fat in a thick-bottomed saucepan and brown the beef slices—not more than two at a time. They must go really dark brown, almost charred-looking. If the bottom of the pan becomes burnt or too dry, pour in a little of the wine, swish it about, scraping off the sediment stuck to the bottom, and pour over the steaks. Then heat a little more fat and continue browning them. As they are browned, lay them in a casserole. When they are all done repeat the *déglaçage* (boiling up with a little wine, and scraping the bottom of the pan). Now melt the butter and fry the onions in it until they are evenly brown all over. Add the mushrooms (sliced, if large) and continue cooking for a few minutes. Stir in the flour, add the rest of the wine and the stock; stir until boiling, again scraping the bottom of the pan. When boiling, pour over the steaks, and add the bouquet made of the bayleaf, parsley, celery and thyme. Season with salt and freshly ground black pepper, cover, and simmer gently for 40 minutes (or until the beef is really tender, but still in firm whole slices). Lift the beef slices into a clean casserole or onto a serving dish, and boil the sauce fast until reduced to a fairly thick, almost syrupy consistency. Stir occasionally during this reduction. Pour over the beef. Remove the bouquet garni (the bunch of herbs and celery).

Creamed potatoes
See page 63.

Courgettes (zucchini) with tomatoes (serves 6)

6 large courgettes
6 large tomatoes
1 clove garlic, crushed
Salt, black pepper
1½ oz/40 grams/3 tablespoons butter

Slice the courgettes thinly. Skin the tomatoes (dipping them into boiling water for five seconds makes this easier). Slice them thickly. Put the courgettes and tomatoes into a casserole. Melt the butter, add the crushed garlic, and pour over the vegetables. Season with salt and pepper and cook in the oven until the courgettes are tender (about 25 minutes at 375°F, gas mark 5).

Walnut and lemon meringue cake (page 54)

Cocktail party, 1930

NONE OF OUR JOYS ARE PERFECT.

Mrs. Sopely (a great Favourite, somehow, with most of our Sex). "No, INDEED, MR. SPARKS! I NEVER, *NEVER* FLATTER! BUT IT WON'T DO TO TELL ME THAT NATURE HAS NOT BEEN UNFAIR IN LAVISHING ALL HER CHOICEST GIFTS UPON YOU ALONE!"

[Sparks is a modest man, but he can't help thinking that if the Lady on his other side, now, were only to talk to him a little in this strain, he could stand a good deal more of it!

A GALLANT REPLY.

Miss Lucy. "HERE'S WHERE YOU AND I ARE TO SIT, MAJOR!"
The Major. "BY JOVE!—A—RATHER A WARM PLACE!"

Miss Lucy. "WHAT—YOU A MAJOR, AND CAN'T STAND FIRE!"
The Major. "NOT AT MY BACK, YOU KNOW, MISS LUCY!"

PUNCH, OR THE LONDON CHARIVARI.—MARCH 6, 1880.

TWO SIDES TO A QUESTION.

IT'S ALL VERY WELL TO TALK OF STICKING TO YOUR OLD FRIENDS, WHETHER THEY BE PROSPEROUS OR THE REVERSE! BUT WHAT IF THEY RESEMBLE BILLY SCATCHERD, FOR INSTANCE? YOU ASK B. S. TO DINNER, TO MEET YOUR RESPECTED FATHER-IN-LAW (THE DEAN), AND GENERAL JENKINSON, AND THE MEMBER FOR HORNSEY, AND, WORST OF ALL, SIR GORGIUS MIDAS AND MRS. PONSONBY DE TOMKYNS—NOT TO MENTION THE BETTER HALVES OF THESE IMPORTANT PEOPLE—AND DEAR OLD BILLY, WHO HATES HUMBUG, AND SCORNS WORLDLY SUCCESS, AND STILL PAWNS HIS WATCH TO PAY HIS RENT, INSISTS ON REMINDING YOU ACROSS THE TABLE OF THE GOOD OLD DAYS WHEN YOU USED TO DO THE SAME; AND AS A PIQUANT SET-OFF AGAINST YOUR PRESENT SPLENDOUR, TELLS THAT CAPITAL STORY OF HOW YOU MANAGED TO GO TICK FOR A WHOLE TWELVEMONTH AT A CERTAIN TRIPE AND TROTTER SHOP IN DRURY LANE, AND THEN SETTLED THE BILL WITH A HAT AND COAT YOUR GRANDMOTHER LENT YOU TO GO TO YOUR GRANDFATHER'S FUNERAL—AND ALL THIS WITH THE SERVANTS IN THE ROOM, CONFOUND HIM! AND THAT SPITEFUL LITTLE BOHEMIAN MINX, MRS. SCATCHERD, GOBBLING AWAY FOR THE WEEK BEFORE AND THE WEEK TO COME, AND REVELLING IN YOUR WIFE'S BLACK LOOKS AT *YOU!*

Annabel's cheesecake (serves 6–8)

For the crust
1 packet babies' rusks or digestive
    biscuits (zwieback or graham
    crackers), crushed (about 16
    biscuits)
3 oz/80 grams/3 tablespoons caster
    (powdered) sugar
3 oz/80 grams/6 tablespoons melted
    butter

For the filling
1 lb/450 grams/2 cups best quality
    soft cream cheese
¼ pint/⅛ litre/5 fl. oz thick cream
2 whole eggs and 1 egg yolk
1½ teaspoons vanilla essence
Sugar to taste (about 6 oz/160 grams/
    6 tablespoons)

For the top
1 carton (about 5 fl. oz) sour cream
1 dessertspoon caster (powdered)
    sugar

Mix the crust ingredients together and line a shallow pie dish or flan ring with the mixture, pressing firmly against the sides and base. Be careful not to get the corners too thick. Bake in a moderate oven (375°F, gas mark 5) for 10 minutes or until hard to the touch.

Mix all the filling ingredients together until smooth, and pour into the pastry case. Return to the oven until the filling has set—about 20 minutes. Take out and allow to cool. Spread with the sour cream mixed with the sugar. The top can be decorated with nuts, sultanas or fresh fruit such as red currants or halved seeded grapes, but it is very good as it is.

On the day before

Smoked trout mousse with smoked salmon can be completed and kept in a cool place, covered with polythene film.

The filet de boeuf à la Bourguignonne can be made well in advance and heated up in the oven or in a saucepan.

Creamed potatoes If the directions on page 63 are carried out this dish can be cooked the day before and reheated in the oven.

Courgettes (zucchini) with tomatoes Prepare the vegetables and put them in the casserole with the butter and the garlic—but do not pre-cook.

Annabel's cheesecake Make the cheesecake the day before. If the sour cream is spread on top, the dish must be covered in polythene film and refrigerated overnight; but if the sour cream is to be added on the day of the party, the cake need not be refrigerated but must be kept in a cool place.

MENU E: DINNER FOR 6

Consommé caviar

Stuffed boned roast duck
Mange-tout peas in onion sauce
Orange and watercress salad

Athol brose

(Preparation on the day before follows recipes.)

Serve sherry with the consommé and a Burgundy, say a Nuits St George, with the duck.

Consommé caviar (serves 6)

2 or 3 cans of consommé (depending
    on the size of the soup cups)
1 large jar of lump fish roe
2 cartons (about 10 fl. oz) sour cream
1 lemon

Chill the consommé well. Chill six soup cups too. Spoon the consommé into the cups, put a large dessertspoonful of sour cream on the top of each, and then add a teaspoon of lump fish roe. Serve with a wedge of lemon at the side of each cup.

Leith's duckling (page 62)

Stuffed boned duck with orange and green olives (serves 6)

One 5–6 lb/2–3 kilos fresh duck
1 onion, finely chopped
1 oz/30 grams/2 tablespoons butter
2 dozen green olives stoned and
  chopped
Finely grated rind of two oranges and
  the juice of one
½ large loaf white bread, made into
  crumbs
1 egg yolk
1 whole egg
1 teaspoon crumbled sage
Salt and pepper
½ clove garlic, crushed (optional)

Some butchers or poulterers in England will bone the duck for you—ask for the giblets and bones as well. If you are doing it yourself you will need a very sharp small knife. It is not a difficult business, but it needs care and patience. Chop off the legs just above the knee joint. Using the little knife, work the skin and flesh loose from the bone, pressing the flesh back all the time to expose the bone. It is a combination of loosening the flesh by inserting the knife, and scraping the bone with the blade of the knife to press back the flesh. When you have gone as far as you can with both legs do the same to the wing joints, starting above the pinion joint. Then work on both ends of the duck, always trying to keep the knife as close to the carcase as possible so as not to pierce the skin. You will find that you can work the carcase loose with your fingers, easing between the skin and bone. When the whole carcase is loose detach it from the legs and wings and draw it out through the large opening—not through the neck. Now turn the whole duck inside out and detach the leg and wing bones. Turn right side out again and stuff it, making sure that any meat still attached to the bones is added to the stuffing.

To make the stuffing melt the butter and add the chopped onion. Fry until transparent. Trim the discoloured part from the duck liver. Chop the liver, and add to the onion. Fry, stirring, for four minutes. Mix the contents of this pan with all the other stuffing ingredients. Add any small pieces of meat from the bones of the duck. Stuff the bird, and roast in a narrow pan that will support it in a duck-like shape (a loaf tin can be placed next to the duck to prevent it going flat if a narrow pan is not available). Cook for 1½ hours at 400°F, gas mark 6, or until the bird is brown and crisp all over.

Mange-tout peas in onion sauce (serves 6)

3 lb/1½ kilos mange-tout peas (they
  are the tender, flat variety, eaten
  pod and all, and only require top-
  and-tailing—US snow-peas)
1 mild onion, finely chopped
1 oz/30 grams/2 tablespoons butter
½ oz/15 grams/1 level tablespoon flour
½ pint/¼ litre/10 fl. oz milk
2 tablespoons cream
Salt and pepper

Melt the butter, add the onion and fry slowly until transparent. Stir in the flour, cook for one minute, then add the milk, stirring until it boils. Boil for one minute, season with salt and pepper, and add the cream. Set aside. Bring a pan of water to a rolling boil. Add salt, and drop in the peas. Boil quickly for about four minutes or until barely cooked. Drain them immediately, swish cold water over them to stop them cooking, and drain them again. Return to the pan, pour on the onion sauce, and reheat just before serving.

Orange and watercress salad
See page 64.

Athol brose (serves 6)
½ pint/¼ litre/10 fl. oz thick cream
¼ pint/⅛ litre/5 fl. oz whisky
3 tablespoons runny honey

Whip the cream stiffly, add the honey, and stir in the whisky. Spoon into very small goblets and serve.

One version of Athol Brose has a cup of soaked oatmeal added to it; the cream is not whipped, and the brose (or brew) is served hot. This used to be served as a warming drink on festive winter nights in Scotland. Our version is a dessert. A dollop on top of hot coffee is delicious too.

On the day before
Consommé caviar Chill the consommé. If you have space in the refrigerator there is no reason why the soup cups should not be filled with the consommé and sour cream, and covered with polythene. The caviar and lemon segment should be added at the last minute, however.
Stuffed boned duck Bone and stuff the duck, but do not cook it. Keep refrigerated.
Mange-tout peas Make the sauce, and prepare the peas but do not cook them until just before dinner.
Orange and watercress salad Slice the oranges and wash the cress. Keep them in plastic bags in the refrigerator. Make the dressing.
Athol brose can be made in advance, put in a bowl and kept covered in the refrigerator until needed, but as it is very quick to make, it could probably be done a few hours before the party.

MENU F: DINNER FOR 6

Iced gaspacho

Poulet François I
Buttered rice
Green salad

Chocolate mousse

(Preparation on the day before follows recipes.)

Serve an Alsatian Traminer or a light Riesling throughout.

Iced gaspacho (serves 6)
1 clove garlic, peeled
4 tomatoes, skinned
1 mild onion, peeled
1 green pepper, seeded
1 cucumber, peeled
Handful of parsley
4 tablespoons olive oil
Juice of ½ lemon
1 pint/½ litre/20 fl. oz tomato juice
Salt, pepper, cayenne

Keep back a little of the tomato, onion, pepper and cucumber for garnishing the soup, and put all the rest with everything else into a liquidizer and blend until smooth. Strain the soup into a bowl and chill well. Correct seasoning if necessary. Chop the reserved vegetables finely, and serve them separately. If the soup is not well chilled, a lump or two of ice should be added to each soup cup.

A little cream can be added to the soup, or small fried croutons of bread may be served with it.

Poulet François I (serves 6)

Two 3 lb/1½ kilos roasting chickens
12 button onions, skinned
½ lb/230 grams button mushrooms
1 oz/30 grams/2 tablespoons butter
½ pint/¼ litre/10 fl. oz chicken stock
¼ pint/⅛ litre/5 fl. oz. thin cream
3 tablespoons brandy
½ oz/15 grams/1 level tablespoon flour
Bouquet garni (sprig each of thyme
    and parsley, a stick of celery and a
    bayleaf, all tied together with a
    piece of string)
Salt and pepper

Joint the chickens. Heat the butter in a large casserole and when it is foaming brown the chicken joints all over in it, frying only a few at a time. As they are browned, remove them onto a plate. Then fry the onions in the same way, and lastly the mushrooms. Replace the chicken, onions and mushrooms and pour over the brandy. Set it alight. When the flames have died down sprinkle in the flour. Then add the stock and the bouquet garni. While the liquid comes to the boil keep agitating it with a wooden spoon, and stirring gently. Add half the cream. Put on the lid, and bake in the oven (375°F, gas mark 4) for one hour, or until the chicken joints are very tender but not broken up. Take the casserole from the oven, lift out the chicken joints, mushrooms and onions, and discard the bouquet garni. Carefully skim the fat from the sauce. Taste, and correct seasoning. (If the sauce is a little thin, a tablespoon of the skimmed fat can be mixed to a paste with ½ oz of flour and put back into the sauce to thicken it; whisk until the sauce re-boils.) Add the rest of the cream, and pour over the chicken pieces.

Buttered rice
See page 70.

Green salad
See page 71.

Chocolate mousse
See page 81.

On the day before
Iced gaspacho can be made the day before, but it must be kept refrigerated. Keep the chopped vegetables for garnish in separate bowls, covered tightly.
Poulet François I Make the day before. Reheating should be done in the oven to eliminate the risk of scorching the bottom.
Buttered rice can be made in advance and reheated in the oven, covered loosely with foil.
Green salad Make the dressing, and if you have the salad ingredients, wash them, shake them dry, and keep overnight in a plastic bag in the refrigerator. Ideally, though, they should be bought on the day of the party.
Chocolate mousse must be made the day before, or at least four hours in advance.

MENU G: DINNER FOR 6

Grape and mint ring

Osso buco
Buttered rice

Walnut and lemon meringue cake

(*Preparation on the day before follows recipes.*)

Serve a light dry inexpensive white wine—a Spanish Rioja, for example—with the first course, and follow with a hearty Italian Barolo for the osso buco.

Jellied grape and mint ring (serves 6)

For the jelly
1 lb/½ kilo green grapes
1 rounded tablespoon gelatine
Juice of three lemons
1 tablespoon finely chopped fresh mint
½ pint/¼ litre/10 fl. oz water
Caster (powdered) sugar to taste –
    about 4 oz/110 grams/4 tablespoons
Green colouring

For the salad
1 cucumber
2 oz/50 grams/½ cup flaked almonds
2 fl. oz/4 tablespoons french dressing
    (page 71)
2 sprigs watercress

To make the jelly plunge the grapes into boiling water to make skinning them easier. Peel, halve and seed them. In a small pan soak the gelatine in two tablespoons of the water. After a few minutes warm the gelatine very slowly until it is dissolved and clear. Put the lemon juice, water, mint and grapes in a bowl. Sweeten to taste. Stir in the gelatine, and add a drop of green colouring. Wet a ring or savarin mould and fill with the mixture. Leave to set in the refrigerator.

Peel the cucumber and cut into match-stick pieces. Mix with the french dressing. Turn out the jelly onto a round plate. To do this, dip the bottom of the mould briefly in hot water, put the plate over the jelly, and turn the whole thing over so that the jelly falls out onto the plate. (This sounds tricky but it is in fact easy to do.) Fill the centre with the cucumber salad, and scatter the almonds over the salad and the jelly. Garnish with a sprig or two of watercress.

Osso buco (serves 6)

Six ½ lb/230 grams pieces of knuckle
    of veal, cut across with the bone and
    marrow in the centre. If the pieces
    do not have enough meat on them,
    get a few extra.
3 tablespoons olive oil
1 large or two small onions, finely
    chopped
1 large carrot, finely chopped
2 cloves garlic, crushed
¾ lb/350 grams ripe tomatoes
1 dessertspoon tomato paste
¼ pint/⅛ litre/5 fl. oz dry white wine
½ pint/¼ litre/10 fl. oz good veal stock
Bouquet garni (a sprig each of parsley
    and thyme, a stick of celery and a
    bayleaf, tied together with string)
1 heaped dessertspoon flour
Salt and pepper
1 dessertspoon chopped parsley

Dip the tomatoes into boiling water for five seconds and skin them. Chop them. Put a tablespoon of the oil into a saucepan, add the onion, carrot and garlic and cover with a well-fitted lid. Leave on a gentle heat to 'sweat' while you brown the meat in the rest of the oil in another pan. Brown the pieces one or two at a time, on both sides. Remove them to a plate as they are browned. When all are done, sprinkle the flour into the pan, add the sweated onion and carrot from the other pan, and stir well. Add the tomato paste, the chopped tomatoes, wine, stock, salt and pepper, and bring to the boil. Replace the ossi buchi, sink the bouquet garni in the liquid and put on the lid. Simmer for 1½ hours or until the veal is very tender, but not quite falling off the bone. Take the veal out, place it on a warmed serving platter with a fairly deep lip. Cover with foil and keep warm while you boil the sauce rapidly until thick. (Stir frequently and watch that it does not catch and burn at the bottom.) Remove the bouquet garni. The sauce should be pushed through a sieve, but it is often served as it is. Osso buco is, and looks, a substantial peasant dish, made brighter by a last-minute scattering of chopped parsley.

Buttered rice See page 70.

Walnut and lemon meringue cake

4 egg whites
9 oz/250 grams/1 heaped cup caster
  (powdered) sugar
5 oz/150 grams/1 large cup walnuts
4 heaped tablespoons lemon curd
  (see page 134)
½ pint/¼ litre/10 fl. oz thick cream

Set the oven at 375°F, gas mark 5. Line the bottom of two sandwich tins (cake pans) with rounds of greaseproof or waxed paper. Brush the paper and sides of the tins with a very little oil or melted lard. Whisk the egg whites until stiff, then add half the sugar. Beat again until stiff. Beat in the rest of the sugar and keep whisking until the meringue is so stiff that it will not flow at all, but holds its shape rigidly. Chop 4 oz of the nuts roughly, and stir into the mixture. Divide between the two pans, smoothing the tops slightly. Bake for 40 minutes. Turn the cakes out on a wire rack, and peel off the paper. Whip the cream and mix half of it with the lemon curd. Sandwich the cakes with this. Use the rest of the whipped cream and the remaining ounce of nuts for decorating the cake (see plate on page 45).

On the day before

Grape and mint ring Make the jelly ring, but not the salad. Prepare the dressing for the salad. The cucumber can be prepared the day before, but it must be salted, rinsed and drained as described on page 133. Mix with the dressing a few hours before the party, when filling and garnishing the jelly ring.
Osso buco Make completely. Reheat in the oven.
Buttered rice can be made even two days in advance. Reheat in the oven on the shelf below the osso buco, covered loosely with foil.
Walnut and lemon meringue cake Make the cakes, but do not fill them until a few hours before the party or they will go rather soft.

MENU H: INEXPENSIVE DINNER FOR 6

Tuna and flageolet salad

Sauté of kidneys Turbigo
Peas
Buttered rice

Latticed apple flan

(Preparation on the day before follows recipes.)

Beaujolais would be excellent with both the first and main courses.

Tuna and flageolet salad (serves 6)

1 onion, finely sliced
1 large can flageolet beans
2 small or one large can tuna fish
1 cup shell-shaped pasta
Salt, black pepper
French dressing (see page 71)
1 teaspoon chopped basil
1 dessertspoon chopped parsley
1 box mustard-and-cress
6 black olives, stoned

Cook the pasta in plenty of boiling salted water until just tender (about 10 minutes). Rinse under cold water and drain well. Rinse the starchy liquid off the flageolets and drain. Gently mix the sliced onion, beans, tuna fish (and the liquid in the can), pasta and chopped herbs in just enough french dressing to moisten the salad. Add salt and pepper if needed. Care should be taken not to over-mix, or an unattractive soggy salad will result. Decorate with the snipped cress and the black olives.

Sauté of kidneys Turbigo (serves 6)

9 lamb's kidneys
½ lb/250 grams small pork sausages
12 baby onions or shallots, peeled
½ lb/250 grams button mushrooms
Butter for frying
2 tablespoons sherry
¾ pint/½ litre/15 fl. oz stock
Salt and pepper
Bouquet garni (a stick of celery, a
    bayleaf, sprigs of parsley and thyme,
    tied together with string)
1 oz/30 grams/2 tablespoons butter
1 oz/30 grams/1 heaped tablespoon
    flour
1 carton sour cream (about 5 fl. oz)

Skin the kidneys; halve them and remove the core. Heat the butter in a frying pan. Brown the kidneys quickly (a few at a time) on both sides. They should cook fast enough to go brown rather than grey. Remove them into a bowl as you go. Now fry the sausages, then the onions, and finally the mushrooms in the same way. Put them onto a plate—not with the kidneys. Pour off the blood that will have run from the kidneys (it can be very bitter). Put everything back into the pan. Pour over the sherry and stock, and sink the bouquet garni in the liquid. Add salt and pepper and cover with the saucepan lid. Cook very gently for about ¾ hour or until the kidneys and onions are tender. Lift the meat and vegetables onto a serving dish and discard the bouquet garni. Work the ounce of butter and the flour together to a paste, and drop about half of it into the sauce. Whisk or stir briskly while bringing slowly to the boil. If the sauce is still on the thin side add the rest of the beurre manié (the butter and flour mixture) in the same way, whisking out the lumps. Boil for 1 minute. Add the sour cream, stir (but do not boil) and pour over the dish. Alternatively, serve the cream separately.

Peas (serves 6)

1½ lb/¾ kilo shelled peas
Bunch of mint
Teaspoon sugar
½ oz/15 grams/1 tablespoon butter
Black pepper and salt

Boil the peas with the mint and sugar in salted water until tender—about 10 minutes if the peas are young. Drain well, and toss them in the butter, adding freshly ground black pepper, and more salt if necessary. Frozen peas need only be brought to the boil and simmered 1–2 minutes.

Buttered rice
See page 70.

Latticed apple flan (serves 6)

¾ lb/350 grams rich short crust pastry
    (see page 88)
3–4 large cooking apples
Caster (powdered) sugar–about
    3 tablespoons
2 cloves
Handful sultanas
Grated rind and juice of one small
    orange

Set oven at 375°F, gas mark 5. Line a pie plate or flan ring with the pastry. Bake blind (see page 105). Peel and finely slice the apples into a bowl and add the other ingredients. Mix well and press into the flan case. Cut the pastry trimmings into thin strips and lattice the top of the flan with them, sticking the ends down with a little water. Brush the lattice with water and sprinkle with caster sugar. Return to the oven until the apple is soft and the pastry pale brown. Serve hot with whipped cream.

On the day before
Tuna and flageolet salad Prepare all the ingredients, but do not combine until a few hours before the party.

Sauté of kidneys Turbigo can be cooked the day before, but do not add the sour cream until the last minute. Reheat the dish in the oven or on the top.

Peas If using fresh peas it is a pity to shell them too far in advance, as they keep their flavour better in the pod.

Buttered rice Make the day before and reheat in the oven.

Latticed apple flan Make completely, and warm in the oven before serving.

MENU I: INEXPENSIVE DINNER FOR 6

Egg mousse

Pigeon casserole with celery and
    walnuts
Buttered leaf spinach
Potatoes boulangère

Blackcurrant fool

(*Preparation on the day before follows recipes.*)

Serve one wine only—perhaps a red Provence.

Egg mousse with anchovies (serves

(for Egg mousse with aspic, see
  below)
6 hardboiled eggs
6 tablespoons mayonnaise (see page 19)
1 dessertspoon anchovy essence
1 dessertspoon gelatine
1 tablespoon water
3 tablespoons cream
1 egg white
Salt, pepper, cayenne

For the garnish
12 anchovy fillets
3 small gherkins
12 radishes
12 thin slices cucumber

Soak the gelatine in the water. Oil a soufflé dish or mould. Chop the eggs and mix them with the mayonnaise, anchovy essence and cream, and season with salt, pepper and cayenne. Dissolve the gelatine over gentle heat and when runny and clear add it to the mixture, stirring briskly. Whisk the egg white until stiff, fold it in, and pour the mixture into the mould or dish. Put in the refrigerator until set. Run a knife round the edge of the mouse to loosen it, and turn out onto a plate. Split the anchovy fillets lengthwise and use them to lattice the top of the mousse. Cut thin rings of radish and gherkin and place them in alternate diamond-shaped spaces of the lattice pattern (see page 132). Decorate the sides of the mousse with thin rounds of cucumber. Trim the rest of the radishes, leaving a few leaves on each, and put them round the mousse.

Egg mousse with aspic (serves 6)

Mousse ingredients as in previous recipe

For the garnish
Aspic powder and boiling water
  (make ¾ pint of aspic according to
  the manufacturer's instructions)
2 hard-boiled eggs, shelled and cut
  into neat slices or wedges
About 10 slices pickled cucumber
About 10 thin slivers of black olive
  or radish
A sprig of watercress

To make an *Egg mousse with aspic* you should start with the decoration. Wet the mould, soufflé dish or bowl, and pour in half the liquid aspic. Refrigerate until it is set. Now arrange the egg pieces, slices of cucumber or radish, pieces of olive and the sprig of watercress in a pattern on the set aspic, bearing in mind that when the mousse is turned out the decoration will be seen from the other side. (See page 132). Dribble enough of the remaining cool liquid aspic over the decorations to stick them down. Put back into the refrigerator until set. Carefully pour enough cooled aspic into the dish or mould to cover the decoration, taking care not to dislodge it. Do not use more aspic than you need to barely cover the decoration as too thick a layer is un-appetising. Refrigerate once again until set.

The basic mousse is the same as in the above recipe. Spoon it carefully into the dish on top of the aspic layer. When it is set, run a knife round the edge of the mousse to detach the sides and briefly dip the bottom of the dish or mould into hot water to loosen the aspic layer (like turning out a jelly). Put a flat serving plate over the top of the mould, making sure that it is dead-centre, then quickly invert both plate and mould. The aspic-covered mousse should fall out onto the plate. If it sticks obstinately, give it a slight shake.

Pigeon casserole with celery and walnuts (serves 6)

6 pigeons
1 head of celery
3 oz/80 grams/¾ cup shelled walnuts
½ pint/¼ litre/10 fl. oz white wine
½ pint/¼ litre/10 fl. oz stock
2 oz/50 grams/4 tablespoons butter
2 slices fatty bacon
½ oz/15 grams/1 level tablespoon flour
Bouquet garni (a sprig each of parsley and thyme, and a bayleaf, tied together with string)

Melt half the butter in a large thick-bottomed casserole. Chop the bacon and fry in the butter slowly for three or four minutes. Remove the bacon and put aside. Brown the pigeons one or two at a time, on all sides, in the butter and bacon fat. Lift out and replace with the celery and walnuts. Fry them until just turning colour, adding the other ounce of butter if necessary. Stir in the flour, then the wine and stock, and stir until boiling. Replace the birds, lying them breast-side down. Sink the bouquet garni in the liquid, add the bacon, and cover the casserole with the lid (wedged with a sheet of greaseproof or waxed paper if it does not fit tightly). Put in a slow oven 325°F, gas mark 3, until the pigeons are tender. If they are very old birds this can take as much as 8 hours (in which case a little more stock would need to be added during cooking), but 3 hours would usually be enough. If the birds are young 1½ hours would do, but young pigeons are seldom available. It is advisable to make the dish the day before, or with plenty of time to spare, as tough pigeon is very disappointing. When cooked, take up the pigeons and put them on a serving platter. Skim any fat off the sauce and remove the bouquet garni. If the sauce is too thin, boil it rapidly until reduced and slightly thickened. Spoon it over the pigeons.

Buttered leaf spinach (serves 6)

3 lb/1½ kilos leaf spinach
Salt and pepper
1 small clove garlic, crushed (optional)
1 oz/30 grams/2 tablespoons butter
Squeeze of lemon
Pinch of nutmeg

Wash the spinach very thoroughly. Remove the tough stalks. Put the wet spinach into a large saucepan, and cover. Cook gently, turning the spinach occasionally, for about 7 minutes or until it is just cooked but still a good green colour.

Drain well, pressing out the water by pushing a plate down on it while in the colander or sieve. Turn the spinach onto a board, and chop roughly. Melt the butter in the pan, add the garlic and fry for one minute. Add the lemon juice, and replace the spinach, turning it gently. Add salt and pepper and a little nutmeg to taste.

Potatoes boulangère

1½ lb/¾ kilo potatoes, thinly sliced
2 onions, thinly sliced
2 oz/50 grams/4 tablespoons butter
½ pint/¼ litre/10 fl. oz chicken stock
Black pepper and salt

Set the oven at 375°F, gas mark 5. Butter a pie dish and arrange the potatoes in layers with the onion, adding a little salt and pepper as you go. Arrange the top layer of potatoes in overlapping slices. Dot with the rest of the butter, and pour in the stock. Bake in the oven for about an hour or until the potatoes are tender and the top browned.

Blackcurrant fool (serves 6)

Fools used to be made with equal quantities of cream and fruit purée, but latterly custard has replaced half the cream, and I find this less rich and cloying. Almost any fruit, fresh or cooked, can be used. The soft fruits (raspberries, strawberries, peaches, apricots, bananas) are perhaps the best.

1½ lb/¾ kilo fresh blackcurrants, or
   2 large cans
Caster (powdered) sugar
½ pint/¼ litre/10 fl. oz thick cream
½ pint/¼ litre/10 fl. oz custard made
   with eggs or custard powder

Drain the fruit if canned. Push through a nylon sieve. Mix the cream and custard together until smooth. Combine the fruit purée and creamy custard, and sweeten to taste. Leave the mixture slightly streaky—do not over-stir. Pour into glasses or china pots and chill well.

On the day before

Egg mousse Make completely, and cover with polythene. Keep refrigerated. Alternatively, make the mousse, but turn out and decorate on the day of the party.
Pigeon casserole Cook the pigeons and leave them in their casserole ready to be reheated the next day. Reheat in the oven.
Buttered leaf spinach can be cooked in advance, but it loses its bright colour. It is better to wash it, and keep in a salad box or plastic bag in the refrigerator overnight. Melt the butter, fry the garlic and add the lemon juice. Set aside to be used when you cook the spinach. The spinach (once buttered) will keep well in a cool oven for an hour or so.
Potatoes boulangère can be made the day before and reheated in the same oven as the pigeons.
Blackcurrant fool Make the fool, pour it into the glasses, and cover each glass with polythene to preserve the flavour and soft texture.

MENU J: INEXPENSIVE DINNER FOR 6

Grapefruit, prawn and almond cup

Curried beef
Fried rice
Side dishes

Apricot slice

(*Preparation on the day before follows recipes.*)

Beer, especially lager, would be best with the curry, though a chilled Portuguese rosé would be refreshing for non-beer drinkers. Slightly dry cider is very good too.

Grapefruit, prawn and almond cup (serves 6)

3 grapefruits
1 dessert apple
12 oz/350 grams/1½ cups cooked
 peeled prawns
2 oz/50 grams/½ cup flaked almonds
1 tablespoon mint
2 tablespoons olive oil
Freshly ground black pepper and salt
9 slices of brown bread and butter,
 cut in half diagonally.

Halve the grapefruits, and using a grapefruit knife remove all the segments. Put them (with the juice) in a bowl. Peel and slice the apple finely and add it to the grapefruit with the prawns, mint, olive oil, a pinch of salt and plenty of coarsely ground black pepper. Pull the membranes from the grapefruit shells and fill the shells with the mixture. Scatter the almonds on top. Serve with brown bread and butter.

Curried beef (serves 6)

Real curry afficionados have their curry powder mixed for them, or mix their own, but this recipe is a basic curry that can be improved upon or altered according to taste.

3 lb/1½ kilos chuck steak, cut in
 2-inch cubes
1 tablespoon oil
1 large onion, finely chopped
1 dessert apple
2 tablespoons tomato paste
3 tablespoons curry powder
1 tablespoon flour
¾ pint/½ litre/15 fl. oz stock
1 tablespoon mango chutney
Salt, pepper
Squeeze of lemon

Melt the oil and fry the steak chunks, a few at a time, until well browned all over, putting them onto a plate as they are done. Fry the onion in the same oil (adding a little more if necessary) until just turning colour, then add the apple. Mix the curry powder and flour together, add it to the pan, and stir for a minute or two. Gradually add the stock and the tomato paste and bring slowly to the boil, stirring all the time. Add salt, pepper, a squeeze of lemon juice and the chutney. Put back the meat, cover with the lid and simmer very slowly until the meat is tender—about 2 hours. Curry is best cooked so slowly that the sauce scarcely moves, or done in a slow oven (300°F, gas mark 2) for 3 hours or so.

Fried rice (serves 6)

6 tablespoons patna type (long grain)
 rice
Salt and pepper
Oil
2 oz/50 grams/½ cup pine kernels
 (optional)
2 spring onions (optional)

Bring a large saucepan full of salted water to the boil, and tip in the rice. Stir, bring back to the boil, and cook for 10 minutes or until the rice is just tender. Rinse plenty of water through the rice to remove the excess starch, and drain well. While it is draining, occasionally turn it over with a spoon to allow trapped steam to escape. Pour 2 tablespoons of oil into the saucepan and put in the rice, now quite dry. Fry the rice, turning it all the time to brown it evenly. Add plenty of pepper, salt if necessary, and the pine kernels. Chop the spring onions finely, and stir them in.

Side dishes for curry

BANANA AND COCONUT
Chop two bananas and squeeze the juice of a lemon over them. Mix in 2 tablespoons of dessicated coconut.

TOMATO AND ONION

Chop a large onion and 3 tomatoes finely, and mix them together with a tablespoon of olive oil, salt and pepper, and a squeeze of lemon.

CHUTNEY AND CUCUMBER

Mix a cupful of sliced or chopped cucumber into the same amount of sweet chutney (such as mango or apple).

POPPADUMS

These are large flat wafers, generally bought in cans. They are heated in the oven or under the grill (broiler), or fried in hot fat until crisp. They can be bought spiced or plain.

GREEN PEPPER, APPLE AND RAISIN CHUTNEY

Chop equal quantities of apple and green pepper finely, or mince them. Add a tablespoon of raisins or sultanas and salt, pepper, lemon juice, cayenne and sugar to taste.

Apricot slice (serves 6)

6 slices of white bread
12 cooked apricots (soaked dried ones if fresh are unavailable or too expensive)
Butter
Brown sugar
Whipped cream or custard

Using a large biscuit cutter, cut a round from each slice of bread. Fry them in the butter on one side only until crisp. Allow to cool, then butter the unfried side. Put them on a baking sheet or in a roasting pan, buttered-side *down*. Cover the fried top with apricots, making sure that the bread is completely covered. Sprinkle heavily with brown sugar and put in a hot oven (425°F, gas mark 7) until the sugar melts and browns on top (about 10 minutes). Serve hot with whipped cream or cold custard.

On the day before

Grapefruit, prawn and almond cup Prepare the grapefruit and thaw the prawns, but do not slice the apple or put the dish together until a few hours before the party.

Curried beef Almost all curries should be made in advance so that the flavour of the sauce has time to soak into the meat.

Rice can be boiled in advance, but is nicer fried not more than two hours before eating. It will keep well in a warm oven after frying.

Side dishes:

BANANA AND COCONUT Squeeze the lemon and mix in the coconut. Add the banana the next day.

TOMATO AND ONION Make, and store covered.

CHUTNEY AND CUCUMBER Prepare the cucumber but do not add it to the chutney until a few hours before the party, or it will lose its crispness.

POPPADUMS If they are to be fried, this should be done just before dinner, but if they are crisped in the oven or under the grill (broiler) they can be done a day in advance, and kept in a large polythene bag overnight.

GREEN PEPPER, APPLE AND RAISIN CHUTNEY can be made two or three days in advance, and stored in the refrigerator.

Apricot slice Fry the bread and cook and drain the apricots but do not put together until half an hour before dinner.

Large Dinner Parties

Food
The prospect of fifty people dining together makes one think gloomily of big hotel banquets: melon balls in dubious liqueur, fish unidentifiable under a tasteless white sauce, a portion-controlled steak, frozen peas artily presented in a frilly tomato, and the *pièce de résistance*—a canned peach, ice cream, and a lump of sponge cake; and then, to drive the point home, the worst coffee you have ever tasted.

Of course it is difficult to cook good food for a crowd. It is also difficult to serve it efficiently (as anyone who has ever wanted to deviate from the menu by so much as a glass of water will know). But neither is impossible. The first thing to remember is that everyone would rather eat good cold food than bad hot food; so, if you are at all nervous, stick to cold food with perhaps hot soup or hot potatoes. If you do want to serve hot food, make only one course hot, and that one in easy-to-serve pieces, preferably in a sauce so that carrying round sauceboats is eliminated, and have a salad instead of vegetables.

Staff (See below for coping without them.)
One trained waiter or waitress can deal efficiently with ten people, but it may be necessary to put the wine on the tables for the guests to help themselves. If one waiter to eight people is allowed, then the staff can pour the wines too. There should be one person in the kitchen dishing up and doing last-minute jobs like making the salad dressing and garnishing the dishes. Most hired waiting staff available from staff agencies or catering firms will wash the dishes, and give a hand in the kitchen if need be. I think round tables each seating six or eight people the most attractive arrangement, but square or long tables can be set apart or in, for example, a U shape. First measure the room, and then draw a seating plan. If the tables are the hired, long trestle type, they come either 2 ft or 2ft 6 ins wide, and 4 ft, 6 ft or 8 ft long. The ideal table-space to allow for each guest is 2 ft, which gives him elbow room and room for a side plate; but at a pinch 18 ins is enough (even less for self-service—see below). He will also need 2 ft 6 ins of space measured at right angles to the table, for his chair and to enable the waiter to pass behind him. This also applies if two tables are set parallel to each other, and guests are therefore seated back to back: there must be 5 ft between the two tables to accommodate the diners, and leave a little alley for the waiters.

Waiters say that it is easier to serve a round table than a square or long one, presumably because there are no corners to get caught on. A 5 ft diameter round table comfortably takes eight people, uncomfortably ten; a 3 ft 6 in. table takes six to eight, and a 3 ft table four to six; a 2 ft 6 in. table holds three to four. As a rough guide, it is possible to seat twenty-four people comfortably in a room 15 ft × 15 ft. Overall, about 10 square feet per guest are needed. This allows for comfortable seating, and a 'service station' (sideboard or table) somewhere in the room for the waiters to rest their trays and plates on. It is essential to have at least one of these, the bigger the better, preferably near the door to the kitchen.

Coping without staff
If little or no help is available, the solution is for the guests to serve themselves from a buffet table. It is then sensible to put the cutlery, glasses, wine, napkins, salt and pepper ready on the dining table: they will have enough to do carrying their plates and handbags. As one never knows how many people will cram around one table when left to themselves, simply put a pile of napkins, cluster of glasses and a dozen or so forks on each table. An ashtray relieves the guest of the embarrassment of using his coffee saucer. Be careful about flowers as they may take up more space than they justify. I have a

curious prejudice against them on the tables anyway because they smack to me of boarding-house gentility; but I agree that this is unreasonable.

If a minimal staff is available, one waiter to every 20 guests would manage to clear the plates as each course is eaten and to serve the coffee at the tables.

Check list for large parties, page 187.

DINNER FOR 30

Smoked trout mousse with
    smoked salmon
Brown bread and butter

Leith's duckling
Creamed potatoes
Orange and watercress salad

Chocolate roulade with cream

(Suitable for a celebration. To be served by three waiters or waitresses)

(*Preparation on the day before follows recipes.*)

With the smoked trout mousse serve a dry Moselle or Rhine wine and with the duck a red Burgundy. Alternatively, serve a white Alsatian wine—e.g. a Gewurtz-traminer—right through the meal.

Smoked trout mousse with smoked salmon (serves 6–8)
(To make enough for 30, quadruple the quantities, and make one small mousse for each table)

6 smoked trout
½ pint/¼ litre/10 fl. oz thick cream
1 teaspoon lemon juice
1 teaspoon creamed horseradish
Black pepper
4 oz/100 grams thinly sliced smoked
    salmon
1 lemon, cut into segments
1 sprig parsley
Brown bread and butter

Take the bones and skin from the trout and put the flesh in a bowl. Pick through it carefully to make sure all the bones have been removed. Add the horseradish, lemon juice and pepper to taste. It is unlikely to need salt, but add a little if it does. Whip the cream and stir in: you should have a moist, but not sloppy paste; if it is too wet, add a tablespoon of fresh white breadcrumbs. Form the mousse into a flat mound on a plate and lay the smoked salmon slices over it, trimming the edges neatly. Decorate with lemon segments and a sprig of parsley. Serve with toast or brown bread and butter. The mousse can be eaten either with a fork or on toast.

Leith's duckling (serves 6–8)
(For 30, cook 10 ducks)
When we opened Leith's restaurant, I needed a speciality duck dish that would not be sweet and sticky and I wanted the duck skin to be crisp, and the sauce light. After some delicious and some frankly forgettable creations, we developed Leith's duckling. As I am sure there is nothing new in cooking, it probably has been done before, and called something else, but I have not seen it. The idea is that the whole dish should be crunchy —the celery, the onion, the almonds and the crisp skin.

Two 5–6 lb/2½–3 kilos ducklings
    (they should never be frozen, and
    should have soft, pliable backbones,
    a dry soft skin—not slimy—and be
    as plump as possible)

Prick the birds all over and put them in a moderately hot oven (400°F, gas mark 6) to roast for one hour. They need no fat, but it is a good idea to lay them legs up for the first half-hour and turn them right side up for the next half-hour.

2 oz/50 grams/2 tablespoons
   granulated sugar
2 tablespoons vinegar
2 celery sticks, finely chopped
1 medium onion, finely chopped
Juice and grated rind of two oranges
½ pint/¼ litre/10 fl. oz stock
1 tablespoon brandy
1 oz/30 grams/2 tablespoons butter
3 oz/80 grams/¾ cup flaked almonds
Salt, pepper
Sprig of parsley
Bayleaf
1 bunch watercress
1 whole orange

Take them out, drain well, and joint them. Put the pieces into a clean roasting pan, skin-side up. Put the sugar and vinegar in a thick-bottomed saucepan. Boil until the sugar caramelizes: it will go darker brown and bubbly, with large slow bubbles. Pour on the stock: it will hiss furiously and steam will billow out, so be careful of your hands. Stir until the caramel lumps disappear. Add the orange rind and juice, and the brandy, and pour over the duck. Return to the oven and continue cooking until the joints are cooked through (another 20 minutes or so). Do *not* baste. Remove the duck joints onto an oven-proof plate and keep warm. (If the skin is not truly crisp the duck can be returned to the oven for 10 minutes like this without the sauce.) Fry the flaked almonds in the butter until golden brown. Scatter over the duck. Skim the sauce to remove any fat, and strain it into a saucepan. Add the finely chopped celery and onion, and boil until the celery is just beginning to soften but is still a little crunchy (about 5 minutes). Taste the sauce and add salt and pepper. You should have a thin, fairly clear liquid with plenty of chopped celery and onion in it. Serve the sauce separately—or poured round, not over, the duck. Cut the orange (with the skin on) in half and slice it. Surround the duck with the orange slices and put a bouquet of watercress at each end of the dish. (See page 48.)

Creamed potatoes (serves 6–8)
These potatoes do not spoil with keeping, even overnight, in the refrigerator. (For 30 people, quadruple the quantities and make one dish for each table.)

3 lb/1½ kilos potatoes
2 oz/50 grams/4 tablespoons butter
Salt, pepper
Milk
1 egg

Boil the potatoes in their skins. Peel them, and remove the eyes. Mash them in a large saucepan over the heat until free of lumps. (If you are doing very large quantities, it is easier to put them through the mincer.) Add the butter, salt and pepper. Heat the milk. Beat in enough to give a fluffy but not sloppy texture. Remove from the heat. Butter a pie dish. Separate the egg, and beat the yolk into the potatoes. Whip the white until stiff and fold into the mixture. Turn into the pie dish and mark the top decoratively with a fork. Dot with butter. Reheat when required in a moderate oven (375°F, gas mark 5) for ½ hour.

Orange and watercress salad (serves 6–8)
(Make four times the quantity for 30 people)

4 oranges
3 large bunches watercress
3 tablespoons oil
1 tablespoon wine vinegar
1 teaspoon sugar
Salt, black pepper

Wash the watercress and drain. Peel the oranges with a knife as though you were peeling an apple. so that the pith is removed with the skin. (It takes practise to do this without involuntarily squeezing the orange too hard. Use a very sharp serrated knife, and hold the orange lightly, not pressing with the thumb. The peeling should be done with more of a sawing than a paring motion. It is easier to peel very thin stripes, working round and round many times, than to try to cut thick pieces off.) Slice the peeled oranges across into rounds. Trim away the thick part of the watercress stalks and put the orange slices and the watercress into a glass bowl. Combine the rest of the ingredients to make a dressing. Pour over just before serving. (If peeling the oranges in the way described proves too difficult, boil them whole for 7 minutes, then peel them conventionally and pick off the pith.)

Chocolate roulade with cream (serves 6–8)
This is a rich, delicious cake made without flour. (Do the recipe four times for 30 people)

5 oz/140 grams dark chocolate, sweetened
½ pint/¼ litre/10 fl. oz water
5 oz/140 grams/5 tablespoons caster (powdered) sugar
5 eggs
1 extra egg white
1 tablespoon rum (optional)
½ pint/¼ litre/10 fl. oz thick cream
Icing (confectioners') sugar

Take a large roasting pan and cut a double layer of greaseproof (waxed) paper slightly bigger than it. Lay this in the tin; don't worry if the edges stick up untidily round the sides. Brush the paper lightly with melted lard and sprinkle with flour. Separate the eggs, and cream the yolks and sugar until pale and mousse-like. Put the chocolate, broken up, in a large saucepan with the water. Stir until it melts and then boils to a thick cream. Add the rum. Cool slightly, then stir it into the yolk mixture. Whip all the whites until stiff, but not dry-looking, and fold them in. Pour into the roasting pan, spreading the mixture evenly over the paper. Bake in a moderately hot oven (400°F, gas mark 6) for 12 minutes or until the top is slightly browned and firm to touch. Remove from the oven, slide the paper and cake out of the tin onto a cooling rack or tray and leave overnight. Next day whip the cream and spread it evenly over the cake. Roll up like a swiss roll, removing the paper as you go. This is rather difficult and the cake is inclined to crack, but it can easily be glued together with cream, and will taste delicious anyway. Put the roll on a serving dish, and just before serving sift a little icing sugar over it.

Coq au vin (page 69)

'Service de table chez une Chatelaine'; from the 15th-century MS *Roman de Renaud de Montauban*

The banquet given by Clement IX to the Queen of Sweden at Monte Cavallo, 1667

Banquet at the Guildhall given by the Lord Mayor of London for the young Queen Victoria,
9 November 1837

On the day before
Smoked trout mousse with smoked salmon can be completed and covered with polythene. Keep refrigerated. The buttered bread (well covered) should be kept in a cool place overnight.
Leith's duckling Make the sauce but do not add the onions and celery. Chop these and keep well covered. The duck *can* be cooked the day before, but care should be taken to undercook it very slightly, so that it will not be overcooked when reheated. I think it preferable to roast the duck just before the guests arrive, and to keep it warm. Better still, have someone in the kitchen to do the last-minute jointing and garnishing.
Creamed potatoes can be made the day before—and kept refrigerated.
Orange and watercress salad Wash and pick over the cress and keep it overnight in a polythene bag in the refrigerator. Slice the orange and keep covered. Make the dressing. Do not combine the salad until the last convenient minute.
Chocolate roulade It is essential to make the cake the day before. Next morning, roll up with the cream but do not sift over the icing sugar until the last minute.

ECONOMICAL DINNER FOR 50

Cauliflower and ham salad

Coq au vin
Buttered rice
Green salad

Chocolate profiteroles

(Preparation on the day before follows recipes.)

The wine should be unpretentious and inexpensive. A Beaujolais or red wine from Bandol in Provence, or a red Rhône such as Châteauneuf-du-Pape, could be drunk with both first and main courses.

Cauliflower and ham salad (serves 8–10)
(For 50 people, do five times the quantity)

1 large or two small cauliflowers
6 eggs, hard-boiled
4 slices ham, cut into thin strips

For the dressing
1 tablespoon chopped mint
1 tablespoon chopped chives
1 dessertspoon chopped fresh tarragon
3 tablespoons olive oil
1 dessertspoon wine vinegar
1 small clove garlic, crushed
Salt, black pepper

Break the cauliflower into sprigs and boil in salted water until barely cooked. Drain well. While still hot, put into a bowl and pour over a dressing made by combining the last seven ingredients. When the cauliflower is quite cold, arrange the sprigs on a dish, with the strips of ham mixed among them. Surround with the hard-boiled eggs, cut into quarters lengthwise, and pour any remaining dressing over.

Coq au vin (serves 4)
This dish is classically made with young cockerels and the blood is used in the sauce, rather as with jugged hare. But a very good coq au vin is made with ordinary chickens, though you should avoid the battery-raised frozen variety.
(If doing this dish for 50 people, double the quantities in the recipe, and then make the dish five times. This means you will need a total of 10 chickens. Do not cook large quantities of hot food all at once. See note on page 8).

Tanger nes in caramel sauce (pa ge 78)

One 3 lb/1½ kilo roasting chicken,
   jointed into eight pieces
Flour
2 oz/50 grams/4 tablespoons butter
¼ lb/100 grams lean bacon, finely diced
12 button onions, peeled
12 button mushrooms
½ pint/¼ litre/10 fl. oz red wine
½ pint/¼ litre/10 fl. oz chicken stock
1 small clove garlic, crushed
Bouquet garni (a bayleaf, a sprig each
   of thyme and parsley, and a stick of
   celery, tied together with string)
1 tablespoon chopped parsley for
   garnish
12 small triangular-shaped croûtons
   (bread fried slowly in butter until
   crisp right through, and evenly
   brown)

Put half the butter in a large heavy saucepan and slowly brown the diced bacon in it. Add the onions, shaking the pan to brown them evenly all over. Add the mushrooms (do not bother to peel them unless the skins are very tough). Fry for a further 2 minutes, then lift out all the onions, mushrooms and bacon. Flour the chicken joints. Add the other ounce of butter to the juices in the pan, and brown the chicken pieces slowly and well on all sides.

Return the vegetables and bacon pieces to the pan. Add the wine, and enough of the stock to half-submerge the chicken pieces. Add the crushed garlic, bouquet of herbs, and salt and pepper. With a wooden spoon move the pieces about and stir the sauce, until it has come to the boil. Cover with a well-fitting lid and simmer slowly until the onions and chicken are tender (about 1 hour). Remove the bouquet garni. If the sauce is too thin, the chicken pieces should be removed to the serving dish and the sauce vigorously boiled to reduce it to a syrupy consistency.

Scatter chopped parsley over the dish at the last minute. Serve with buttered rice and croûtons.

Buttered rice

Take 1 tablespoon of patna-type (long grain) rice for each person. If it is to be a very large party (such as this one for 50) estimate 1 dessertspoon per person instead of 1 tablespoon.

Every cook has a favourite method of cooking rice, and I have been told mine is no good for preserving the nutritional value of rice. But it is fool-proof, and produces fluffy separate grains.

Take the largest saucepan you have, and fill it with salted water. When the water is boiling fast, tip in all the rice. (1 cup of rice will need at least six cups of water, but the exact quantities do not matter—as long as there is plenty of water.) Stir until the water re-boils. Boil for exactly 10 minutes and then test. The rice should be neither hard nor mushy, but firm to the bite (*al dente*). It may need one more minute. Drain the rice in a colander or sieve, and swish plenty of water through it. Stand the colander on the draining board. With the handle of a wooden spoon make a few 'draining' holes through the pile of rice to help the water and steam escape. Alternatively, every few minutes turn the mass of rice over with a spoon. Butter a fireproof dish. Return the rice to the empty saucepan and fork in ¼ ounce of butter per person with pepper to taste, and salt if necessary. (Buttering the rice prevents the grains sticking together.) Spoon the rice into the fireproof dish. Reheat in the oven when needed, lightly covered with foil, forking the rice occasionally so that the middle gets as hot as the edges.

Green salad

Use any salad you like, the only criteria being that it should be green and very fresh. For 10 people one lettuce (preferably curly endive, or Cos), a few slices of cucumber, green pepper, and celery would be about right. You could add half a dozen spring onions, a bunch of watercress and 2 heads of chicory. Cooked green vegetables, especially beans and peas, are good in a tossed salad. Very nearly anything goes. Remember never to 'wring' lettuce when breaking it—this bruises the leaves. Pull each leaf to pieces separately.

The salad should be as dry as possible before mixing with the french dressing. Use a large bowl. Mix at the last minute.

For the french dressing
4 tablespoons oil (a fifty-fifty mixture of olive and corn oils, or all olive oil)
1 tablespoon wine vinegar
½ teaspoon salt
½ teaspoon black pepper or six twists of a pepper mill

Put all these ingredients in a jar and shake them together. Other flavourings, such as crushed garlic, chopped onion, mustard, sugar, or chopped herbs can be added to the basic dressing according to taste, and depending on what sort of salad the dressing is for: e.g., mustard is good with cabbage; garlic with tomatoes. I dislike sugar in a dressing unless the salad contains fruit such as apples or oranges.

For a salad for 50 people you might use the following:

5 large lettuces, washed and picked into small pieces
2 cucumbers, sliced
1 head of celery, chopped, plus a few young leaves, chopped
2 green peppers, seeded and finely sliced
1 bunch spring onions, washed and peeled
2 lb/1 kilo chicory, wiped and picked
2 bunches watercress, washed and picked
Three times the amount of french dressing given above

Chocolate profiteroles (serves 10)
(Make the recipe 5 times for 50 people)
Make the profiteroles according to the recipe on page 23, but make each profiterole about the size of a ping-pong ball before it is cooked. They will take slightly longer to cook than those in the recipe. Split them. Fill with whipped cream, flavoured with caster (powdered) sugar and a few tablespoons of marsala wine. For profiteroles for 10 people you will need about ¾ pint (½ litre or 15 fl. oz) thick cream; for 50 people about 3 pints (2¼ litres).

Put the profiteroles in a glass dish, and make this chocolate sauce (for 50 people you will need *three*, not five, times the quantity):

Chocolate sauce

1 lb/½ kilo dark sweetened chocolate
½ pint/¼ litre/10 fl. oz water

Break the chocolate up and put it in a heavy saucepan with the water. Stir until the chocolate has melted and thickened to the consistency of thick cream. Pour half the sauce over the profiteroles (or dip the top of each one carefully into the sauce). Serve the rest piping hot. If it has been allowed to cool and harden again before serving, a little more water may be added when re-melting it.

On the day before

Cauliflower salad Make the day before, but keep refrigerated and well covered. A few more chopped herbs scattered over at the last minute will brighten the appearance if it should look at all dull.
Coq au vin Make completely. Reheat in the oven (400°F, gas mark 6) for 20 minutes. Fried bread croûtons are better done in butter at the last minute, but they will reheat satisfactorily if they have been fried till crisp right through, cooled, and kept in an airtight container until the next day. Reheat them on a plate in the oven.
Buttered rice Reheat in the oven on the shelf below the coq au vin.
Green salad Make the dressing. If you have bought the salad, pick it over and keep refrigerated in a plastic bag. Ideally salad should be bought on the day of the party.
Chocolate profiteroles The profiteroles keep well in a plastic bag overnight in the refrigerator. If they are to be kept for longer periods they should be frozen. Filling and coating with chocolate can be done on the morning of the party.

Unusual Dinner Parties

An amusing change is Chinese or Indian cookery, or for that matter, Mexican, Russian, Hungarian, Danish, or anybody-else's. This is particularly so if you are entertaining people you often have to dinner. And it can be added fun if they come dressed in something like the relevant national costume. But cooking foreign recipes is generally more work for the hostess, who must shop for unfamiliar ingredients and learn completely new dishes, requiring special concentration.

Books on almost any cuisine can be bought quite inexpensively. Embassies and trade centres are generally delighted to advise on how to make the party as authentic as possible, and most of them publish pamphlets—with recipes and pictures—about foods available.

Among the easiest national dishes are the Swiss fondues. They are simple to organize and are cooked at the table. A fondue burner and pot are essential unless you have an electric frying pan which would do equally well; but there is no need to buy an expensive set of bowls and long forks, which can be improvised. Fondue parties are best for small numbers of people, four or six, and the guests must be the sort that will not *mind* doing the work: some people—crusty colonel or gentle aunt—might think the whole thing a messy business, and might secretly have preferred a sandwich.

FONDUE BOURGUIGNONNE

The oil is heated in the fondue pot in the middle of the table. Each guest spears cubes of meat with a fork and cooks them in the sizzling oil. After slightly cooling them on his plate he dips them into one of the sauces and pops them into his mouth. A salad is a good idea (e.g. beetroot and onion salad with horseradish cream, page 90; or mixed bean, page 80). You will need salt, pepper, mustard and the oil for frying; and each person should have:

6 oz/150 grams fillet, sirloin or rump steak cut into bite-size cubes
3 small bowls of sauce, one curried mayonnaise, one garlic cream and one tomato dip
  (see recipes below)
1 long fork or steel knitting needle for spearing and cooking the meat
1 ordinary fork for eating it (the long one gets too hot)
A plate
Plenty of paper napkins for mopping up drips

Curried mayonnaise

¾ pint/½ litre/15 fl. oz mayonnaise
1 large onion, finely chopped
1 dessertspoon curry
2 tablespoons olive oil
1 teaspoon apricot jam
2 tablespoons red wine
1 dessertspoon lemon juice
Salt and pepper

Put the oil and onion into a frying pan and cook slowly until the onion is just beginning to colour. Stir in the curry powder, and fry for one minute. Add the lemon juice, jam and wine and simmer for 2 minutes. Take from the heat and stir into the mayonnaise. Add salt and pepper to taste.

Garlic cream

¾ lb/350 grams/1½ cups cream cheese
2 tablespoons cream
¼ pint/⅛ litre/5 fl. oz. milk
2 tablespoons chopped chives
1 clove garlic, crushed
Salt and pepper

Combine all the ingredients and mix until smooth.

Tomato dip

¾ pint/½ litre/15 fl. oz tomato ketchup
  (or one large bottle)
Large handful of parsley
1 large mild onion
1 teaspoon french mustard
1 clove garlic, crushed (optional)

Wash the parsley stalks and leaves and chop them finely. Chop the onion. Mix everything together. Alternatively put all the ingredients into an electric blender and liquidize them.

On the day before

Make the three *sauces or dips*. Keep them covered in a cool place.
The meat is best cut up into chunks only a few hours before the party as it tends to look less fresh and lose some of its blood if done too much in advance. However, the fat and any skin or gristle can be trimmed off the day before.
If a *salad* is to be served the dressing for it should be made the day before. If it is to be a salad of cooked ingredients (such as the beetroot or the mixed bean salads suggested) these can be prepared too. Assemble all the utensils and ingredients for the fondue.

SWISS CHEESE FONDUE (serves 6)
This is much simpler than the fondue bourguignonne (above) but it is only suitable for a light supper or lunch. The preparation takes no time at all. Classically the fondue is made at the table, but many people start the process in the kitchen. The fondue is set in the middle of the table, and guests dip small chunks of bread (on their forks) into it. Each guest will need a plate, a fork, a napkin and plenty of coarse crusty bread. Follow the fondue with a green salad (page 71).

1 clove garlic, peeled and bruised
½ pint/¼ litre/10 fl. oz dry white wine
1 dessertspoon lemon juice
1 lb/½ kilo cheese, preferably gruyère
  or Emmenthal cut in wafer-thin
  slices or coarsely grated
1 level dessertspoon cornflour
Black pepper
Pinch of grated nutmeg
1 liqueur glass of kirsch

Rub the garlic all round the fondue pot. Put the wine and lemon juice into the pot, and heat gently. Add the cheese gradually, stirring all the time until all the cheese is incorporated and melted. In a cup mix the cornflour with the kirsch, and pour, stirring, into the hot fondue. Add pepper and nutmeg to taste. Keep the heat low—the fondue is liable to curdle if it boils fast —and cook for 3 more minutes. It should be thick and creamy.

Fondue can be made with cheddar and cider instead of gruyère and wine.

On the day before
Assemble all the utensils and ingredients for the fondue.

Apart from perhaps grating the cheese, no preparation for the fondue is needed as the cooking is done at the table. If a salad or dessert is to be served after the fondue, these may need some advance work.

4 · Buffet Parties

To my mind this is much the most pleasant way of entertaining a lot of people at once—much more civilized than cocktail parties, where everyone ends up shouting harder than everyone else; and more fun than a big sit-down dinner, where escaping from a boring neighbour is not possible. But it is important that there should be *some* seating—if one has enough for half the guests, that will do: many men prefer to stand anyway, and with to-ing and fro-ing to the buffet, seats are constantly vacated and slipped into by other guests. There should also be somewhere (mantelshelf, window seat, coffee table) for guests to rest their glasses while they deal with their plates.

Seating and space A room about 15 ft × 12 ft with a large sofa and four chairs can hold fifteen to twenty people for a party with the buffet table set up in one corner, or slightly more if the dining room is used for the buffet. A room 25 ft × 15 ft comfortably holds forty people, but a few small chairs to supplement the seating might have to be hired. I say 'a few' because I have often seen back stairs and landings crammed with unwanted hired chairs (and they are not cheap) because the hostess has felt that a chair per person is vital—and then found that they made her house look like a church hall. It is a good idea to clear the room of all *unnecessary* objects like the television and record stands, and to take out any large chairs that only one person can use. Chesterfield chairs should stay because three people can sit on one chair without danger of capsizing.

Hiring china etc Anything from candelabra to ashtrays can be hired, but if this can be avoided a lot of money is saved. Anyway, unless the party is extraordinarily grand, nothing need match—if the food looks good, no-one will look at the plates. If you are hiring cutlery (silverware) be careful that some of your own silver does not go back with the hire contractors'.

Planning the menu It is not worth wearing yourself out stuffing a turkey with a goose stuffed with a duck stuffed with a chicken stuffed with a pigeon stuffed with a quail, and other gastronomic follies, so in this book I have not included anything more elaborate than a decorated salmon. As long as the *pièce de résistance* is beautifully cooked, I think a little 'padding' in the way of bought salamis, patés, and liver sausage is fine. Food snobs have become so dreary, one would believe that *nothing* bought ready-made is permissible.

Hot food, unless there is staff and plenty of hot-cupboard space, is not practicable for more than about thirty people. But a hot soup (which, if hot enough, can be served in unheated cups) or hot potatoes will take the slight feeling of bleakness off a completely cold table.

Calculating the quantities If two or three dishes are to be offered, calculate how many people each dish would serve. Add up the helpings and as long as they come to more than your guest list, you have catered well. Too much food is a much more usual problem than too little, with the family eating cold turkey for a week after the party. It is not necessary for every guest to have every dish. He will not want to anyway, and if he does have a little of everything, it will have to be a very little or he will not get it all on his plate. The one exception to this rule is that if there is to be a *hot* dish, almost everyone will have a fair helping of that, and may then go on to the cold food.

I would not reckon on more than one plate and fork to each person. Even if two or three different sorts of food are on the buffet (say fish mousse, cold chicken, salads), people seldom bother with a clean plate, simply helping themselves to a bit of everything onto one plate.

Check lists, page 187.

SIMPLE INEXPENSIVE BUFFET FOR 20

Frankfurter, tomato and baked
  bean casserole
Salad Niçoise
Stuffed courgettes (zucchini)
Watercress and chicory salad
Hot new potatoes with chive and
  sour cream dressing
Coffee rum tipsy cake
Tangerines in caramel sauce

(Preparation on the day before follows recipes.)

See also *Calculating the quantities*, page 75.

Beer, particularly lager, would be the perfect drink, but for non-beer drinkers a rosé from the Tavel district of Provence would be excellent.

Frankfurter, tomato and baked bean casserole (serves 5)
(Do four times the quantity for 20)
8 frankfurters
3 slices lean bacon
1 lb/½ kilo can baked beans
1 large onion
3 tomatoes, skinned and sliced
1 teaspoon curry powder
Salt and pepper
1 oz/30 grams/2 tablespoons butter

Slice the onion and fry in butter until soft and transparent, and just beginning to colour. Add bacon, cut in pieces, and fry for one more minute. Stir in curry powder; fry another minute. Add the frankfurters, sliced, and the baked beans. Season with pepper and a little salt if necessary. Tip everything into a casserole, arrange the tomato slices on top, and bake at 300°F, gas mark 2 for ½ hour.

Salad Niçoise (serves 6)
(Do three times the quantity for 20)
3 tomatoes, skinned and quartered
½ mild onion, thinly sliced
1 green pepper, seeded and sliced
12 radishes, washed, and topped and
  tailed
1 lettuce heart
2 sticks celery, sliced
½ lb/250 grams cooked french (green)
  beans
1 small can tuna fish
6 anchovy fillets, split lengthwise
2 hard-boiled eggs, quartered
  lengthwise
8 black olives

Dressing
1 tablespoon wine vinegar
4 tablespoons olive oil
Salt, black pepper; ½ clove garlic,
  crushed
12 leaves fresh basil, roughly chopped
  (or 2 teaspoons dried basil)

Put all the dressing ingredients into a bowl and whisk well. Reserving a few olives, radishes, tomato quarters and anchovy fillets for the top, put all the rest of the salad ingredients into a large salad bowl. Turn them gently in the dressing. Do not over-mix. Put the reserved olives, radishes etc., on top.

76

Stuffed courgettes (zucchini) (serves 4)
(Do five times the quantity for 20)

4 large courgettes
1 onion, chopped finely
1 small green pepper, finely chopped
4 tomatoes, skinned and chopped
¼ lb/100 grams minced beef, pork or veal
½ glass white wine
2 tablespoons fresh white breadcrumbs
Salt and black pepper
Olive oil

Set the oven at 350°F, gas mark 4. Oil the bottom of a roasting pan. Cut courgettes in half lengthwise and scoop out most of the flesh, leaving boat-shaped skins. Heat a dessertspoon of olive oil in a frying pan and fry the onion gently until transparent. Add the green pepper and the meat. Fry for 5 minutes, stirring. Add the courgette flesh, chopped, and the skinned and chopped tomatoes. Pour in the wine and boil fast, stirring until you have a fairly moist but not liquid mixture. Fill into the courgette-halves, and lay them in the roasting pan. Sprinkle the tops with the breadcrumbs, and with olive oil. Bake for ½ hour, or until the courgette skins are soft and the crumbs brown. Serve hot or cold.

Watercress and chicory salad (serves 6)
(Do three times the quantity for 20)

2 bunches watercress
1 lb/½ kilo chicory
4 tablespoons French dressing (see page 71)

Wash the watercress, discarding the tough stalks. Drain well. Wipe the chicory and separate into leaves. At the last minute toss the salad in the dressing.

Hot new potatoes with chive and sour cream dressing (serves 6)
(Do three times the quantity for 20)

3 lb/1½ kilos new potatoes, scrubbed
1 bunch chives, chopped
1 carton sour cream (about 5 fl. oz/⅛ litre)
Salt, black pepper

Combine the sour cream with the chives, and plenty of salt and black pepper. Boil the potatoes in salted water, and when tender, drain them. Toss them in the sour cream just before serving.

Coffee rum tipsy cake (serves 6)
(Do four times the quantity of cake, and twice the quantity of butter icing and cream, for 20 people)

2 plain sponge cakes or 2 packets small sponge cakes
3 heaped tablespoons instant coffee
4 tablespoons sugar
6 fl. oz/a good ¼ litre boiling water
1 tablespoon rum
3 oz/80 grams/6 tablespoons butter
5 oz/150 grams/1 cup icing (confectioners') sugar
½ pint/¼ litre/10 fl. oz thick cream
2 oz/50 grams/½ cup whole blanched almonds

Break up the cakes roughly and put in a large bowl. Boil the water, pour onto the coffee and sugar, and stir until the sugar has dissolved. Add the rum, and pour over the cake. Do not mix it in too much (the cake should retain a 'marbled' look, half white, half brown) but turn with a metal spoon. Press the cake into a mixing bowl, and leave it with a weight on top (a 2 lb can of fruit standing on a side plate will do) while you make the icing. Beat the icing sugar and butter together until very light and creamy. Whip the cream until just firm enough to hold its shape. Brown the nuts under the grill. Unmould the cake onto a plate. Using a pallet-knife dipped in hot water, spread the butter icing over the cake. Then spread a layer of whipped cream over the icing, and stick the almonds into the cream.

Tangerines in caramel sauce (serves 6)
(For 20 people use 40 tangerines and twice the amount of sauce in the recipe)

12 satsumas, tangerines, or mandarin
    oranges
8 oz/250 grams/1 cup granulated sugar
1 pint/¾ litre/20 fl. oz water

Peel the tangerines and remove as much pith as possible, while keeping the fruit whole. Put them into a glass bowl. In a heavy saucepan melt 4 oz of the sugar slowly. When it is bubbly and brown, pour on the water. It will fizz dangerously, so take care. Add the rest of the sugar. Re-boil, stirring, and then boil the sauce until it is of a syrupy consistency. When cool pour over the tangerines, and chill before serving. A tablespoon of liqueur such as Cointreau, Van der Hum or Grand Marnier is a magical addition. (See page 68.)

On the day before

Frankfurter, tomato and baked bean casserole Make completely, and keep in a cool place.
Salad Niçoise Prepare all the salad ingredients, but keep them separately wrapped in polythene or in plastic boxes in the refrigerator. Make the dressing. Do not put everything together and toss in the dressing until the last convenient moment.
Stuffed courgettes (zucchini) Make completely, and keep in a cool place.
Watercress and chicory salad Make the dressing, but do not mix the salad until the day of the party. It can be prepared about eight hours in advance and the dressing added an hour or two before the arrival of the guests.
Hot new potatoes with chives and sour cream dressing Scrub the potatoes, and leave them in a polythene bag or in cold water overnight. Make the dressing. Boil the potatoes at the last minute if you can. Alternatively, they can be boiled, cooled, and reheated in the oven in a little butter when needed. Add the dressing when serving.
Coffee rum tipsy cake Make the cake, cover with icing, and keep overnight in the refrigerator or a cool place. Brown the almonds. On the morning of the party, cover the cake with the cream and add the almonds.
Tangerines in caramel sauce Make completely. Before serving, gently turn the tangerines over in the syrup to get the shiny sides up.

BUFFET FOR 30, SLIGHTLY GRANDER

Crab and celery cup
Canneloni with spinach and
    mushroom filling
Chicken Elizabeth
Rice salad Niçoise
Mixed bean salad with almonds

Raspberry vacherin
Chocolate mousse

(*Preparation on the day before follows recipes.*)

See also *Calculating the quantities*, page 75.

Serve a Riesling or an Italian red wine, or both.

Crab and celery cup (serves 6)
(For 30, do five times the quantities given)

½ lb/250 grams white cooked crab
    meat (canned or frozen is fine)
2 sticks celery
½ eating apple

Drain the crab, reserving the juice. Mix together the mayonnaise, cream and enough of the crab liquid to make a soft but still fairly thick sauce. Season with tabasco, salt and pepper. Chop the

¼ pint/⅛ litre/5 fl. oz mayonnaise
  (see page 19)
2 tablespoons cream
Finely grated rind and juice of half
  a lemon
Black pepper, salt
Dash of tabasco sauce
Paprika

apple and celery finely, and mix with the crab. Stir in the lemon juice and rind, and salt and pepper to taste. Spoon into goblets, and top each with a large dessertspoonful of sauce. Sprinkle with paprika.

Canneloni with spinach and mushroom filling (serves 6)
(Do four times the quantity for 30 people)

12 canneloni (the bought ones can be
  very good, and thin pancakes are an
  excellent substitute)
2 lb/1½ kilos fresh spinach, well
  washed, with stalks removed
½ lb/250 grams flat black mushrooms,
  sliced
2 oz/50 grams/½ cup grated cheddar
  cheese
½ pint/¼ litre/10 fl. oz cream (or
  creamy white sauce)
2 oz/50 grams/4 tablespoons butter
Salt and pepper

Put the wet spinach in a large saucepan and put on the lid. Cook gently for 5 minutes, stirring occasionally. Drain well, pressing out the moisture. Turn onto a board and chop roughly. Melt the butter, add the sliced mushrooms, and fry gently until tender. Add the spinach, salt and pepper. Fill the mixture into the canneloni, or roll up in the pancakes. Lay them in a buttered fireproof dish, pour over the cream, and sprinkle the cheese on top. Bake in the oven until the canneloni are tender (about 35 minutes at 350°F, gas mark 4). If using pancakes you need only reheat the dish and get the cheese slightly browned (about 15 minutes).

Chicken Elizabeth (serves 8)
(Do three times the quantity for 30 people)
This dish (often called Coronation Chicken) was devised by the London Cordon Bleu Cookery School when asked to cater for 300 international guests at a lunch on Coronation Day. It is quite delicious if carefully made; but every ingredient matters, and taking short cuts will produce a less delicate and subtle flavour.

Two 3 lb/1½ kilo roasting chickens
Bunch of watercress
¾ pint/1½ litre/15 fl. oz Elizabeth sauce
  (see below)

Elizabeth sauce
1 tablespoon oil
1 small onion, chopped
1 dessertspoon curry powder
1 teaspoon tomato purée
1 wine-glass red wine
½ wine-glass water
Bayleaf
2 slices lemon, and a dessertspoon
  lemon juice
1 tablespoon apricot jam
¾ pint/½ litre/15 fl. oz mayonnaise
4 tablespoons lightly whipped cream

Gently poach the chickens in chicken stock until tender. Then make the Elizabeth sauce as follows.

Cook the onion gently for 4 minutes in the oil. Add the curry powder and fry gently for another minute. Add tomato purée, wine, water, bayleaf, salt, pepper, jam, lemon slices and juice, and simmer for 8 minutes. Strain, pushing as much as possible through the sieve. Use this sauce to flavour the mayonnaise to the desired strength, lightening it by adding the whipped cream. Adjust seasoning.
Take the flesh from the chicken bones, and when it is cold mix with the sauce, keeping a little sauce back for evenly coating the top. Serve surrounded by a rice salad, and garnished with watercress.

Rice salad (serves 8)
(Do three times the quantity for 30)
Almost any vegetables can be added to cold cooked rice to make a salad, but it is important to have approximately equal quantities of rice and vegetables, or the result may be lifeless and stodgy. The dressing should moisten, not soak, the dish.

1 large cupful patna-type (long grain) rice
1 small green pepper, seeded and chopped
1 stick celery
½ cucumber peeled
2 tomatoes
Few black olives
1 small packet frozen mixed vegetables or peas
Finely chopped parsley, mint, chives or dill

For the dressing
3 dessertspoons salad oil
1 dessertspoon vinegar
1 onion, finely chopped
Salt and pepper

Boil the rice in plenty of water until just tender (about ten minutes). Rinse under the cold tap, and leave to drain well. Cook the packet of vegetables. Chop the pepper, celery and cucumber. Plunge the tomatoes into boiling water for 5 seconds so that they will peel easily. Peel them and cut into quarters. Put the dressing ingredients into a screwtop jar and shake well. Mix everything together and add salt and pepper if necessary. Pile onto a dish and decorate with the olives and tomato pieces. (If not used round a main dish, rice salad looks pretty when turned out of a ring mould, jelly mould, or even a mixing bowl: push it down firmly in the oiled mould, then invert it onto a dish.)

Mixed bean salad with almonds (serves 10)
(Do three times the quantity for 30 people)

1 large can flageolet beans
1 lb/½ kilo cooked broad (Lima) beans (frozen or canned are fine)
1 can butter beans
1 lb/½ kilo fresh french (green) beans
2 oz/50 grams/½ cup flaked almonds
1 tablespoon olive oil
French dressing (see page 71)
1 dessertspoon each chopped chives, parsley and mint
1 small clove garlic, crushed

Drain the canned beans well. It may be necessary to rinse the flageolets in cold water to remove some of the starchy liquid. Cook the french (green) beans in salted water until just tender. Drain them and allow to cool. Fry the almonds in the oil until brown. Cool. Add the herbs and garlic to the french dressing. Gently combine all the beans and put them into a salad bowl. Pour on the dressing, and scatter over the almonds.

Raspberry vacherin (serves 8)
(Make three for 30 people)

4 egg whites
8 oz/230 grams/1 cup caster (powdered) sugar
1 lb/½ kilo raspberries
Icing (confectioners') sugar
½ pint/¼ litre/10 fl. oz thick cream
¼ pint/⅛ litre/5 fl. oz thin cream
1 tablespoon Cointreau

To make the meringue base set the oven at 250°F, gas mark ½. Oil a large sheet of greaseproof (waxed) paper and put it on a baking tray. Whip the whites until very stiff, fold in half the caster sugar, and beat again until the mixture is thick, very glossy, and will hold its shape stiffly. Fold in the rest of the caster sugar. Spread two even-sized rounds of meringue on the oiled paper, not more than 1 in. thick. Bake for about 2 hours, or until the meringue is quite dry and the paper will peel off the underside easily. Remove, and allow to cool. Whip the thick cream, stir in the thin cream, and whip again until thick. Sandwich the two meringue rounds with half the cream, and pipe the other half in rosettes round the edge of the top layer. Pile the raspberries in the middle. At the last minute dust the top with icing sugar.

Chocolate mousse (serves 6)
(For 30 people, make four times the amount, but in two separate lots)

8 oz/250 grams sweetened chocolate
¼ pint/⅛ litre/5 fl. oz water
1½ oz/40 grams/3 tablespoons butter
1 tablespoon rum
4 eggs

Break up the chocolate and put in a saucepan. Add the water. Boil, stirring until it is smooth and has the consistency of thick cream. Cool slightly and stir in the rum and the butter. Separate the eggs. Beat the yolks into the chocolate. Whisk the whites until stiff but not dry-looking, and fold into the mixture. Pour into individual pots, glasses or coffee cups. Refrigerate overnight. The mousses can be decorated with whipped cream or chopped nuts, but classically they are served as they are. For a lighter, less rich mousse, leave out the egg yolks.

On the day before
Crab and celery cup Make the mixture without the celery, and keep it covered in the refrigerator. Chop the celery and leave in a bowl of cold water. Next morning drain the celery and finish making the cup. Cover each glass with polythene and keep chilled until just before the party.
Canneloni with spinach and mushroom Make completely and keep in a cool place. Reheat in the oven when needed.
Chicken Elizabeth Prepare the chicken and the sauce, but do not combine them or arrange them for serving until the day of the party. Then cover the dish with polythene to prevent the mayonnaise forming a skin.
Rice salad Niçoise Make the salad and the dressing, but do not combine until the morning of the party.
Mixed bean salad with almonds Make the salad and the dressing, but do not combine until the next morning.
Raspberry vacherin Make the meringue rounds. If possible buy the raspberries only on the day of the party. The vacherin can be filled eight hours before it is to be eaten.
Chocolate mousse This is best made the day before, and in any case should be made at least four hours in advance.

CLASSIC BUFFET FOR 80

Sugar-baked (glazed) ham
Roast stuffed turkey
Filet de boeuf en croûte
Roast crown of lamb
Cold duck à l'orange
Boiled tongue
Salmon mayonnaise
Pork pie
Green salad
New potato salad with mustard
   dressing and olives
Tomato, onion and pimento salad
(*continued overleaf*)

(*Preparation on the day before follows recipes.*)
Serve hock or claret, or both.

Trifle
Treacle tart
Fruit salad

If this menu is exactly followed, with each *main* dish done precisely as in the recipe, there will be the right amount of food for 80 people—with a decent but not extravagant amount left over. The salads and puddings must be quadrupled. 4 pints of cream would be adequate for the desserts and the coffee. If variations on the menu are undertaken (or if the number of guests is substantially greater or less than 80), quantities should be carefully calculated. See page 75.

Sugar-baked (glazed) ham (serves 12)

One 14 lb/8 kilo raw ham or gammon, green or smoked
1 carrot, sliced
1 onion
1 sprig or pinch thyme
1 bunch parsley
1 bayleaf
1 stick of celery
Small handful of peppercorns (about 20)
½ lb/250 grams/1½ cups demerara (granulated brown) sugar
Cloves

Put the ham into a very large saucepan or fish kettle and cover completely with water. If the ham is very salty it should be soaked overnight, and the water changed the next day; if it is mild it should not need preliminary soaking (if you are unsure, ask the grocer's opinion when you buy it). Add the onion, carrot, thyme, parsley, bayleaf, celery and peppercorns. Cover, and bring slowly to the boil. Simmer for 3½ hours, or until the meat has shrunk back from the bone and a skewer will penetrate the ham easily. Allow to cool in the liquid. Before the ham is quite cold, lift it out and skin it, leaving the fat on. With a knife cut a criss-cross pattern all over the fat. Press a layer of sugar over the top and sides of the ham and stick a clove into each of the diamond shapes formed by the criss-cross marking. Lift into a roasting pan, and pour 1 pint water in at the side to stop the sugar burning and sticking to the pan. Put into a hot oven (450°F, gas mark 8) for 10 minutes, or until the sugar has slightly melted and browned. Remove and allow to cool. Tie a ham frill (bought or home-made—see page 10) round the bone before serving.

Roast stuffed turkey

See recipe on page 172, omitting the gravy as the bird is to be served cold.

Filet de boeuf en croûte (serves 10)

4 lb/2 kilos piece of fillet, from the thick end
2 oz/50 grams/4 tablespoons butter
½ lb/250 grams flat mushrooms, sliced
1 large onion, chopped
Small clove garlic, crushed (optional)
French mustard
½ lb/250 grams puff pastry (see next recipe—or buy it frozen)
1 egg, beaten

Skin the fillet and put it in a hot oven for ½ hour (450°F, gas mark 8). Take out and allow to cool but do not turn the oven off. Melt the butter in a large saucepan and add the chopped onion. Cook gently until transparent. Add the mushrooms (and the garlic if used) and fry for a further 6 minutes, stirring. Allow to cool. Spread the fillet thinly with the mustard. Roll out the pastry into a large rectangle about 15 ins × 13 ins. This will

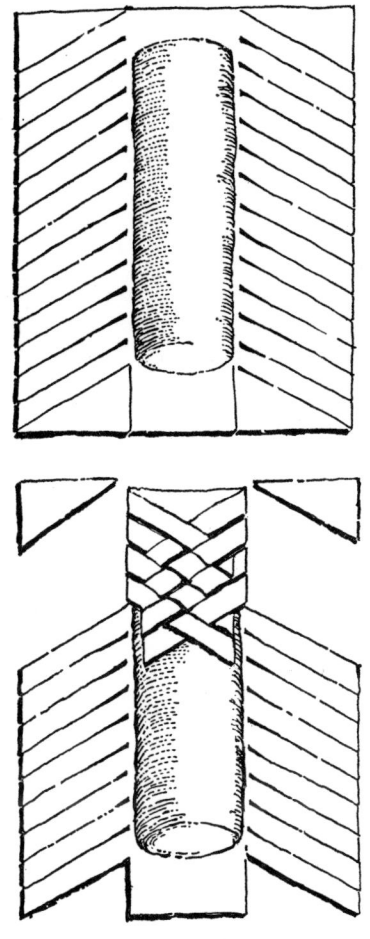

mean the pastry is very thin. Now cut through the pastry as indicated in the diagram. Then lay the fillet down the middle of the pastry (on the uncut portion). Carefully spoon the mushroom and onion mixture onto the top of the fillet, taking care not to drop it on the side strips of pastry. Now plait (braid) the strands of pastry over the top of the fillet, as in the diagram. It may be necessary to 'patch' the ends with a solid piece of pastry. Do not be concerned if the result is not very neat, or if there are gaps between the ribbons of pastry—it will look fine when it comes out of the oven. Brush all over with egg and return it to the same hot oven for twenty minutes, or until the pastry is very deep brown and shiny. Serve hot or cold. (This recipe assumes that rare beef is desired, but longer cooking in the first instance—without the pastry—will ensure a more well-done fillet. For medium beef give it a further 10 minutes; for well-done beef a further twenty, making 50 minutes in all. If the beef is to be served cold, it looks attractive surrounded by chopped aspic: see plate on page 132. If served hot it should be carved at the table, or the juice will be lost and the meat may have a grey unappetising look.

Puff pastry

8 oz/230 grams/1¾ cups plain flour
1 oz/30 grams/2 tablespoons lard
5–7 oz/140–200 grams/1–1½ cups butter
Just under ¼ pint/⅛ litre/5 fl. oz water

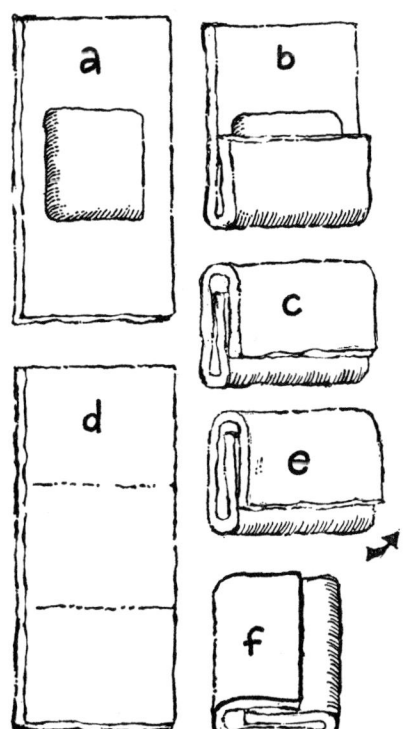

If you have never made puff pastry before, use 5 oz butter: this will give a normal pastry. If you have some experience, 7 oz will produce a lighter, very rich pastry.

Sift the flour with a pinch of salt. Rub in the lard. Add the cold water and mix with a knife to a doughy consistency. Turn onto the table and knead until smooth. Wrap in a cloth and leave in the refrigerator for 30 minutes to relax.

What follows is illustrated here. Lightly flour the table and roll the dough into a rectangle about 5 ins × 10 ins. Tap the butter lightly with a rolling pin to get it into a flattened block about 4 ins × 3 ins. Put the butter on the rectangle of pastry (a) and fold both ends over to enclose it (b and c). Press the sides together to prevent the butter escaping. Now tap the pastry parcel sharply with the rolling pin to flatten the butter a little; and then roll out, quickly and lightly, until the pastry is three times as long as it is wide (d). Fold it very evenly in three (e), and give it a 90° turn to the right so that the folded, closed edge is on your left (f). It should now look rather like a closed book with the loose flap of pastry on your right. Roll out again as before, fold in three as before and give it a turn to the right as before. Now the pastry has had two 'rolls and folds' and it should be put to rest in a cool place for 30 minutes or so. The rolling and folding must be repeated twice more, the pastry again rested, and then again given two more rolls and folds. This makes a total of six. If the butter is still very streaky roll and fold it once more.

Roast crown of lamb (serves 8)

One 21-bone crown of lamb (ask the butcher to use three 7-bone best end racks)
2 oz/50 grams/4 tablespoons butter
Good sprig of rosemary
Watercress
(21 paper cutlet frills)
(1 ham frill, page 10)

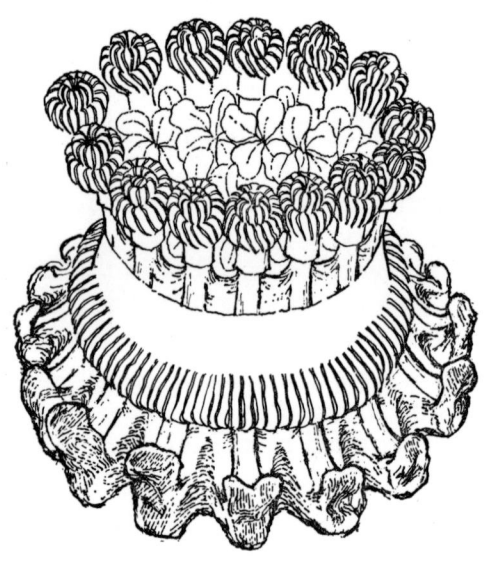

Crown roasts are often filled with a veal force-meat stuffing, but they need not be, and I prefer to cook them without stuffing because the force-meat takes so long to cook that the lamb is generally overdone by the time the middle of the stuffing is cooked. Ask the butcher to use the trimmings from the best-ends (instead of the stuffing) to hold the crown in place. Set the oven at 400°F, gas mark 6. Melt the butter. Add the crumbled rosemary. Put the crown into a roasting tin and pour over the butter. Wet some grease-proof (waxed) paper and wrap the exposed bones with it, using tin-foil over the top to hold it on—this is to prevent the bones burning. It is easier to wrap 6–7 bones at a time than to cover the whole crown. Roast, basting occasionally, for 1 hour. Now remove the supporting fat and meat from the middle. Return the empty crown to the oven for a further $\frac{1}{2}$–1 hour. After $\frac{1}{2}$ hour it will be pink, but many people prefer lamb well-done. When cooked to the desired degree, gravy can be made in the usual way (see Arabian Lamb recipe, page 128). If it is for a cold meal, gravy is not necessary, but the crown should be carved and re-formed into a crown shape and kept together with a ham frill. When carving the crown all the fat should be cut away, as cold lamb fat is un-appetising. Keep the cutlets in their correct order when trimming them, or it will be difficult to get them into the crown shape again. Re-form the crown on the plate it is to be served from, for moving it may prove hazardous. Encircle with the ham frill and put the paper frills on the cutlet bones. Fill the centre with a large bunch of water-cress.

Cold duck à l'orange (serves 8)

Two 6 lb/3 kilo ducklings, roasted and
cooled (see notes on roasting ducks
in the recipe for Leith's duckling,
page 62)
French dressing (see page 71)
2 oranges
1 bunch watercress

Joint the birds, and lay the pieces on a flat dish. Sprinkle the juice of one orange over them, and then spoon a teaspoon of french dressing onto each piece of duck. Halve the other orange and cut it into slices—with the skin on. Surround the duck with them. Break the stalks from the watercress and plant the sprigs between the joints of duck.

Boiled tongue (serves about 10)

1 large or two small salted ox tongues
1 carrot, sliced
1 onion, sliced
1 stick celery, sliced
1 bunch parsley
Sprig or pinch of thyme
1 bayleaf
About 20 peppercorns
Cucumber slices and black olives for
garnish

Soak the tongue overnight in cold water. Place in a deep saucepan, and cover with fresh water. Add the other ingredients (except the garnishes). Bring to the boil, skim, cover and cook gently for 2 hours or until the tongue is very tender. Allow to cool in the liquid, but while still just warm remove the skin. Arrange the tongue on a plate, with a few slices cut from it and the rest uncut, ready to be carved as needed. Garnish with a few black olives and cucumber slices.

Salmon mayonnaise (serves 12)

1 whole fresh salmon, about 8 lb
(4 kilos) weight, gutted, and with the
fins trimmed off

For the courtbouillon
1 pint/¼ litre/10 fl. oz malt vinegar
1 carrot, sliced
1 onion, sliced
1 stick celery
1 bunch parsley
1 pinch or sprig thyme
2 bayleaves
About 20 peppercorns
Salt
¼ pint/⅛ litre/5 fl. oz oil

For garnish
1 cucumber
2 lemons
1 bunch watercress

Half fill a fish kettle, large enough to take the whole salmon, with water. Add the courtbouillon ingredients. Bring to the boil. Boil fast for 10 minutes, and allow to cool. Put in the salmon. Reheat gently, never allowing the water to boil again. Poach the salmon until tender—about an hour, depending on the size of the fish. Test with a skewer: it should glide easily in, and the fish should feel firm to the touch. Cool the salmon in the water. When cold, lift out and place on a salmon dish. Skin one side first, and then carefully turn the fish over and skin the second side. Many people object to the brownish flesh near the bones, but its taste is indistinguishable from the pink, and scraping it off often spoils the smoothness of the fish. Decorate the salmon with alternate overlapping slices of cucumber and lemon, and put a line of watercress down the belly to hide the rather untidy slit where the fish has been cleaned. (See plate on page 132.) Serve with mayonnaise (page 19). If the mayonnaise is really stiff, and the weather not too warm, it can be piped down the centre of the fish instead of, or as well as, the cucumber and lemon garnish.

 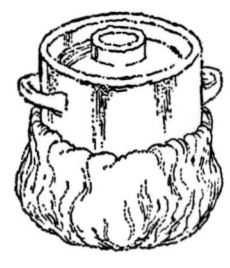 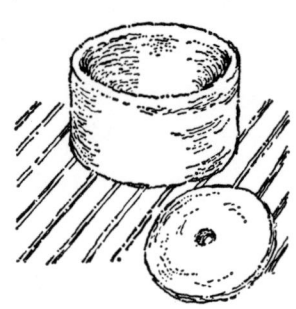 

Pork pie (serves 8)

This pie must be started at least a day in advance and will come to no harm if made several days before, and kept in the refrigerator.

For the jelly
1 lb/½ kilo broken pork bones
3 pints/2¼ litres water
1 onion, sliced
1 stick celery
1 pinch or sprig of thyme
1 bunch parsley
1 bayleaf

For the filling
2 lb/1 kilo fresh pork, containing
   some fat
1 pig's kidney
1 small teaspoon salt
Pinch cayenne pepper
Plenty of freshly ground black pepper

For the crust
2 lb/1 kilo/6½ cups plain flour
¼ pint /⅛litre/5 fl. oz milk
Just under ¼ pint/⅛ litre/5 fl. oz water
½ lb/230 grams/1 cup lard
Beaten egg

Prepare the stock for the jelly the day before making the pie. Put the bones in a saucepan and cover with the 3 pints of water. Bring to the boil and skim carefully. Add all the other jelly ingredients, cover and simmer very gently all day, skimming occasionally. When it is reduced to about 1 pint liquid, strain and allow it to cool. When cold and set, remove the fat from the top. Cut the meat, including the kidney, into small squares and mix with the seasonings. Put aside.

Warm the flour in the oven; then rub in half the lard. Heat the rest of the lard with the milk and water in a saucepan. When the lard has melted, cool to blood temperature. Pour onto the flour mixture and, first with a knife and then with one hand, mix to a soft dough. Reserve a small piece of pastry for the two lids, and keep it covered and in a warm place. Working quickly, divide the rest into two, and mould each piece into a pork-pie shape: it can be shaped round the bottom of a large glass jar or small straight-sided saucepan, and the dough will stay soft if the jar or saucepan is warmed (see drawing). When each pie 'cup' is shaped, remove it from the jar or saucepan and place on a baking sheet. As the pastry cools it will get firmer.

Fill the pies with the seasoned meat and cover with the pastry lids, pressing the edges together and making a neat hole in the middle of each lid. Brush with the beaten egg. Bake for 2 hours in a low oven (325°F, gas mark 3). After the first hour it may be necessary to cover the pies with damp greaseproof paper to prevent too much browning. Take the pies out of the oven, and allow them to get quite cold. Warm the jelly just sufficiently to melt it—no more—and, using a funnel, fill up the pies through the hole in the crust. (If in melting the jelly you have allowed it to become at all warm, cool it by standing the saucepan in cold water.) Put the pies into the refrigerator for the jelly to re-set.

Green salad

See page 71.

New potato salad with mustard dressing and olives (serves 10)

4 lb/2 kilos very small new potatoes,
  well scrubbed
1 oz/30 grams/¼ cup black olives,
  stoned
1 oz/30 grams/¼ cup green olives,
  stoned

For the dressing
1 tablespoon brown sugar
1 dessertspoon flour
1 teaspoon salt
1 dessertspoon french mustard
¼ pint/⅛ litre/5 fl. oz malt vinegar
3 tablespoons water
1 oz/30 grams/2 tablespoons butter
¼ pint/⅛ litre/5 fl. oz creamy milk

To make the dressing, mix the dry ingredients together in a heavy saucepan. Mix in the mustard, then gradually stir in the vinegar and water. Bring to the boil, stirring, and simmer for at least 10 minutes, adding more water if the mixture is so thick it is likely to burn. It should have the consistency of half-whipped cream. Remove from the heat and stir in the butter. When cold, add the milk, and beat until smooth.

Boil the potatoes in salted water until just tender and drain them. As soon as they are dry, but still very hot, toss them in the dressing. When cold turn them into a salad bowl, and scatter the olives on top.

Tomato, onion, and pimento salad (serves 10)

4 lb/2 kilos tomatoes
1 large spanish onion
1 can red pimento caps
¼ pint/⅛ litre/5 fl. oz french dressing
  (page 71)
1 teaspoon sugar

Plunge the tomatoes into boiling water for 5 seconds. Skin them, and cut them into quarters. Slice the onion into thin rings, using a stainless steel knife to prevent discolouration. Drain the water from the can of pimento and reserve it. Mix the sugar, french dressing and pimento liquid together. Slice the pimentos. Put the tomatoes, onions and pimento into a bowl and pour over the dressing.

Trifle (serves 5)

(For 80 people, provided there are to be two other desserts as well, make 6 trifles)
The French and Italians rather rudely call this delicious pudding 'English Soup'—but they eat it almost as much as the English. The best trifle *is* a little soupy—soft and creamy. As with Pêche Melba, bad cooks have spoilt its good name and now one is nervous that some stodge containing red jelly, canned fruit and packet custard will appear. But a classic rich trifle, with a hint of sherry or brandy, is sublime.

1 sponge cake, preferably stale
4 tablespoons sherry
2 tablespoons brandy
Raspberry jam
1 pint/¾ litre/20 fl. oz milk
4 egg yolks
2 tablespoons sugar
2 drops vanilla essence
½ pint/¼ litre/10 fl. oz thick cream
1 oz/30 grams/¼ cup split almonds
A few ratafia biscuits (optional)
Angelica
6 glacé cherries

Cut the sponge cake into thin pieces. Spread each sparingly with jam. Pile them into a glass dish. Pour over the sherry and brandy, and leave to soak while you prepare the custard. Put the milk, sugar and vanilla into a saucepan and bring to the point of boiling. In a large bowl lightly beat the yolks with a fork. Pour the scalding milk onto them, stirring with a wooden spoon. Return the custard to the pan, and carefully re-heat it, stirring all the time, until it thickens enough to coat the back of the spoon. Care must be taken not to boil the custard, lest it curdle. Strain onto the cake and leave to get quite cold. Whip the cream until fairly stiff and spread or pipe over the trifle. Decorate with the blanched almonds, glacé cherries, angelica cut into diamond-shapes, and the ratafia biscuits.

Treacle tart (serves 6)
(For 80 people, provided there are to be two other desserts as well, make 4 tarts)

For the rich shortcrust pastry
8 oz/230 grams/1¾ cups plain flour
Pinch salt
5 oz/140 grams/10 tablespoons butter
1 dessertspoon caster (powdered)
    sugar
Squeeze lemon juice
2–3 tablespoons very cold water
1 egg yolk

For the filling
4 heaped tablespoons golden syrup
3 heaped tablespoons fresh white
    breadcrumbs
Grated rind of ½ lemon and a
    dessertspoon of the juice

Sift the flour with the salt. Rub in the butter until the mixture looks like fine breadcrumbs. Add the sugar. Mix the yolk with half the water and the lemon juice, and add to the flour. Mix to a firm dough—first with a knife, and finally with one hand. It may be necessary to add the rest of the water, but the pastry should not be too damp. (Though crumbly pastry is more difficult to handle, it produces a shorter, less tough result.) Roll the pastry out to ¼ inch thick, and line a pie plate or flan ring with it. Prick the bottom with a fork. Sprinkle the crumbs evenly on the bottom. Heat the syrup with the lemon juice and rind to make it a little runny. Pour into the pastry case. Bake in a moderate oven (375°F, gas mark 5) for about 30 minutes or until the filling is almost set, and the edge of the pastry is brown. The filling should be a little on the soft side if the tart is to be eaten cold, because it hardens as it cools.

Fruit salad (serves 10)
(If this is to be the only dessert, calculate between 2 and 3 pieces of fruit per head. If you are catering for 80 and there are to be two other desserts as well, make three times the quantity in the recipe)

2 oranges
1 bunch black grapes
1 bunch white grapes
1 small melon
1 small pineapple
4 plums
4 apricots
2 dessert apples
2 pears
4 bananas
½ lb/¼ kilo strawberries
1 lb/½ kilo/2 cups sugar
1 pint/¾ litre/20 fl. oz water
1 tablespoon kirsch (optional)

Thinly pare the outside rind of one orange and put this rind into a saucepan with the sugar and water. Bring to the boil, and cook until a little of the syrup feels sticky between the thumb and forefinger. Strain and allow to cool. Prepare all the fruit, leaving till last the apples and bananas (which would go brown if left in the air). By the time you get to them, the syrup should be cool enough for the fruit to be put straight into it. Peel the oranges with a knife as you would an apple, making sure all the pith is removed, and slice them. Halve and seed the grapes (peel them only if they have spotty or very tough skins); cut the melon into cubes or balls, and the pineapple into thin strips—removing the woody middle. Cut the plums into segments, leaving the skin on, and finally peel and slice the apricots, pears, apples and bananas. Turn everything over in the syrup, making sure all the fruit is well coated. Lastly hull the strawberries, and place them on top. If the fruit salad is too sweet a little lemon juice may be added. Kirsch is a good addition, as it both cuts the sweetness and gives the dish a luxury 'lift'.

On the days before

Most of this menu can be done well in advance. The *pork pies* need to be started two days before the party, and providing there is enough refrigeration or cold larder space, the *ham, turkey, beef, tongue* and *crown of lamb* could also be cooked two days ahead. When they are quite cold, wrap them well in polythene to prevent any drying out. *The duck* should be cooked the day before, and the dressing made. Carve the duck the next morning, and arrange on a plate with the watercress. Cover with polythene. (Do not pour on the dressing until setting out the food on the buffet). *The salmon* should be poached the day before, and left in its liquid overnight. It may be decorated in the morning and covered in polythene until the last minute. Everything can be arranged on the buffet table an hour or so before the guests are due.

Green salad Make the dressing the day before, but prepare the salad on the day of the party. Add the dressing at the last convenient moment.

New potato salad with mustard dressing and olives Make the salad the day before, but dish up and garnish with olives on the day of the party. Keep covered until setting out the buffet.

Tomato, onion and pimento salad Prepare the salad and the dressing but do not combine until the day of the party. Keep the salad covered and refrigerated.

Trifle can be made but the decoration should be left until the morning.

Treacle tart Make one or two days in advance. No need to refrigerate.

Fruit salad Make the day before, but leave out the strawberries and bananas, which should be added the next day. Make sure all the cut up fruit is well coated in the syrup, and put it into a bowl; cover tightly with polythene, and refrigerate overnight.

QUICKLY-PREPARED BUFFET FOR 40

In anticipation of the inevitable catering emergency it is worth walking round the best grocery shop in the area and looking at the ready-prepared foods. The sad fact is that the nicest are usually Continental and expensive. I can buy at my local delicatessen:—mackerel in white wine, stuffed vine leaves, pasta in tomato sauce, chile-con-carne, sardines, frankfurters, fresh cole slaw, and much else. With a few black olives and slices of tomato these make a more exciting hors d'oeuvre platter than the all-too-usual offering of baked beans, pickled onions and anchovies.

For the following menu I have assumed that with little warning the hostess is confronted by the prospect of 40 people for supper—just time to shop, hire or borrow the plates, order the drink, and with two hours to throw everything together.

Cold meats and salamis (*Assiette anglaise*)

Hot baked potatoes with sour cream, walnuts and chives

Cole slaw with raisins

Beetroot and onion salad with horseradish cream

Watercress and apple salad, french dressing

Whole white peaches in brandy

As this party is designed for someone catering in a hurry, it may be a question of drinking whatever is in the cupboard—a Portuguese Rosé would be admirable but chilled lager would be a good alternative.

Platters of cold meats and salamis

Allow ¼ lb (100 g) of cold meat per person, and have the delicatessen slice it very finely. For each person, you might buy one small slice of ham, one of tongue, one of garlic sausage and one of Italian salami. Buy a pound or two of liver sausage and the same of rough paté or terrine, and slice them yourself. Arrange the slices in overlapping rows on a large platter or tray, and garnish with black olives and radishes, and a few sprigs of watercress. Cover the whole platter with polythene until you are about to put it on the buffet.

Hot baked potatoes with sour cream, walnuts and chives

For each guest you will need:
1 large but not enormous potato, well scrubbed
2 tablespoons sour cream
2 walnuts, chopped
1 teaspoon of chopped chives
Salt and pepper

Prick the potatoes with a fork, to eliminate any risk of them bursting in the oven. Wet them and rub them all over with salt. Bake in a fairly hot oven (400°F, gas mark 6) for an hour or until a skewer glides easily through the largest potato. Mix all the other ingredients together. Split the potatoes without cutting them quite in half, and fill them with the sour cream mixture. Serve immediately. If guests are helping themselves from a buffet, leave the potatoes whole, and let everyone do his own splitting and filling.

Cole slaw with raisins (serves 10)
(For 40, use four small or three large cabbages, and 3 lb/1½ kilos carrots)

1 small hard white cabbage
6 small carrots
½ pint/¼ litre/10 fl. oz mayonnaise
3 tablespoons cream
1 teaspoon french mustard
1 teaspoon sugar
Salt and pepper
Handful raisins or sultanas

Shred the cabbage as finely as you can. Grate the carrot coarsely. Mix the mayonnaise with all the other ingredients, and then combine it with the cabbage and carrots. (Mixing with the hand is the quickest way to get all the cabbage coated.)

Beetroot and onion salad with horseradish cream (serves 10)
(Do four times the quantity for 40)

3 lb/1½ kilos cooked beetroot
1 large spanish onion, very finely sliced
1 carton (5 fl. oz/a good ⅛ litre) sour or fresh cream
1 dessertspoon horseradish cream or sauce
1 dessertspoon lemon juice
Pepper and salt
3 or 4 spring onions, chopped

Combine the sour cream with the horseradish and lemon juice. Season with salt and pepper. Slice the beetroots thinly, mix with the onion slices, and then turn gently in the cream dressing. Put into a salad bowl, and scatter the chopped spring onions on top.

Watercress and apple salad (serves 5)
(For 40 you will need 7 or 8 bunches of cress and 4 lb/2 kilos apples)

1 large bunch watercress
2 dessert apples
3 tablespoons french dressing
1 teaspoon sugar

Mix the sugar into the dressing. If the apples are red, do not peel them; if they are green, peel them or not as you prefer. Core and slice them very finely, using a stainless steel knife. Immediately toss them in the french dressing. Wash the cress and cut off the long stalks. Just before serving mix nearly all the cress in with the apples, and put into the salad bowl. Cut the remaining cress very short (with no stalk at all) and scatter on the top.

Whole white peaches in brandy
Certain canned fruits make excellent emergency desserts. I think Japanese or South African white peaches, and Greek or Israeli figs are among the best. If using the peaches, pour off half the syrup and add a tot of brandy to the peaches in the remaining syrup. Serve with cream. The figs are delicious with a wine glass of marsala added to them. A healthy dash of kirsch greatly improves canned pineapple rings, and canned black cherries are excellent as they are, or with a tot of brandy or rum. Reckon on five people to a 2 lb/1 kilo tin.

QUICKLY-PREPARED BUFFET FOR 20

Sweet and sour ham rolls
Tongue and egg rolls
Hot boiled potatoes with hot
    french dressing
Green salad

Apples baked in cider

(Preparation on the day before follows recipes.)

Inexpensive claret from St Emilion or Graves would be suitable—and easy to buy in a hurry.

Sweet and sour ham rolls (serves 10)
(Double the quantities for 20 people)

10 slices ham
½ lb/250 grams cooked sweetcorn,
    off the cob
½ lb/250 grams/1 cup cottage cheese
2 oz/50 grams/¼ cup gherkins, chopped
2 oz/50 grams/½ cup sultanas
1 stick celery, finely chopped
Salt and pepper

Lay the ham slices out on a board or tray. Mix all the other ingredients together. Taste and season. Put a large spoonful of mixture onto each ham slice, and roll it up. Lay the rolls on the serving dish, and garnish with a few sprigs of watercress.

Tongue and egg rolls (serves 10)
(Double the quantities for 20 people)

10 large thin slices tongue
8 hard-boiled eggs
1 cucumber, peeled and chopped
4 oz/100 grams/1 cup walnuts,
    chopped
¼ pint/⅛ litre/5 fl. oz sour cream
1 small teaspoon ready mixed English
    mustard
Salt, black pepper
Radishes

Put the chopped cucumber into a bowl and sprinkle with salt. Leave to stand for ½ hour. Rinse with cold water and drain, and then dry well on a cloth. Mix the sour cream with the mustard, salt and pepper. Slice five of the hard-boiled eggs. Mix with the chopped cucumber, walnuts, and sour cream. Lay the tongue slices out on a board or tray and divide the mixture between them. Roll them up round the spoonful of filling. Lay the rolls on a serving dish and decorate with the remaining three hard-boiled eggs cut lengthwise into quarters, and a few trimmed radishes.

Hot boiled potatoes with french dressing (serves 8–10)
(Double the quantities for 20)

3 lb/1½ kilos new potatoes
¼ pint/⅛ litre/5 fl. oz french dressing
 made with slightly less vinegar than
 usual (see page 71)
1 teaspoon french mustard
1 tablespoon chopped parsley
1 teaspoon chopped dill

Peel the potatoes. Boil them in salted water until just tender. Drain them. Stir the mustard well into the french dressing and toss the potatoes, still hot, in this. Scatter over the parsley and dill. Serve hot or cold.

Green salad
See page 71.

Apples baked in cider (serves 10)
(Double the quantities for 20)

10 dessert apples
1 pint/½ litre/20 fl. oz cider
½ lb/230 grams/1 cup brown sugar
Handful sultanas
Juice and finely grated rind of one
 orange

Set the oven at 375°F, gas mark 5. Dissolve the sugar in the cider, heating it without boiling. Peel the apples, leaving them whole with the stalks on. Put them into a large pie dish, pour over the cider syrup, and add the sultanas, orange rind and juice. Poach in the oven until the apples are quite soft—about one hour. If a thicker syrup is wanted it can be boiled down in a saucepan until reduced to the required thickness. Serve hot with cream or custard.

On the day before
Sweet and sour ham rolls Make the filling and keep it in the refrigerator, well covered, until needed. The rolls can be put together several hours before the party.
Tongue and egg rolls are less successful if made as much as a day in advance. They are quick to make, and ideally should be done not more than five hours before the meal.
Hot boiled potatoes with french dressing Prepare the dressing and peel the potatoes, but do not cook them.
Green salad Make the dressing. If you have already bought the salad, wash it and pick it over, and put it in a plastic bag in the refrigerator. Ideally salad should be bought on the day of the party.
Apples baked in cider Complete the dish. Reheat in the oven or in a saucepan with the lid on.

5 · After-Theatre Suppers

There are few things more frustrating than to be invited to an after-theatre supper and then to wait, starving for food and panting for a drink, while the host fiddles about with the ice-tray and the hostess sets the table between making forays into the kitchen. The essential, as always, is planning ahead—and also, in this instance, choosing food that can be on the table when you get home, or heated quickly while you have one drink. If the party is at all formal, any of the buffet menus (Chapter 4) or dishes from them would be suitable. However, one often wants only a simple snack, easily digestible and unlikely to keep everyone there till 2 a.m.

Unless it is the height of summer, I have a leaning towards fattening food in the middle of the night. There is something very comforting about garlic bread or pasta. Perhaps because one is tired, soup seems welcoming and reviving too. My idea of a perfectly horrid after-theatre supper is chilled melon, cold chicken and ice cream.

AFTER-THEATRE SUPPER FOR 8

Mushroom soup

Hot meat loaf
Salad of chicory and endive

Ginger syllabub

(Preparation on the day before follows recipes.)

A good Burgundy, soft and full, would be perfect for drinking late at night with this menu.

Mushroom soup (serves 8–10)
1½ lb/750 grams flat mushrooms
4 oz/100 grams/½ cup butter
1 large clove garlic, crushed
½ loaf white bread with the crusts cut off
Pinch of ground nutmeg or mace
3½ pints/2¼ litres good chicken stock
Salt and plenty of freshly ground black pepper
½ pint/¼ litre/10 fl. oz cream
4 heaped tablespoons chopped parsley

Melt the butter in a very large thick-bottomed saucepan. Chop the mushrooms fairly finely and add to the butter. Cook gently, stirring, until soft and mushy. Add the garlic and the bread, broken into bits. Stir until the bread and mushrooms are well mixed, then add the stock, nutmeg or mace, and salt and pepper to taste. Bring to simmering point and cook slowly for 10 minutes. Liquidize the soup in an electric blender, or put through a vegetable mill. Return to the pan, add the chopped parsley and the cream, and reheat. If the soup is to be served cold, reheating is unnecessary, but in this case the cream and parsley should be added only when the soup is cold.

Hot meat loaf (serves 8)

1 lb/½ kilo puff pastry (see page 83)
2 lb/1 kilo belly of pork, minced
1 teaspoon dried basil
2 eggs
1 level teaspoon salt
1 teaspoon ground black pepper

Roll out the pastry to an oblong 10 ins × 14 ins. Mix the minced pork, basil, salt and pepper with one whole egg and one yolk, reserving one egg white. Form the mixture into a roll and place down the centre of the pastry. Fold one side of the pastry over the meat, brush the edge with lightly beaten egg-white, and fold the other side over, pressing the join lightly to seal it. Put the pastry roll, centre join underneath, onto a baking sheet and brush with the rest of the egg white. Bake in a moderately hot oven (400°F, gas mark 6) for 40 minutes.

Chicory and endive salad (serves 8–10)

There is always great confusion about which is which—chicory or endive. In France the white plump heads with pointed leaves in a bud-shape are called *chicorée*, although when cooked they are sometimes called *endive*. In England they are chicory, and the frilly lettuce-like plant is endive. In France this is *chicorée frisée*. However, as this recipe calls for both, buying should be easy enough.

1 lb chicory heads, plump, white, and tight closed (the ones with green tips are too bitter)
1 endive
French dressing (page 71)

Discard the outside leaves of the endive, and thoroughly wash the others, breaking them up into easily manageable sprigs. Wipe the chicory heads with a clean damp cloth, remove any outside leaves that are discoloured at the edges, and break the leaves apart. Discard the bitter core. Mix the endive and chicory leaves in a salad bowl and toss with sufficient french dressing to moisten without over-wetting. In France this salad is often dressed well in advance of the meal to allow the dressing to soak into the leaves, but this slightly spoils the fresh crispness of the salad, and on the whole I think it better not tossed more than an hour before the meal.

Ginger syllabub (serves 8–10)

1 pint/¾ litre/20 fl. oz thick cream
1 gill/⅛ litre/5 fl. oz advocaat liqueur
4 heaped tablespoons ginger marmalade
2 or 3 pieces preserved ginger

Whip the cream stiffly and stir in the advocaat and the ginger marmalade. Spoon into small glasses or little china pots or coffee cups. Put two or three thin slivers of preserved ginger on top of each syllabub.

On the day before

The mushroom soup can be made completely, and put into a cool place until needed. Reheat gently, without boiling.

The hot meat loaf can be completed the day before, and reheated in a fairly hot oven (400°F, gas mark 6) for 20–30 minutes.

Salad of chicory and endive Prepare salad ingredients and dressing. Keep the salad well wrapped in a cool place. Mix the salad not more than two hours in advance.

Ginger syllabub can be made the day before but should be well covered with polythene, as cream is inclined to absorb the flavours of other foods in the refrigerator. However, as it does not take five minutes to make, it could be done during the day of the party.

AFTER-THEATRE SUPPER FOR 10

Chicken liver pâté
Thick fish soup or stew
Garlic bread
Lady Elizabeth Anson's spiced
  peach brûlée

(Preparations on the day before follows recipes.)
White Provence wine is good with fish soup. So is
white Beaujolais.

Chicken liver pâté

This is a basic pâté, very delicious, and easy to do. It keeps well—at least a week—if kept in the refrigerator. I think it is best made with a mixture of duck and chicken livers, but duck livers are more difficult to obtain, and chicken livers do very well.

1 lb/½ kilo chicken livers
  or ½ lb duck livers and ½ lb chicken
  livers (250 grams of each)
10 oz/275 grams/1¼ cups butter
1 large onion, very finely chopped
1 large clove garlic, crushed
Salt and plenty of freshly ground
  black pepper
2 tablespoons brandy, or one each of
  brandy and sherry

Melt 4 oz of the butter in a large thick frying pan, and in it fry the onion gently until soft and transparent. Add the crushed garlic and continue cooking for a further minute. Discard all the discoloured bits from the livers as they are very bitter. Add the livers to the pan, and cook, turning them to brown on all sides, for 8 minutes or so, when they should be cooked but still pink inside. Add salt and pepper. Mince or liquidize the mixture in an electric blender. Work in the rest of the butter and the brandy. If the pâté is to be kept more than three days put it into an earthenware dish or pot, and cover the top with a layer of clarified butter.

To clarify butter

Put 3 oz butter in a pan with a cupful of water, and heat until the butter is melted and frothy. Allow to cool and set solid, then lift the butter, now clarified, off the top of the liquid. It will need to be melted to pour over the pâté.

Serve the pâté with a few leaves of watercress or lettuce, and freshly-made thick toast. Butter should be offered, though many people consider pâté so rich as not to need any.

Hot thick fish soup or stew (serves 10)

2 lb/1 kilo fishheads, skin and bones
1 large onion
Large bunch parsley
1 bayleaf
4 pints/2 litres chicken stock, or
  4 pints water and 2 chicken stock
  cubes
1 oz/30 grams/2 tablespoons butter
2 large cloves garlic
Pinch of thyme
Black pepper
Salt
4 lb/2 kilos fresh fish—
  haddock, hake, whiting, cod, or a
  mixture of any of them
  (continued overleaf)

Put fishheads, skin and bones into a large saucepan with half the onion, sliced; half the bunch of parsley, bruised; and the bayleaf. Add the chicken stock or the water and stock cubes, and bring to the boil. Simmer gently for 20 minutes, then strain.

Melt the butter in a large saucepan. Chop the rest of the onion very finely and cook it gently in the butter. When it is soft and transparent, pour on the stock, add the tomato paste, crushed garlic, thyme, ground black pepper and salt. Bring to simmering point. Add the filleted fish in fairly large chunks. Cover the saucepan, and poach very gently for 15 minutes. The water should not be allowed to bubble at all. Dip the tomatoes into

8 tomatoes
4 slices white bread
Olive oil
6 oz/175 grams cooked peeled prawns

boiling water for five seconds; then skin and slice them. Chop the rest of the parsley finely. Cut the bread into small triangles and fry in the olive oil until crisp. Just before serving the soup, throw in the parsley, prawns, and tomato slices. Reheat and serve with the croûtons handed separately.

Garlic bread

For 10 people use one large or two small french loaves or any lozenge-shaped bread with a crisp crust. Slice the loaf at an angle, but without going right through to the bread board. Mix a crushed clove of garlic into 4 oz (120 grams) softened butter. Spread each slice of bread with the garlic butter on one side only, taking care not to break the slices away from the loaf as you push them apart to butter them. Put the loaf on a piece of foil and draw up the sides of the foil round the loaf, leaving it open at the top (closing the packet completely results in soggy bread with no crisp crust). Bake the bread in a fairly hot oven for 10 minutes or until the top is crisp, the whole loaf hot, and of course, the butter melted.

Lady Elizabeth Anson's spiced peach brûlée (serves 10)

1½ pints/1 litre/3½ cups thick cream
1 large tin spiced peaches (if these are unobtainable plain white peaches make a delicious, though different, dessert)
1 oz/30 grams/¼ cup preserved ginger, chopped, and two tablespoons of syrup from the ginger jar
4 oz/100 grams/1 cup chopped blanched or flaked almonds
8 oz/230 grams/1 cup caster (powdered) sugar

Drain the peaches well, and slice them finely. Whip the cream until stiff. Put the peach slices at the bottom of a soufflé dish, and spread half the cream over them. Then sprinkle on the chopped ginger, the almonds, and the ginger syrup. Cover completely with the rest of the whipped cream, and put the dish into the refrigerator for at least three hours or overnight.

Turn the grill to maximum heat. Stand the dish on a large sheet of greaseproof (waxed) paper on the kitchen table. Using a sieve or strainer, shake an even layer of caster sugar all over the top of the pudding. (The paper under the dish is to catch the sugar falling wide.) The sugar should be about ¼ inch thick, and perfectly flat. When the grill (broiler) has been heating for at least 10 minutes, put the dish close under the heat. Use oven gloves or a thick towel if you need to turn the dish during grilling, and to remove it when the top has caramelized to an even golden brown. Cool, then return to the refrigerator until serving. The top should be like glass when cold.

On the day before

The chicken liver pâté can be made days ahead and kept in the refrigerator, or made the day before and kept in the larder. Toast should be made at the last minute.

The fish soup can be made the day before and kept refrigerated. The croûtons should be fried until crisp right through if they are to be made in advance.

Garlic bread can be buttered hours before the party, or even the day before (in which case it should be well wrapped and kept in the refrigerator overnight).

Lady Elizabeth Anson's spiced peach brûlée can be made the day before, and anyway it should be made several hours before the party. Do not keep it in a steamy or damp atmosphere or the caramel top will go sticky, and finally liquid.

6 · Dances and Balls

Whatever the difference between a dance and a ball (to me a ball goes on all night or is very grand, and a dance generally stops at 1 a.m. or so), both can end with breakfast, and both involve music, so I am treating them together.

A hostess' first job is to book the band, group, discothèque, or jukebox; or—for a small informal affair—make sure she has a good record or cassette player with enough amplification to compete with a room full of dancers. If a marquee and/or dance floor is to be hired, this too should be done at once (contractors get booked up well ahead, especially for midsummer Saturdays). When ordering a marquee, reckon on 12 square feet per person. This allows for dancing, sitting-out and milling-about space, and for a buffet and bar. The dance flooring need not cover the whole tented area, but should be calculated at one square yard per couple. A hundred people will therefore need a tent 30 ft × 40 ft, with a dance floor of 15 ft × 10 ft (assuming that only half the guests will be on it at once).

The next task is the sending out of invitations, which is usually done four to six weeks before the party.

As soon as the menu is decided, all china, silver, tables, chairs, linen and glass should be ordered. Next, the hiring of staff—waiters, waitresses and someone to help in the kitchen. Allow one for every 25 guests.

Then write out a programme of the preparations in the weeks before the party. This should include:—the arrangements settled with a florist if flowers are needed, what day the china is being delivered, when the tent (if any) is to be set up, when the band will arrive (they will spend hours setting up their amplifiers and lights, plugging in electric guitars and so on). It should cover in great detail all cooking jobs to be done in the week before the party, on the day before, and a few hours before the guests arrive.

Once upon a time, in the more opulent households, the hostess invariably had a dinner party for her 10 or 20 house guests before the ball, while everyone else dined at the houses of her co-operative friends. The ball then started at about 10 p.m., and dancing continued with few intervals until supper was served, around midnight. 'Supper' was a vast buffet, heavy with salmon, boar's head, stuffed turkey and the like, traditionally followed by strawberries and cream. After coffee the dancing was resumed until about 4 a.m. when a sustaining breakfast of kedgeree, kippers, eggs and bacon, rolls and butter was served, with more coffee. Guests then began to drift off, the last few generally being helped on their way with a sobering cup of hot soup.

Grand affairs of this kind are still occasionally held, sometimes with imaginative innovations by the host. When Prince Richard of Gloucester was an architectural student at Cambridge he determined to improve on the celebrated May Balls there. At his parental home various rooms, tents and barns were devoted to a discothèque, a steel band, bagpipers, and a conventional band. Innumerable amusements were laid on in case guests should tire of dancing. There was croquet on the floodlit lawns, movies in the tennis court, and moonlit swimming. There were great coal braziers throughout the grounds. Tables and chairs dotted the barnyard, in the middle of which was a huge step-pyramid of freshly gathered hay in bales: comfortable and fun to sit on, the haystack filled the whole yard with the smell of harvest.

For most of us, a party on that scale is a pipedream—and needs a castle to hold it in anyway. But modest versions of the grand ball can produce as great a success.

In recent years the custom of serving what amounts to three huge meals during the night has fallen away. Guests are given *either* the private dinner before they come, and then breakfast at 1 a.m. or so; *or* just the buffet supper during the dance. The hostess may arrange hot soup or coffee, and perhaps croissants and butter, for the small hours. Obviously it depends on how long the party is to last. If the buffet has been served at about 10.30 p.m. and the dancers are still going strong at 4 a.m., a plate of kedgeree or a cup of steaming soupe à l'oignon is most welcome.

Even a smallish house need not preclude the host's imaginative touches. My catering firm recently arranged a party for 100 in a Hampstead house with about a quarter of an acre of garden that had a small swimming pool at the end of it. We arranged lighting (hired) for the garden, a barbecue at the pool-side where a hired chef cooked chops and sausages, and a large buffet in the dining room. The guests drifted about playing croquet on the lawn, listening to a strolling guitarist, and at one point watching a water-polo match in the pool. And we had a fortune teller, and a group playing for the dancers in the hall. (Adults are just as excited by fortune tellers and croquet games as children, and if they are to be with you for six or eight hours of festivity, some diversion is sensible.)

Remember that hired staff and musicians cost a great deal more after midnight than before, so it is important to decide *before* the party how long you want it to last, and plan accordingly. And do not forget about feeding the staff and musicians, who will have worked a ten-hour shift before the night is out. For this reason too, and for variety, two bands were always essential; today one band and a discothèque are more usual—or just the discothèque.

Check list page 187.
See Buffet Parties (Chapter 4) for buffet suppers, and Dinner Parties (Chapter 3) for dinners before the dance. The following menus are for breakfast after a dance. I am assuming that there is no-one to fry eggs, so all food is going to be cooked in advance and re-heated.

SIMPLE BREAKFAST FOR 200

Creamy vegetable soup	(*Preparation on the day before follows recipes.*)
Kedgeree	*Champagne or Buck's Fizz (one-third fresh orange juice, two-thirds champagne) are extravagant but delicious breakfast drinks.*
Croissants	

Creamy vegetable soup (serves 10)
This soup can be cooked in large quantities, but should be cooled as quickly as possible —pour into small containers to cool (see *Cooking in quantity*, page 8). At a dance not everyone will want soup: it is safe to assume that only two-thirds of the guests will. If coffee is offered as an alternative, you need only provide soup for half the guests.

1 lb/½ kilo leeks, well washed
1 lb/½ kilo onions, very finely sliced
1 small head of celery, finely sliced
2 large potatoes, peeled and finely sliced

Finely slice the leeks, both white and green parts, but discarding any tough outside leaves. Melt the butter in a very large pan and gently cook the sliced onions, leeks, celery, and potatoes in it, stirring occasionally, until the whole mass is soft

2 oz/50 grams/4 tablespoons butter
1 heaped tablespoon flour
2 pints/1¼ litres/5 cups chicken stock
1 pint/¾ litre/2½ cups creamy milk
Salt, pepper, ground nutmeg
3 tablespoons port (optional, but
  amazingly good)
3 tablespoons thin cream

and cooked (about 20 minutes). The vegetables should not be allowed to brown at all. Do this 'sweating' of vegetables with the saucepan lid on, as the juices run more easily from the vegetables in a steamy atmosphere and they are less likely to fry brown.

Stir in the flour, then add the stock. Bring to the boil, stirring, and boil for one minute. Add the milk, reheat without boiling and add salt, pepper and nutmeg to taste. Simmer gently for 20 minutes. Liquidize the soup in an electric blender. or pass through a vegetable mill. Reheat, and add the cream and port. Use white port if you would prefer the soup not to go faintly pink.

Kedgeree (serves 10)

(For large numbers reckon on one dessertspoon raw rice, half an egg and 2 oz/50 grams of fish per person.)

Kedgeree is best made with lots of butter but no cream. Cream tends to stick the rice together and make a rather soggy dish. For a good kedgeree you need at least as much fish and eggs as rice, and the rice should not be overcooked (see page 70 on boiling rice).

10 oz/275 grams/1½ cups long grain
  rice, boiled (weighed before cooking)
1½ lb/¾ kilo smoked haddock fillet,
  cooked, skinned and boned
  (or cooked fresh salmon if
  preferred)
6 hard-boiled eggs, coarsely chopped
4 oz/100 grams/½ cup butter
Salt, pepper and cayenne pepper

Melt the butter in a large shallow pan, and add everything else. Stir gently until very hot. If making it in large quantities, heat it in the oven instead of on the top. Kedgeree will not spoil in a low oven (250°F, gas mark ½). Stir occasionally to prevent the sides getting hot before the middle.

Croissants (makes 10–12)

(It would be foolish to attempt to make croissants for a party of 200. Order them well in advance from your baker or grocer, and if possible have them delivered on the day of the party.)

Croissants are a sort of cross between puff pastry and bread, but they are not as complicated as they would seem from reading the recipe, and they are very satisfying to make.

The dough must be made the day before baking.

12 oz/340 grams/2½ cups plain flour
½ oz/15 grams/1 tablespoon yeast
  (rather less if the yeast is dried)
¼ teaspoon salt
6 oz/170 grams/¾ cup butter
¼ pint/⅛ litre/5 fl. oz warm milk and
  water mixed

Sift the flour onto the middle of the table. Take about one quarter of it, and make a well in the centre. Put the yeast in a cup and add a few spoonfuls of warm water—just enough to dissolve the yeast, and mix well. Pour this into the well in the middle of the flour, and mix the flour gradually into it, forming a soft dough (you may need to add a few drops more water). Fill a bowl with luke-warm water, and drop the ball of dough you have just made into it.

Take the remaining 9 oz (approximately) of flour that you have already sifted; make a well in the

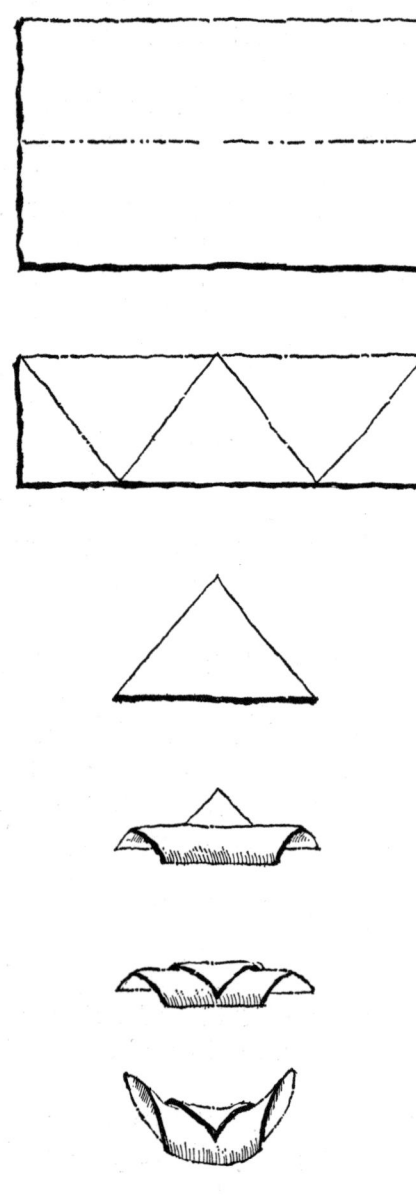

centre of it. Put into the well half the butter, softened. Using the fingers of one hand, work the butter and gradually draw in the surrounding flour, adding the warm-water-and-milk mixture gradually when necessary to make a stiff dough. Now beat the dough for 10 minutes, either by bashing it with a rolling pin or by picking it up and throwing it down hard on the table in a slapping motion: this makes the pastry very elastic. Now take the yeast ball from the water, where it should have become spongy and swollen, and work it into the beaten paste until completely incorporated. Flour a large mixing bowl and drop the dough into it. Cover with a saucepan lid, plate or piece of polythene, and refrigerate overnight.

Then roll the dough to an oblong 8 ins × 5 ins. Put the remaining 3 oz butter in the middle, and wrap up like a parcel. Now read the instructions in the puff pastry recipe (page 83) and give the paste six rolls and folds. The butter should by now be completely incorporated, and barely visible as streaks in the paste. Sometimes five rolls and folds are enough. If the paste becomes at all warm or sticky during rolling, it should be rested, covered, in the refrigerator between rollings.

To make the croissants, roll out the pastry into the thinnest possible rectangle, cut this in half lengthwise, forming two thin strips (see drawing). Cut each of these strips into five or six triangles. Roll them up, starting from the base and rolling towards the apex. Stick the point down with a little beaten egg, then curl the roll into a crescent shape, keeping the stuck-down point on top. Put the croissants a little apart on a damp baking sheet and set them somewhere warm and out of draughts to prove (i.e., rise). In half an hour or so they should be risen and puffy. While they are proving, heat the oven to 450°F, gas mark 8. Bake for about 25 minutes or until well browned. In France buttering croissants is thought to be gilding the lily, but do not let this deter you.

On the day before

Creamy vegetable soup Make the soup and keep it in a cool place.

Kedgeree can be made and put into buttered roasting pans for re-heating. Keep in a cool place—though not necessarily refrigerated.

Croissants Preparations must start the day before baking. They should be eaten as soon as possible after baking.

Solomon and his wives at table. Engraving by Anton Koburger, Nuremburg, 1491

From *Banchetti compositioni di Vivande et apparecchio generale* (Cristoforo de Messisburgo, 1549)

THE FESTIVE SEASON.

(*Mrs. Ponsonby de Tomkyns at Home—"Early and Late."*)

Mr. P. de T. (to the Waiters). "WOULD YOU MIND, ONE OF YOU, BEING SO VERY KIND AS JUST TO GIVE ME THE LEG OF A FOWL, OR SOMETHING. I'M—I'M THE MASTER OF THE HOUSE."

HEARTY BREAKFAST FOR 60

Bacon and egg flan

Sausages with onions and tomato
sauce

Wholemeal baps

(Preparation on the day before follows recipes.)

*Champagne is the traditional wine for all hours
but beer is good with breakfast after a party, when
people are thirsty and tired. An eccentric combination of the two is Black Velvet (see page 15).*

Bacon and egg flan (serves 10)
(This is classically known as quiche lorraine)

¾ lb/350 grams rich short crust pastry
  (page 118) with sugar omitted
2 whole eggs
2 extra egg yolks
2 oz/50 grams/½ cup grated cheese
  (cheddar or gruyère)
Salt, pepper, cayenne
A little under ½ pint/¼ litre/10 fl. oz
  creamy milk, or cream and milk
  mixed
1 large onion, finely sliced into rings
1 oz/30 grams/2 tablespoons butter
¼ lb/100 grams bacon slices, without
  rind, coarsely chopped

Line a large flan ring with the short crust pastry, and bake 'blind' (see below) for 20 minutes in a moderate oven (375°F, gas mark 5). Melt the butter in a frying pan, and add the bacon and onion. Fry gently until the onion is transparent and the bacon cooked. Take off the heat. Grate the cheese into a mixing bowl and add the yolks, whole eggs, milk, cream, plenty of pepper, a pinch of cayenne and a little salt (remember that the bacon and cheese are salty). Add the contents of the frying pan. Pour the filling into the pastry case, and return to the oven for a further 20 minutes or until the custard has set and is slightly browned on top.

For a quiche that will cut more easily than the above into thin slices for a first course, or into little pieces as a cocktail savoury, the onion and bacon should be finely diced.

Baking blind This is done to cook the pastry slightly before the filling is added to it. When the flan ring or pie dish is lined with the pastry, a piece of tin foil or a double layer of greaseproof (waxed) paper is laid inside, on the pastry. It is then filled with 'blind beans' (dried beans, rice grains, even pebbles or pennies) which prevent the pastry bubbling up as it cooks. The foil or paper makes it easier to lift out the blind beans. The same beans can be used for years.

Sausages and onions in tomato sauce (serves 10)
(Allow one sausage per head for large parties)

2 lb/1 kilo pork sausages, preferably
  big ones
6 large onions, sliced
3 oz/80 grams/6 tablespoons butter
1 large can tomatoes (about 2 lb or
  1 kilo)
1½ oz/45 grams/3 level tablespoons
  flour
Salt and pepper

Grill the sausages without overcooking them, and place in the bottom of a casserole. Fry the sliced onions gently in the butter, stirring every now and then, until they go first transparent and then a gentle even brown. They will reduce greatly in bulk and have a melted soft look. Stir in the flour, add the tomatoes, and bring to the boil, stirring. Add salt and pepper, and pour over the sausages. Reheat in the oven when needed.

Wholemeal baps (soft rolls) (makes about 8)

(Unless you have plenty of freezer space, it would be inadvisable to make more than a few dozen baps. But they do freeze well if you have the time to make them gradually in the weeks before the party.)

8 oz/230 grams/1¾ cups wholemeal flour
8 oz/230 grams/1¾ cups plain flour
1 level teaspoon salt
1 level dessertspoon sugar
1 oz/30 grams/2 tablespoons yeast (half the amount if using dried yeast)
2 oz/50 grams/4 tablespoons lard
2 tablespoons warm milk (about blood-heat)
½ pint/¼ litre/10 fl. oz warm milk and water mixed

Mix the yeast well with the sugar, and then add the 2 tablespoons of warm milk. If using dried yeast this mixture should now be left to stand for 15 minutes, until it looks bubbly, but this is not necessary if fresh yeast is used.

Sift the white flour and the salt into a large bowl and add the wholemeal flour. Rub in the lard. Pour the yeast liquid into the milk and water, and add it to the flour. First with a knife and then with one hand, work to a soft dough, adding a little more warm water if necessary. Turn onto the table and work until the dough is quite smooth.

Flour the board or table lightly and knead the dough for a few minutes. Flour a warm (not hot) bowl, and drop the ball of dough into it. Stand the bowl over a saucepan of warm water, making sure that the bottom of the bowl does not touch the water—the water should not be hotter than your hand can bear comfortably. Cover the bowl with a plate or baking sheet. After 20–30 minutes the dough should have risen to about double its original size. Remove and roll it out on a floured board to about half an inch thick. Stamp out rounds with a pastry cutter (a 3-inch or 3½-inch cutter is usual but it can be smaller if preferred). Place them on a floured baking tray. Cover with a floured cloth or sheet of polythene (oiled so that when the dough rises it will not stick to the polythene). Leave in a warm, draught-free place until the rolls have risen to about double their height (about ½ hour). Dust lightly with wholemeal flour, and bake in a hot oven (450°F, gas mark 8) for 15 minutes. The baps should not brown much, but they will feel firm to the touch when done.

On the day before

Bacon and egg flan Make completely.
Sausages with onions and tomato sauce Complete the dish and keep in a cool place.
Wholemeal baps Make the baps well in advance and store frozen until needed.

106

7 · Children's Parties

Children mostly ignore the meringue swan floating on a green jelly lake and the birthday cake shaped like Batman, and demand sausages on sticks and packets of potato crisps. The birthday boy scorns his presents and retires with his ancient teddy, and most of the guests go home quarrelsome and sulky. It is almost impossible to send them all away happy, but some pitfalls can be avoided to ensure maximum pleasure for the maximum number.

First of all the fewer children the better. For a small child, six people is a party—and less overwhelming than a crowd of half-strangers in their Sunday best. Another good rule is to make the party short: say, games from 3.30, food at 4.15, a story or some entertainment (even children's television if you time the party right) for half an hour, and then home before anyone has had time to get weepy. Almost all the food should be simple, almost pedestrian. Sandwiches, especially savoury ones like sardine or egg, are more popular than dainty iced cakes. This is less work and expense for the cook, and better for the children's teeth. However, when it comes to drinks, most eight-year-olds will not be fobbed off with healthy milk or fresh orange juice. They want, and actually enjoy, fizzy red and green drinks, and of course Coca-Cola. Milkshakes might be acceptable alternatives; but when I was a child, our favourite drinks were 'Brown Cow' (ice cream floating in Pepsi) and 'Green Mamba' (ice cream in green soda pop).

About games: the four to seven-year-olds will be quite happy with traditional party games, and perhaps a treasure hunt, if it can be swung so that everyone finds a treasure. The eight to eleven-year-olds prefer boisterous games like tug o'war, sardines, musical chairs and leap-frog.

And they all like presents to take home. These need not be expensive but they have become *de rigueur*: packets of crayons or toy watches for the small children, perhaps ball-point pens or modelling wax for the older ones. The golden rule is to dispense the presents only as the children are leaving—partly to stave off tears of exhaustion, and partly because if there *are* tears (of exhaustion or disappointment at your offering) you will not have to cope with them.

As the food is to be very plain, the table should be pretty. The easiest way to achieve this is to buy matching paper sets of napkins, tablecloths, plates, cups and dishes. Red is still the most popular colour. Messy chocolate bars are a bad idea if the children are very young (as are toys that go bang with frightening loudness).

Some gloomy words of warning: stock the first-aid cupboard with adhesive dressings and antiseptic, and check that you know your doctor's telephone number—just in case anyone falls over or gets biffed.

Check list for children's parties, page 189.

PARTY FOR 12 FIVE-YEAR-OLDS

Checkerboard of sandwiches
Sausages on sticks
Cheese and pineapple on sticks
Cheese pictures
Gingerbread men
Jelly boats
Chocolate hedgehog birthday cake

(*Preparation on the day before follows recipes.*)

Checkerboard of sandwiches

8 slices white bread
8 slices brown bread
Various meats and spreads for the
  sandwiches—e.g., ham, cream cheese,
  cucumber, beef extract, yellow
  cheese, canned salmon, chopped
  egg. (The idea is to have as many
  contrasting colours as possible.)

Butter the bread. Apply the various toppings, and cut off the crusts. Cut each slice into four squares. Arrange the squares on a board or tray, side by side, as a checkerboard (try to get contrasting colours next to each other). Surround with a border of parsley sprigs, and keep covered with a piece of polythene, or an inverted tray, until they are to be eaten.

Sausages on sticks

Children eat more of these than anything else at a party, so allow about 6 cocktail sausages per head. Follow the instructions on page 20. Chipolata sausages or big ones are good too, but children seem to find cocktail ones more exciting. Frankfurter sausages are also popular.

Cheese and pineapple on sticks

Squares of mild cheddar and a cube of canned pineapple stuck on a wooden cocktail stick are well liked by most children. Canned pineapple chunks are cheaper than the pineapple rings, and are perfect for this snack. One can of pineapple and ¾ lb of cheese will be enough for 12 children.

Cheese pictures (makes 12)

12 slices bread
12 slices luncheon meat or ham
6 slices processed cheese
Butter

Butter the bread and lay the meat slices on top. With animal biscuit cutters stamp out shapes from the middle of each slice of processed cheese. Put the six animal shapes on half the open meat sandwiches, and the cheese frames—the surrounds left after cutting out the middle—on the other six.

Gingerbread men (makes 12)

12 oz/340 grams/2½ cups plain flour
1 level teaspoon bicarbonate of soda
2 level teaspoons ground ginger
4 oz/110 grams/½ cup butter
6 oz/180 grams/¾ cup soft brown sugar
4 tablespoons golden syrup
1 egg
Currants

Sift the flour into a bowl. Add the ginger and the bicarbonate of soda. Rub in the butter until the mixture looks like breadcrumbs. Mix in the sugar. Warm the syrup slightly to make it runny, add the beaten egg, and stir this into the flour mixture. You should now have a soft dough. With one hand knead until quite smooth, then roll out on the table or board as thinly as possible (about ¼ in.). With a gingerbread-man cutter, stamp out the men. If you haven't a cutter, do the best you can cutting round a gingerbread-man paper cut-out. Using the currants, give each man a row of buttons, two eyes and a mouth. With a fish slice, lift the shapes onto a greased baking sheet and cook them in an oven set at 375°F, gas mark 5, for about 12 minutes or until just coloured. Lift onto a cooling rack. They will become crisp as they cool.

Jelly boats (makes 12)

2 medium-sized melons
Different coloured jellies (jellos)
    —orange, red, yellow, green
(Cocktail sticks and coloured paper)

Make up the jellies as instructed on the packet, but using one-third less water than recommended (this is to make a firmer jelly). While the jellies are cooling, cut the melons in half lengthwise, and scoop out the flesh. (This is not required for the boats, so it can be eaten either on its own or in fruit salad.)

When the jellies are cool pour each into a melon skin, and refrigerate until firmly set. Now cut each melon-half into three long segments so that you have boat-shaped pieces filled with jelly. The jelly should be firm enough to stand up.

Make flags and masts from coloured paper and cocktail sticks, and write each child's name on a flag. Stick these into the jelly just before putting everything on the table. (See plate on page 102.) Smaller boats can be made with orange skins.

Chocolate hedgehog birthday cake

For the cake
3 eggs
3 oz/80 grams/3 tablespoons caster
    (powdered) sugar
2½ oz/75 grams/ 2 heaped and 1 level
    tablespoon plain flour
2 teaspoons cocoa powder
Pinch of salt

For the icing
2 tablespoons sweetened condensed
    milk
3 oz/80 grams sweetened dark
    chocolate
Few drops coffee essence
4 oz/110 grams/¼ cup butter

For the decoration
½ lb/250 grams chocolate buttons or
    split almonds
1 glacé cherry
1 currant
1 chocolate candy bar, preferably log-
    shaped
(Cake candles and holders)
(Fresh flowers, leaves or ferns)

Set the oven at 400°F, gas mark 6. Put a small disc of greaseproof (waxed) paper in the bottom of a 2½ pint mixing bowl, and brush out the paper and sides of the bowl with melted lard.

To make *the cake*, put the eggs and sugar together into a mixing bowl, and whisk until the mixture is very light and so thick that a ribbon of mixture is left on the surface when the whisk is withdrawn. (This process is speeded up if the mixing bowl is placed over a saucepan of simmering water during the whisking—the bottom of the basin must not come into contact with the water, however; and when thick the mixture should continue to be whisked until cool before you proceed.) Sieve the flour, cocoa and salt together and fold into the mixture, using a large metal spoon, and lifting rather than stirring the mixture with it. Turn the mixture into the greased bowl, and bake for 40 minutes or until the cake feels firm and springy to the touch. Turn out onto a cooling rack.

To make *the icing* put the condensed milk and coffee essence into the top of a double boiler. If you do not have a double boiler stand a mixing bowl (containing the milk and essence) over a saucepan of simmering water. Grate or chop the chocolate and put it in too. Stir until melted. Allow to cool. Beat the butter until light and creamy. Beat the cooled chocolate mixture into the butter. Put into the refrigerator to harden slightly before using.

Turn the cake out onto a flat round plate, and cover with the fudge icing, forking the icing as in the drawing.

Form the hedgehog's snout with the icing. Cut all the chocolate buttons in half and stick them or the almonds into the icing to form the hedgehog's spines. Make a nose with the currant. Cut the glacé cherry in half and use it to make the eyes.

Stick the candles, in their holders, into the log-shaped chocolate bar. Put the log next to the hedgehog and decorate with the leaves or flowers.

On the day before

The checkerboard of sandwiches can be completed, covered with polythene and kept in a cool place.

The sausages on sticks can be completed. When reheating put them in a low oven 250°F, gas mark ½, for 20 minutes. They can be reheated with the sticks in place.

Cheese and pineapple on sticks Make them and put in a plastic container. Cover well and refrigerate.

Cheese pictures can be made, covered well and kept in a cool place.

Gingerbread men can be made up to a week before and stored in an airtight container.

Jelly boats are better made the day before and kept overnight in the refrigerator. This ensures that the jelly will be really well set. Make the flags but do not stick them into the boats until setting the table.

Chocolate hedgehog birthday cake can be made completely. Keep in a cool place.

PARTY FOR 12 TEN-YEAR-OLDS

Locomotive birthday cake
Open sandwiches and rolls
Miniature kebabs
Hot dogs
Shortbread fingers
Toffee apples

(*Preparation on the day before follows recipes.*)

Locomotive birthday cake

3 chocolate swiss rolls (they may be the chocolate-covered kind, or made to the recipe below)
1 chocolate flake bar for the chimney stack

Put the cakes, a little apart, in a line on the cardboard. With a sharp knife cut out a piece of the top of the first cake (half a slice, 1½ inches wide, towards one end of the cake—see drawing opposite). With a cocktail stick to support it, fix

110

13 small round chocolate-covered biscuits (cookies) for wheels
1 glacé cherry, cut in half, for head-lights
¼ lb/110 grams toffees
¼ lb/110 grams miniature liquorice-all-sorts
Icing (confectioners') sugar
Water
(Wooden cocktail sticks)
(A piece of strong cardboard about 2 ft 6 ins long and 6 ins wide)

the chunk of cake over the gap to form a cab roof. If your piece of cake is too fragile to be supported on a cocktail stick, use a flat piece of chocolate, a chocolate bar, a rectangular chocolate biscuit or a piece of cardboard.

Hollow out the top of both the second and third cakes to make the freight wagons. Fill the hollows with toffees, miniature liquorice cubes, or coloured candy beans.

Mix a cupful of icing sugar with a very little water—just enough to make an icing of piping consistency. Using a fine nozzle and forcing bag, ice lines for wheel spokes (as in the drawing) onto 12 of the biscuits (cookies). Use half a cocktail stick to pin them into place. The remaining biscuit should be secured to the front of the train.

Stick the chocolate flake bar on the engine for a chimney stack. Using icing as adhesive, stick the cherry halves onto the front biscuit as headlamps. Outline these with icing. Pipe the birthday child's age or name, or both, onto the side of the engine. Take care when cutting the cake to remove the pieces of cocktail stick holding the wheels in place.

If candles are wanted they can be stuck onto one of the wagons or around the chimney stack.

Chocolate swiss roll (serves 6)

For the cake
3 eggs
3 oz/80 grams/3 tablespoons caster (powdered) sugar
2½ oz/75 grams/2 heaped and 1 level tablespoons plain flour
2 teaspoons cocoa powder

For the filling
¼ pint/⅛ litre/5 fl. oz thick cream and/or 3 tablespoons raspberry jam

Lay a shallow roasting pan or Swiss roll tin on a double sheet of greaseproof (waxed) paper larger than the area of the pan. Snip the corners and fold them as shown in the diagram so that the paper will line the pan with a good edge standing up all round. Pin the paper as shown if necessary. Brush out the paper with melted butter or lard. Set the oven at 400°F, gas mark 6. Put the eggs and sugar into a mixing bowl, and using a rotary whisk, whisk the mixture until it is light and thick enough to hold the impression of the whisk for a

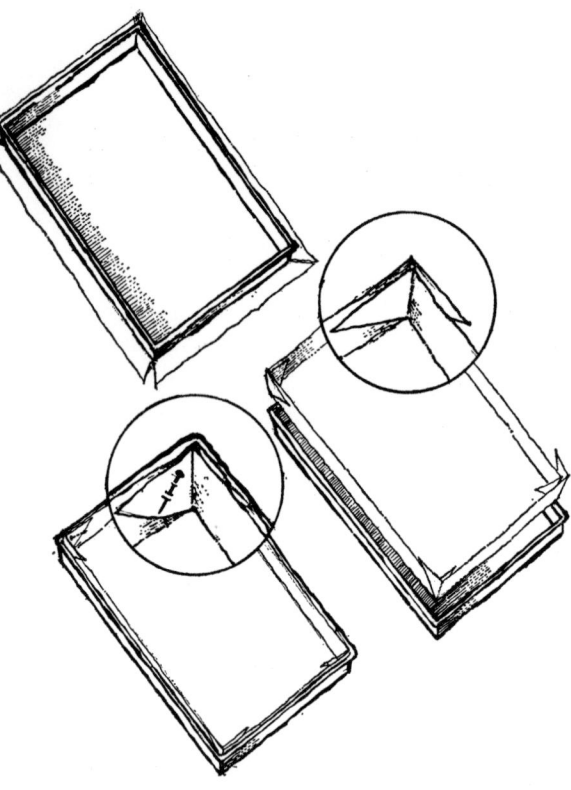

few seconds. (The process is greatly speeded up if the bowl is set over a pan of simmering water, but care should be taken that the bottom of the bowl does not touch the water. An electric mixer makes very light work of the job.)

Sift the flour with the cocoa and the salt. Fold it into the egg mixture, using a large metal spoon, and taking care not to over-stir. Pour the mixture into the paper-lined pan, spreading it evenly. Bake for 10 minutes or until the top of the sponge feels resistant to the touch.

Lay a clean cloth on the tabletop. Dust it lightly with caster (powdered) sugar. Turn the pan over onto the cloth, so that the cake falls out. Remove the paper. Roll the cake and cloth up together, starting at one of the shorter sides. Allow to cool. When the cake is cold, carefully unroll it, spread it with the jam and/or the whipped cream, and roll up again—this time without the cloth.

Open sandwiches and rolls (makes about 36)

6 small brown rolls
6 slices white bread
Butter
2 hard-boiled eggs
1 large tablespoon mayonnaise
1 can sardines
Salt and pepper
1 box mustard and cress

Split the rolls in half and butter them. Mash the eggs and mix with the mayonnaise. Spread each roll thickly with this.

Butter the slices of bread. Drain the sardines and mash them with a little more butter, pepper and salt. Spread on the bread. Cut the crusts off, and cut the slices into fingers.

Arrange the rolls piled in the middle of a large plate with the sardine fingers round the edge, pointed outwards like sunrays. Cut the cress with scissors and scatter it over.

Miniature kebabs (makes about 40)

$\frac{1}{2}$ lb/250 grams chipolata or cocktail
    sausages
16 long strips of fatty bacon
20 button mushrooms
1 green pepper (optional)
(Wooden cocktail sticks)

Fry the sausages, and if using chipolatas cut them each into five small pieces when cold. Cook the mushrooms in the fat from the sausages until soft, then drain them. Cut each in half. Cut each strip of bacon into pieces about two inches long, and roll up into tiny rolls. Pack them side by side in a roasting pan (very close together to prevent unravelling). Cook them for about 12 minutes in a fairly hot oven (400°F, gas mark 6) or until just beginning to brown.

Cut the green pepper into 40 half-inch squares. Skewer a piece of bacon, green pepper, mushroom and sausage (in that order) onto each of the cocktail sticks. Do not push everything too well onto the stick: it is easy for a child to scratch the back of his throat if the tip of the stick is exposed. If the sausage is skewered last, it will hold everything else in place.

Job feasting with his children

Company shocked at a Lady getting up to Ring the Bell by James Gillray

Hot dogs (makes 12)

I think hot dogs are nicest made with crisp french bread and pork sausages, but some prefer frankfurters and soft rolls. In either case the bread should be hot.

12 fat frankfurter or pork sausages
12 long soft rolls, or 4-inch lengths of thin french bread
Mustard
Tomato ketchup or relish

Heat frankfurters in water, or fry till hot. Fry or grill pork sausages until cooked through. Heat the bread in the oven for about 10 minutes at 400°F, gas mark 6. Split the rolls down one side and lay a hot sausage inside. Close the roll as far as possible over the sausage. With french bread, poke a hole through the middle of the length of bread with the handle of a wooden spoon, discarding some of the soft bread from the inside of the loaf. Push the sausage into the hole. The hot dogs can be kept warm in a cool oven (250°F, gas mark ½). Serve with mustard, ketchup or relish.

Shortbread fingers (makes about 18)

4 oz/110 grams/½ cup butter
2 oz/50 grams/2 tablespoons caster (powdered) sugar
6 oz/180 grams/1 cup plain flour
1 oz/30 grams/¼ cup split almonds

Set the oven at 370°F, gas mark 5. Beat the butter and sugar together until soft and creamy. Work in the flour by degrees, with a minimum of beating. Pat the paste into a smooth ball, then into a square about ½ inch thick. Slide a floured baking sheet under the paste; cut it into fingers; decorate with split almonds, pressing them in gently. Bake to a pale biscuit colour (about 20 minutes).

Toffee apples (makes 12)

12 small red or green dessert apples
1 lb/½ kilo/2 cups granulated or lump sugar
½ pint/¼ litre/10 fl. oz water
(Wooden skewers)

Wash and dry the apples. Oil a baking sheet, tray or large plate. Stick the skewers firmly into the apples (near the stalk). Heat the sugar and water slowly in a small thick-bottomed saucepan until the sugar melts and then boils to an even brown. (Do not stir, as this causes bubbles in the caramel. If the sugar is caramelizing unevenly hold the saucepan by the handle and *carefully* swill the contents round.) Make sure the apples are quite dry. Holding the skewer, dip each apple into the caramel, turning it to coat evenly, then put it on the oiled surface. Work fast so that all the apples are done before the caramel cools and thickens. Do not let the apples touch—they stick together like limpets.

On the day before

Locomotive cake Make completely the day before. Cover lightly with polythene.
Open sandwiches and rolls With the exception of the final scattering of mustard and cress, these can be done a day in advance, and kept covered in polythene in a cool place.
Miniature kebabs Make them and keep in a cool place.
Hot dogs are best freshly made; the sausages can be cooked and reheated in the oven.
Shortbread fingers Make up to a week in advance and store in an airtight tin.
Toffee apples can be made several hours ahead of the party but (especially in damp weather, when they tend to get sticky) it is unwise to make them much earlier.

8 · Young Teenagers' Parties

The temptation to quit the house altogether while the teenagers are deafening the neighbours should be resisted—although your offspring will very likely *implore* you to leave, and insist that everyone else's Mum always does. But sitting in the cinema worrying about what is happening back home can be worse than consoling broken-hearted Amanda because Jim is dancing with Mary. And anyway, the knowledge that a grown-up is in the house somewhere might restrain the wilder excesses of the children (which, whatever they say, they still *are*).

The guest-list and most of the arrangements can be left to the young host, who will anyway have very clear ideas of what he wants. It is certain to involve noise, so the neighbours should be warned. Drinks should look grown-up, even though non-alcoholic (see Teetotaller's Tipple, page 15): a fruit cup or apple juice are good ideas too, as well as the usual cokes, ginger ales, etc. (for quantities see page 16). Decorating the room can be left to the children, as can arranging the music, fixing the record player, etc.

A firm time-limit is helpful to other parents collecting their children (say 10.30 p.m.) and it establishes a bargaining point with the young host ('All right, ten minutes extra then').

Supper can be set out on a table, which teenagers might like to decorate with silver foil or tissue paper.

The food should, indeed must, *look* very sophisticated, but need not really be. A good menu would be the Cocktail Lunch/Supper (page 22) if it is to be eaten without plates, or the simple Inexpensive Buffet (page 76).

Teenagers are generally more enthusiastic than adults about unusual parties like beach picnics and barbecues, and a lot of the work—like building the barbecue—can be fobbed off on to them if you decide to risk the weather. (See *Outdoor Parties*, page 138 and *Hallowe'en Parties*, page 169.)
General check list, page 184.

9 · Garden Parties

Assemblies redolent of the British raj still rule the lawns in some countries. I recently catered for such a party given by a High Sheriff in England. The guests drifting round the sward presented a picture from another age, all large white floppy hats on silk-clad county ladies, gentlemen in formal attire, and a red-coated brass band booming away from the pavilion bandstand.

High Sheriff or not, if you are going to give a summer party in your garden you need a large barn, cleaned out, or a huge tent—for trusting the weather, with possibly hundreds of people on your hands, is folly. (I know that in England, at least, the Queen trusts to luck, but she is the Queen, and people are prepared to stand under their umbrellas for her.) If the weather is fine, the sides of the tent can be raised, turning it into a summer pavilion.

Well polished thermal tea-urns are acceptable on the buffet table, but if teapots are to be used, allow enough for some to be filled while others are in use—to avoid obliging the guest to hold a half-filled cup while the waitress disappears into the service tent. The water urns are boiled on gas rings (hired). The tea should never be made in them but in thermal urns or large teapots. Milk or cream, sugar and cups are set out on the buffet table in the main tent, the urns being carried in by the staff. It is a good idea to have two or three serving points to avoid too much waiting, and the food should be set out between these points.

If there is a band, they will need feeding too. Fruit drinks, milk and coke are necessary for the children. Strawberries and cream are a tradition at garden parties, and I think iced coffee should be. If the milk is kept in bottles, sunk in ice in a large bowl or washtub (like chilling champagne), iced coffee is not too much trouble to make, using iced-coffee-mix. A blob of whipped cream and a straw are added just before the guests arrive. This takes a lot of pressure off the tea servers.

Quantities When calculating the amount of milk required for tea, reckon on getting 20 cups per pint. If iced coffee is served a pint is only enough for three glasses. Generally about half the guests have tea; half iced coffee. Surprisingly, a pound of tea will easily do 100 cups, and teabags make for speed. Allow four little cakes or sandwiches per head and a quarter of a pound of strawberries. A pint of cream is enough for 20 helpings of strawberries, or for rather more if it is whipped. Alcohol is not usually served at a garden party but there is always the chance that a few guests will linger on and come back to the house expecting drinks. Garden parties generally start at about 2.30 or 3 p.m., and are over by 5 p.m.

Check list for large parties, page 187.

GARDEN PARTY MENU FOR 100

Sardine and lemon sandwiches   (*Preparation on the day before follows recipes.*)
Salami on rye
Fruit tartlets
Bakewell tart
Strawberries and cream

Sardine and lemon sandwiches

Make sandwiches with white or brown bread, using the filling below. For 100 miniature sandwiches you will need 2½ loaves of sliced bread, about a pound of butter, and twice the quantities in this recipe.

1 large can sardines (about ¾ lb/350 grams)
6 oz/175 grams/¾ cup butter
Juice of half a lemon
½ teaspoon french mustard
Salt and black pepper
1 egg white (optional—will make the pâté lighter and softer)

Put the butter in a large bowl and beat it with a wooden spoon until soft. Add the sardines with their oil and beat all together. Add the mustard and lemon juice, salt and plenty of freshly ground black pepper, and mix well. (For a soft creamy pâté, beat the mixture very well, preferably in an electric machine. Whisk the egg white stiffly and fold it in.)

(This sardine pâté served with toast is delicious as a first course for dinner and looks pretty served in scooped-out lemon skins, or little china pots. The above quantities would serve about 10.)

Salami on rye

For 100 small canapés you will need about six loaves of sliced rye bread, 2 lb /1 kilo butter and 100 slices of salami. Choose a very fat salami and if possible get the grocer or delicatessen to skin it and to slice it thinly on a slicing machine.

Using a pastry cutter the same size as the salami, cut a round out of each slice of bread, butter it thickly, and cover with the salami. Keep well wrapped in polythene until needed.

Fruit tartlets

For 100 tartlets you will need to make four times the recipe for rich short crust pastry on page 88. It is easier to make the recipe four times than to quadruple the quantities and have to deal with an unwieldy bulk.

Shortcrust pastry
Fresh fruit such as cherries, strawberries, bananas or grapes and perhaps canned black cherries or canned mandarin oranges. For the 100 tartlets I would use:
100 black grapes (about 2 lb/1 kilo)
About 6 bananas
100 small strawberries (about 3 lb/ 1½ kilos)
100 segments of canned mandarin oranges (about 3 large cans)
Crème pâtissière (see below)
2 lb/1 kilo apricot jam
Juice of one lemon

Roll out the pastry and line into deep tartlet pans. Bake blind (see note on page 105) for 12 minutes at 400°F, gas mark 6, or until the pastry is quite cooked. Allow to cool.

Put a spoonful of crème pâtissière into each tartlet, and arrange the fruit on top. Each tartlet should contain a black grape (halved and seeded), two slices of banana, a segment (well drained) of canned mandarin, and a hulled strawberry, cut in half. (The grapes and strawberries are placed cut-side down.) Melt the apricot jam, add the lemon juice, and sieve. While it is still runny, paint a thin glaze over the fruit to prevent the banana discolouring and to make the tartlets shiny.

Crème pâtissière

(Do four times the quantity for 100 tartlets.)

2 egg yolks
2 oz/50 grams/¼ cup caster (powdered) sugar
½ pint/¼ litre/10 fl. oz milk
1½ oz/45 grams/1 heaped and 1 level tablespoon cornflour

Put the egg yolks in a bowl with the sugar and mix well. Put the cornflour into a cup with a little of the milk and mix to a smooth paste. Add this to the yolk mixture. Boil the rest of the milk, and pour it onto the mixture, stirring. Pour this into the milk saucepan and stir over gentle heat until

1 egg white
2 drops vanilla essence

thick. During the cooking the custard will form alarming lumps, but they will disappear when the whole custard is thick and well beaten. Draw the saucepan aside while you whip the egg white and fold it in. Return to the heat, and cook, stirring all the time, until thick and smooth. Add the vanilla and turn the mixture into a bowl to cool.

Bakewell tart (serves 5)
(For 100 small slices you will need 10 tarts, but if the thought of making so many is daunting, good ones can be bought. Order them well in advance from the baker.)

½ lb/230 grams rich shortcrust pastry (page 88)
2 oz/50 grams/2 heaped tablespoons ground almonds
2 oz/50 grams/2 tablespoons caster (powdered) sugar
Juice and grated rind of 1 lemon
2 oz/50 grams/4 tablespoons butter
1 egg
1 oz/30 grams/3 heaped tablespoons cake crumbs
Raspberry jam
2 drops almond essence

Set the oven at 400°F, gas mark 6. Line a flan ring or shallow cake pan with the pastry and leave to rest while you make the filling. Keep the pastry trimmings. Beat the butter and sugar together until light and creamy. Add the lemon juice and rind. Beat in the egg, then add the cake crumbs, the almond essence and the ground almonds. Cover the pastry sparingly with jam, and spread the filling on top. Roll the trimmings of pastry out and cut into thin strips. Lattice the top of the tart with them, sticking the edges down with a little water. Bake for 30–40 minutes, or until the top is pale brown and the pastry cooked. You may need to cover the tart with foil or paper half way through cooking to prevent the pastry becoming too brown before the filling is set.

Strawberries and cream
Hulling a pound or two of strawberries presents no problem, but strawberries and cream for 100 is rather more tricky. Allow 1 lb of strawberries for four people if they are to eat off flat plates. If glasses, sundae cups or small glass bowls are used, the same amount of strawberries will serve five. For 100 people, a gallon of runny cream or 5 pints of whipped cream is adequate, and you will need about 3 lb of caster (powdered) sugar. If the strawberries are bought the day before (it is risky to rely on getting them on the day—especially if it is a Saturday—and there may not be time for the long job of hulling them on the day of the party), prepare them in advance: hull them and put them into shallow containers. (If they are piled into a bucket the ones underneath get badly squashed.) Sugar them lightly, and sprinkle with orange juice. Some of the juice will run from the strawberries, but they will not go mouldy and will be even more delicious after macerating in the orange juice. Keep in a cool place, but on no account freeze them.

On the day before
Sardine and lemon sandwiches should be completed the day before and kept well wrapped in polythene in a cool place.
Salami on rye Make them, and put in a box or on a tray with sheets of polythene or paper between them. Cover the box tightly or wrap the tray with polythene. Keep cool.
Fruit tartlets Make the pastry cases and the crème pâtissière; sieve the jam and prepare all the fruit except the bananas—which would go brown if cut. The tartlets should not be put together more than eight hours before the party.
Bakewell tart Make up to five days in advance and keep in an airtight container.
Strawberries and cream See notes above.

10 · Breakfast Parties ('Brunch')

A breakfast party on a Sunday mid-morning can be marvellous. It relieves one's friends of the chores both of breakfast and that Victorian institution, Sunday Lunch. The only snag is the probability of your friends staying on for drinks, and even for tea after that. So it is sensible to lay in at least some white wine or beer lest Sunday inertia prevents anyone going home. Incidentally, champagne is delicious at breakfast, as is Buck's Fizz (page 98).

If you have someone to do the cooking you cannot do better than serve the classic English Breakfast—eggs, bacon, kidneys, sausages, tomatoes, toast and marmalade. Without help you had best plan a menu that requires little more of you than to keep filling the toaster. Kedgeree, egg-and-bacon flan, sausages with onion and tomato sauce, or baked bean casserole (pages 99, 105 and 76) can all be made the day before and reheated. Because the meal is partly lunch it should be hearty enough to last everyone till supper.

Of the two menus below, the first can mostly be prepared in advance; the second calls for more last-minute cooking—which is fun if the party is in the kitchen, with everyone giving a hand. Alternatively, buy an electric frying pan and do the cooking on the sideboard in the dining room.

BRUNCH PARTY FOR 8

Orange and tomato juice
Muesli with fruit and yoghurt
Soft eggs with cheese
Croissants

(Preparation on the day before follows recipes.)

Serve plenty of coffee first, then either lager or a sparkling hock.

Orange and tomato juice (serves 8)

2 pints/1½ litres/5 cups canned tomato juice
2 pints/1½ litres/5 cups orange juice (fresh is best, but frozen or unsweetened canned orange juice is acceptable)

Mix the juices together, add sugar if necessary, and chill well.

Muesli with fruit and yoghurt (serves 8)

8 tablespoons flaked oats
4 tablespoons lemon juice
4 grated apples
4 sliced bananas
4 tablespoons runny honey
4 tablespoons hazelnuts, chopped
4 tablespoons seedless raisins
2 pints/1½ litres/5 cups milk
2 small cartons yoghurt

Soak the oats overnight in a pint of water. Mix all the ingredients together, except the milk and the yoghurt. Serve these separately. Most people add milk to their muesli, but it is sometimes eaten dry. A dollop of yoghurt on top is delicious.

Soft eggs with cheese (serves 8)

8 eggs
3 oz/80 grams/¾ cup grated cheddar
cheese
3 oz/80 grams/6 tablespoons butter
Salt and black pepper

Boil the eggs for 5–6 minutes and put immediately into cold water. Shell them straight away, plunging them into the cold water frequently to prevent burning your fingers. Once they are shelled put them into hot (not boiling) water to keep warm. Warm eight coffee cups, and drop an egg into each. With a knife break the eggs open and sprinkle with grated cheese, pepper and salt. Melt the butter in a pan, and heat it until it just begins to go brown and look granular. While sizzling pour over the eggs and serve immediately. The browned butter gives a nutty rather rich taste to the eggs, but you may prefer a knob of plain butter.

Croissants

See recipe on page 99.

On the day before

Orange and tomato juice Mix the juices and keep overnight in the refrigerator.
Muesli with fruit and yoghurt Soak the oatflakes, prepare the fruit, nuts and raisins and mix with the sugar, honey and lemon juice.
Soft eggs with cheese Grate the cheese. The eggs can be boiled and shelled the day before, for re-heating in hot water, but this is as much trouble as boiling them just before eating.
Croissants are best baked before breakfast, although the dough is made the day before. But they are still delicious if baked the day before and kept well wrapped in a cool place. They are particularly good hot.

BRUNCH PARTY FOR 8

Spiced marmalade apples with
   cream
Framed eggs with tomatoes and
   mushrooms
Wholemeal baps, butter and
   honey
Oatcakes

(Preparation on the day before follows recipes.)

Serve a sweet, fruity hock—a spätlese. Unusual but delicious.

Spiced marmalade apples with crème chantilly (serves 8)

12 eating apples, peeled, cored and
   quartered
4 oz/100 grams/½ cup butter
4 large tablespoons golden syrup
2 tablespoons brown sugar
2 tablespoons bitter marmalade (or
   ginger marmalade)
1 tablespoon mixed spice
Juice of one orange and one lemon

For the crème chantilly
¼ pint/¼ litre/10 fl. oz thick cream
2 dessertspoons caster (powdered) sugar
2 egg whites

Melt the butter in a large thick-bottomed frying pan. Add the syrup, brown sugar and apple pieces and cook until the apple is brown on all sides. Add the marmalade and mixed spice, and boil fast until the toffee is a good brown. Tip the apples into a shallow ovenproof dish; pour on the orange and lemon juice, and any remaining toffee from the pan. Whip the cream and stir in the caster sugar. Whip the egg-white until it is stiff, and fold into the cream. Just before serving spread this crème chantilly over the hot apples.

121

Framed eggs with tomatoes and mushrooms (serves 8)

8 eggs
8 large slices of white bread
4 large tomatoes
8 large flat mushrooms
Oil for frying
Butter

With a large round biscuit (cookie) cutter remove the middle from the bread slices. Do not throw away the rest of the bread. Fry the rounds in oil until brown on both sides. Dot the mushrooms with butter and grill them. Cut the tomatoes in half; grill them until just cooked. Set each mushroom on a round of fried bread, and put a tomato-half on top. Keep them warm. Now fry the bread frames—i.e., the pieces left after the middle was removed from the bread slices—on one side. Turn them over, and break an egg into the middle of each. Fry until the whites are set, spooning over some of the hot fat to help the process. Serve each guest with a framed egg and with the mushroom and tomato on fried bread. Have salt and pepper ready for those who want it. Unless you have two or three large frying pans it is impossible to fry more than two framed eggs at once, so unless the party is very small, guests should be encouraged to eat as you finish frying, rather than waiting for everyone to be served.

Wholemeal baps (soft rolls)
See page 106.

Oatcakes

1 lb/450 grams/3 cups medium oat-meal
1 oz/30 grams/2 tablespoons lard or margarine
½ teaspoon bicarbonate of soda
Big pinch of salt
½ pint/¼ litre/10 fl. oz hot water

Melt the margarine in the water. Mix the oatmeal, salt and bicarbonate of soda together in a large bowl. Make a well in the middle, and pour in the water and margarine. With a knife, mix to a soft dough. Dust a board or table top with oatmeal and roll the dough out into as thin a round as possible. To prevent the dough sticking, keep dusting liberally with more oatmeal. Slide a baking sheet under the dough, and when in place cut into segments (called farls in Scotland) and separate them slightly. Bake at 370°F, gas mark 5, for about 20 minutes or until the oatcakes are crisp. They should be turned over once or twice during baking. Cool on a wire tray. Store in an airtight container.
Serve hot with butter and marmalade.

On the day before
Spiced marmalade apples Cook the apples, but do not add the crème chantilly until just before serving. Reheat the apples in a hot oven (450°F, gas mark 8) for 10 minutes.
Framed eggs with tomatoes and mushrooms Prepare the bread, tomatoes and mushrooms, but cook nothing until the guests are assembled. The eggs must be eaten as soon as cooked.
Wholemeal baps (soft rolls) can be made a day or two before and kept in a breadbox or well wrapped in the refrigerator.
Oatcakes can be made at least a week in advance, and kept in a cake tin.

11 · Lunch Parties

Most lunch parties fall into one of three categories—the businessmen's (where the prime object is to talk money, so that anything like artichokes would be an unwelcome distraction); the ladies' lunch, where a bit of competitiveness and showing-off is no bad thing (though the food should not be too fattening); and the family affair like Sunday lunch, which is the weekly blow-out for the children and must be 'good plain cooking'.

BUSINESSMEN'S LUNCH FOR 6

Soused mackerel with mustard
    sauce

Tranche d'agneau à la catalane
Vegetable mornay

Rum baba

Stilton

(*Preparation on the day before follows recipes.*)

Serve a light claret—a St Emilion or a red Graves.

Soused mackerel with mustard sauce (serves 6)

6 small mackerel, cleaned

For the court bouillon
1 carrot, sliced
1 onion, sliced
2 bayleaves
Bunch of parsley
12 peppercorns
A pinch of ground mace or nutmeg
1 teaspoon salt
1½ pints/1 litre/3¾ cups cider
Juice of one lemon

For the sauce
1 oz/30 grams/1 heaped tablespoon
    flour
1 tablespoon french mustard
1 teaspoon sugar
¼ pint/⅛ litre/5 fl. oz thin cream
Salt and pepper
1 egg white

Put all the court bouillon ingredients into a saucepan and bring to simmering point. Simmer for 20 minutes. Lay the mackerel in a roasting pan or shallow dish. Strain over the liquid, cover and cook in a slow oven (300°F, gas mark 2) for 45 minutes or until the fish are very soft. Cool in the liquid.

To make the *mustard sauce* put the flour, sugar and mustard in a thick-bottomed saucepan and mix well together. Add two tablespoons of the court bouillon from the cooked fish, and when smooth add ½ pint more, stirring all the time. Put over gentle heat and slowly bring to the boil, stirring. Boil for 10 minutes, stirring all the time. Allow to cool. Beat in the cream. Season with salt and pepper to taste. Whip the egg-white stiffly, and fold into the sauce. Lay the mackerel on a dish, and serve the sauce separately.

Tranche d'agneau à la catalane

6 lamb steaks, about ½ in./1¼ cm.
  thick, cut from the leg
Bunch of watercress

For the marinade
½ pint/¼ litre/10 fl. oz olive oil
6 cloves garlic, crushed
1 tablespoon dried, or a good handful
  fresh, thyme
1 large onion, finely sliced
24 peppercorns, slightly crushed
Salt

Lay the lamb steaks in a roasting pan or shallow dish. Pour over the oil and add all the other marinade ingredients. Leave the steaks to marinate for at least eight hours, preferably twenty-four, turning them over two or three times—unless they are left in the refrigerator, where the oil solidifies and can simply be spread with the slices of onion etc. over the top of the steaks. Get a thick frying pan or griddle really hot. Alternatively pre-heat the grill (broiler) for at least 10 minutes. Strip most of the oil from the steaks and immediately put them in the hot pan, or under the grill. Grill or fry, turning once, until both sides are a good brown. Like beef steaks they can be eaten in any state from blue to well done, but I think they are best slightly pink. Overcooking tends to toughen the meat, and the juiciness is lost. Serve immediately with a sprig or two of watercress.

Vegetable mornay (serves 6–8)

1 small cauliflower
3 tomatoes
½ lb/250 grams shelled peas, or 1 small
  packet frozen peas
1 lb/½ kilo carrots
1 pint/¾ litre/20 fl. oz milk
1 oz/30 grams/2 tablespoons butter
1 oz/30 grams/1 heaped tablespoon
  flour
3 oz/80 grams/¾ cup grated cheese
Salt and pepper

Break the cauliflower into sprigs and cook them in boiling salted water until just tender, but not soft. Cook the peas. Peel and slice the carrots, and boil in salted water until just tender. Skin the tomatoes (plunge them into boiling water for five seconds to loosen the skins) and cut them in half. Put all the vegetables into a fireproof dish.
Melt the butter; stir in the flour; cook, stirring, for one minute, then draw the pan off the heat. Add the milk slowly, beating out the lumps as you go. Return the pan to the heat and stir until boiling. Boil for 2 minutes. Add the cheese, and mix well. Season with salt and pepper, and pour over the vegetables. Put in a fairly hot oven (400°F, gas mark 6) for about 15 minutes to reheat and to brown the top.

Rum baba with raspberries and grapes (serves 6)

For the baba
4½ oz/125 grams/¾ cup plain flour
½ teaspoon salt
½ oz/15 grams/1 tablespoon yeast
  (less if dried yeast is used)
½ oz/15 grams/½ tablespoon granulated
  sugar
½ gill/2½ fl. oz warm milk
2 eggs
1¾ oz/45 grams/3 tablespoons butter

For the syrup
½ lb/230 grams/1 cup granulated
  sugar

To make *the baba* sift the flour with the salt into a warm dry bowl. Mix the yeast and sugar together in a cup, and add the milk. (If using dried yeast, use half the quantity given. Reconstitute it by mixing with 2 tablespoons of tepid milk or water and sprinkling with 1 teaspoon of sugar. Allow to stand for 15 minutes. When it is frothy add it to the milk.) Beat the eggs in a small bowl, add the yeast mixture to them, and pour onto the flour. Using the fingers of one hand, mix and beat the mixture well for about 5 minutes. Stand the bowl, with a cloth or sheet of polythene across the top, in a warm place to rise: it should double

½ pint/¼ litre/10 fl. oz water
3 tablespoons rum
½ lb/250 grams fresh raspberries
½ lb/250 grams black grapes
½ pint/¼ litre/10 fl. oz thick cream
1 egg white

its bulk in about ¾ hour. Now beat the softened butter into the dough, and beat for another five minutes. Butter a large savarin mould or cake tin and pour in the mixture. Leave in a warm place for 15 minutes to prove (i.e. rise again). During this time the oven should be heating to 400°F, gas mark 6. When the baba is well risen, bake it to a golden brown (25–30 minutes). Turn out onto a large plate with a good lip.

To make *the syrup* bring the sugar and water slowly to the boil, stirring occasionally. Boil fast until the syrup is very tacky and will form a short thread between thumb and forefinger (first dip your fingers into cold water to prevent burning them). Add the rum, and pour carefully over the baba, saving a few tablespoons to add to the cream. Whip the cream stiffly. Stir in enough syrup to sweeten it, but not to make it at all runny. Whip the egg white, and fold it in. Pile the cream into the centre of the baba.

Halve the grapes and remove the seeds. Mix with the raspberries, and spoon round the baba.

On the day before

Mackerel with mustard sauce Cook the mackerel. Leave overnight in the liquid. Make the mustard sauce—it need not be refrigerated.

Tranche d'agneau à la catalane The steaks must be marinated the day before, but they should not be cooked until the last minute.

Vegetable mornay As long as all the vegetables are slightly undercooked, this dish can be completed the day before, and simply heated up in the oven. It will take about 25 minutes to heat through if it is quite cold when put in the oven.

Rum baba with raspberries and grapes Make the baba, but only pour over half the syrup. Prepare the fruit and put it into some of the rest of the syrup. (This will help preserve the fruit.) Remember to save a little syrup for adding to the cream. The cream should be whipped, and the baba filled, only a few hours before the party.

LADIES' LUNCH FOR 6

Filets de sole Dugléré

Lemon chicken
Glazed onions
Mixed green salad

Yoghurt, honey and dates

(*Preparation on the day before follows recipes.*)

Serve a good white Burgundy—a Meursault or a Montrachet—right through the lunch.

Filets de sole Dugléré (serves 6)
18 small or 12 large fillets of sole,
   skinned
The skin, heads and bones from
   the fish
1 onion, sliced
9 peppercorns
(*continued overleaf*)

Set the oven at 350°F, gas mark 4.
Put the fish heads, skin and bones in a saucepan with the water, onion, peppercorns, bayleaf, parsley and thyme. Cover and simmer for 20 minutes.
Lay the fillets, with their ends tucked under, in an ovenproof dish or roasting pan. Strain over the

1 bayleaf
Bunch of parsley
1 sprig or pinch of thyme
$\frac{1}{2}$ pint/$\frac{1}{4}$ litre/10 fl. oz water
$\frac{1}{2}$ pint/$\frac{1}{4}$ litre/10 fl. oz white wine
1 oz/30 grams/2 tablespoons butter
1 oz/30 grams/1 heaped tablespoon
   flour
$\frac{1}{4}$ pint/$\frac{1}{8}$ litre/5 fl. oz cream
2 large tomatoes, skinned, seeded and
   chopped
1 tablespoon chopped parsley
1 tablespoon chopped chives
Salt and pepper

Lemon chicken (serves 6)
Three 2-portion poussins (broilers)
   or two 3 lb (1$\frac{1}{2}$ kilo) roasting
   chickens
3 oz/80 grams/6 tablespoons butter
Juice of two lemons
2 teaspoons sugar
Paprika
Black pepper
Salt
Watercress

Glazed onions (serves 6)
36 button onions or shallots
2 oz/30 grams/4 tablespoons butter
1 level dessertspoon sugar
Salt and pepper

Green salad
See page 71.

fish stock. Add the wine, cover with foil, and put in the oven for about 20 minutes or until the fish is cooked. (The fish will be firm to the touch, and have a creamy look when done, but if unsure, cut the thickest one open and look.) Melt the butter in a saucepan, add the flour and stir for $\frac{1}{2}$ minute. Draw off the heat, strain in the liquor from the fish, whisk out any lumps, and reboil, stirring. Add salt and pepper to taste, and the cream. Add the tomatoes, parsley and chives, but do not cook any more. Lay the fillets of fish in a serving dish, and pour over the sauce.

Melt the butter in a large saucepan (or two if necessary) and add the lemon juice. Lay the chickens whole in the saucepan, and cover with the lid. Cook on a gentle heat for $\frac{1}{2}$ hour, turning the chickens to brown slightly on all sides. After $\frac{1}{2}$ hour the chickens should be partially cooked, and the butter and lemon juice in the pan should be brown but not burnt. Take out the birds, and split them in two or joint them if large. Heat the grill (broiler). Lay the portions of chicken, cut-side-up on the grill tray. Brush them with some of the lemon juice and butter from the saucepan(s). Sprinkle with half the sugar, plenty of paprika and black pepper. Grill slowly until a really good brown. Turn the joints over, and again brush with lemon juice and butter, and sprinkle with sugar, paprika and pepper. Grill until cooked through and very dark—almost but not quite charred. Sprinkle with salt. Arrange on a heated dish, pour over the juices from the grill pan, and garnish with bouquets of watercress.

Peel the onions, taking care not to cut the root back too far (the onions unravel if you do). Boil them in salted water for 6 minutes. Drain well. Melt the butter in a large thick-bottomed pan and put in the onions. Sprinkle with the sugar. If the onions are still very undercooked put on the saucepan lid; if they are nearly done leave it off. Shake the pan occasionally, and cook the onions until an even brown all over. The cooking should be very slow to prevent burning, and to ensure that the onions are tender right through. Test with a skewer.

Yoghurt, honey and dates (serves 6)
This is a childishly simple dessert but delicious and very light.

1½ pints/1 litre/3½ cups natural
   unsweetened yoghurt
6 tablespoons runny honey
1 box best dates
6 tablespoons thick cream
Juice of half a lemon
Jordan almonds (optional)

Take six pudding bowls or large goblets, and spoon the yoghurt into them. Squeeze a little lemon juice onto each. Remove the stones from the dates and chop them. Scatter them onto the yoghurt. Trickle a tablespoon of honey over each helping, and add a good tablespoon of cream. A few Jordan almonds, shelled but with the inner skins left on, are a good addition, or they can replace the dates for a less sweet result.

On the day before
Filets de sole Duglére The dish can be made the day before and heated in the oven, though this generally results in the tomatoes (which should be firm and raw in the sauce) becoming cooked and colouring the sauce pink. The best method is to cook the fish, lay it in a fireproof dish, brush it with melted butter and cover it well with foil. Put in the refrigerator. Make the sauce, but do not add the tomato, parsley or chives. Prepare these and keep them in a cool place. Before lunch put the fish in the oven set at 300°F, gas mark 2, for about 15 minutes to heat up. Heat the sauce in a pan, adding the tomato and herbs just before pouring over the fish.
Lemon chicken Do the preliminary cooking in the saucepan, and grill (broil) one side of the chicken very well. It should be very nearly cooked when you stop. Turn the joints over, brush them with the butter etc., and keep them in the refrigerator. Do the final grilling just before the meal.
Glazed onions can be cooked completely and left in the pan when done. Simply re-heat by putting back on the heat.
Mixed green salad Make the dressing, and if you have bought the salad, prepare it and put in a polythene bag in the refrigerator. Salad is best bought on the day it is eaten.
Yoghurt, honey and dates Stone and chop the dates.

FAMILY SUNDAY LUNCH FOR 8

Mussel soup

Arabian stuffed lamb
Fantail potatoes
Mixed spring vegetables

Iced bombe with black cherry
   sauce

(*Preparation on the day before follows recipes.*)

A Burgundy, preferably a Beaune, would go well with the soup and the lamb.

Mussel soup (serves 6)
1 quart/1½ litres fresh mussels
2 medium onions, finely chopped
1½ oz/45 grams/3 tablespoons butter
1½ oz/45 grams/1 heaped and 1 level
   tablespoon flour
1 bayleaf
Bunch of parsley
Sprig of thyme
1 stick celery, sliced
(*continued overleaf*)

Scrub the mussels, removing the 'beards' and discarding any open or broken ones. Put them into a large saucepan or fish kettle, pour on the wine, and shake over fierce heat, turning them with a wooden spoon until all are opened. Allow to cool sufficiently to handle, then remove the mussels from the shells, reserving the shells and liquid. Discard the 'rubber band' around each mussel. Put the mussels aside. Pour the water and

127

1 glass white wine
¾ pint/½ litre/15 fl. oz milk
¾ pint/½ litre/15 fl. oz water
¼ pint/⅛ litre/5 fl. oz cream
Salt and pepper, ground nutmeg

milk into the pan on top of the shells, and add the bayleaf, parsley, thyme and celery. Simmer for 10 minutes. Melt the butter in another saucepan, and add the onion. Cook very gently until the onion is soft and transparent. Stir in the flour, and cook for a further minute, stirring. Strain on the liquid from the other pan, and stir until boiling. Add the mussels, and simmer for 5 minutes. Liquidize the soup in an electric blender, or push through a sieve. Add salt, pepper and nutmeg to taste, and the cream. Reheat without boiling.

Arabian stuffed lamb (serves 8)
1 shoulder of lamb, boned
1 oz/30 grams/2 tablespoons butter
2 slices fatty bacon, diced
¼ lb/100 grams lamb's liver, diced
1 large onion, finely chopped
4 oz/100 grams mushrooms, sliced
2 cloves garlic, crushed
1 tablespoon mixed chopped herbs
   (basil, thyme, parsley and rosemary)
Grated rind of ½ lemon
2 tablespoons sultanas
1 cup cooked rice

For the gravy
1 tablespoon tomato paste (optional)
1 dessertspoon flour
½ pint/¼ litre/10 fl. oz stock

Set the oven at 375°F, gas mark 5.
For *the stuffing* melt half the butter in a frying pan and put in the diced bacon and onion. Fry gently until the onion is soft. Add the liver, and turn the heat up. Fry fairly fast to brown the liver on all sides. Add the mushrooms, crushed garlic, herbs and lemon rind and cook gently until the mushrooms are soft. Season with salt and pepper. Remove from the heat and mix into the cooked rice. Add the sultanas. Push this stuffing into the shoulder of lamb, sewing up the edges with thin string. Use a darning needle if you do not have a kitchen larding needle. Spread the remaining butter over the lamb, and roast for about 2 hours, basting occasionally.
To make *the gravy.* Lift the meat from the roasting pan and keep it warm on a serving platter in the switched-off oven. Pour off most of the fat from the roasting pan, and then stir in first the flour and then—if using it—the tomato paste. Add the stock, and stir over the heat until it boils, scratching the brown bits from the bottom of the pan as you go. Taste and add salt and pepper if necessary.

Fantail potatoes (serves 8)
8 medium-sized potatoes
2 oz/50 grams/4 tablespoons butter
2 oz/50 grams/½ cup grated cheese

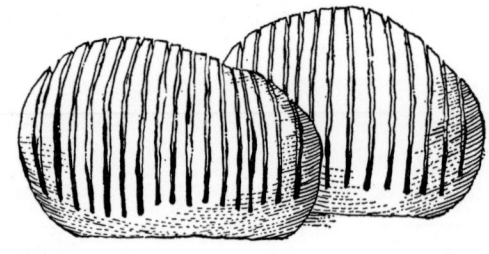

Peel the potatoes. Cut them as if you were slicing them but without cutting right through. (See the drawing.) Shave off a piece from the underside of each potato, to prevent them rolling over. Spread with butter. Put them into the oven at 375°F, gas mark 5, and roast for 1¼–1½ hours, basting occasionally. After ¾ hour sprinkle them with the cheese. Take them out when they are brown, and soft inside.

Mixed spring vegetables (serves 8)

8 small beetroots
1 small cauliflower
8 young leeks
½ lb/250 grams peas
8 small tomatoes

or

8 small courgettes (zucchini)
1 lb/½ kilo leaf spinach
3 sticks salsify
1 lb/½ kilo broad (Lima) beans
8 young carrots

or

Any other fresh vegetables

You will also need chopped parsley, chopped mint, and melted butter, and perhaps rosemary, nutmeg and lemon juice (depending on the vegetables you have chosen)

Prepare and cook each vegetable separately and carefully. The beetroots can be bought cooked, and simply heated up in a little melted butter. The cauliflower, leeks, peas, courgettes, salsify, beans or carrots can be boiled until just tender, then tossed in melted butter. The tomatoes can be grilled or baked in the oven. The white vegetables like cauliflower and salsify are often browned in butter after boiling. When all the vegetables are done, drain them and keep them warm in the saucepans they were cooked in with the lid on; or on a hot-plate or in a cool oven; or in vegetable dishes or casseroles in the oven. Keep them covered if they are boiled, uncovered if they are to be slightly crisp—fried cauliflower, for example.

Arrange the vegetables on a large platter, taking care to separate the colours by putting white or red next to green, etc. Brush them with melted butter, grind some pepper over them, and sprinkle with appropriate herbs or flavourings, e.g. chives on the beetroot, mint on the peas or carrots, parsley on the leeks or salsify, lemon juice or nutmeg on cabbage or sprouts, rosemary on the tomatoes. Boiled cauliflower is delicious if sprinkled with brown butter (butter melted until just brown but not yet burnt).

If space on the stove (or for keeping things warm) is limited, the vegetables can be mixed together in the dish, but in that event beetroot, which would colour everything red—or tomatoes, which would break up—should not be used. A mixture of broad beans, carrots, peas, chopped leeks and fleurets of cauliflower is good.

Iced bombe with black cherry sauce (serves 8)
A mixing bowl can be used instead of the traditional bombe mould.

1 pint/¾ litre/20 fl. oz thick cream
 or 1½ lb/¾ kilo vanilla ice cream
1 can morello cherries
1 can raspberries
Sugar to taste
1 tablespoon brandy or kirsch
 (delicious, but should be omitted if the bombe is for children)

For the sauce
1 dessertspoon arrowroot
1 tablespoon brandy or kirsch
 (optional)

Drain the cherries and raspberries well, reserving the juice. Chop them into small pieces. Whip the cream until stiff, add the liqueur and sweeten to taste. If using ice cream allow it to soften but not to melt. Mix in the chopped fruit. Spoon into the bombe mould or mixing bowl, and put immediately into the freezer. It will take at least 2 hours, and probably 4, to harden. It can then be turned out onto a plate and put back in the freezer until needed.

To make *the sauce* mix the arrowroot with a little water in a cup. Heat the mixed cherry and raspberry juices in a saucepan, pour some of the hot juice onto the arrowroot, stirring, and then pour back the arrowroot and juice into the saucepan. Bring to the boil, stirring. Allow to simmer 1 minute after boiling. Add the brandy or kirsch, and serve hot with the bombe.

This bombe can be made with fresh or frozen strawberries, pineapple or peaches, but the fruit should be chopped rather than left whole or in large pieces.

On the day before

Mussel soup Make the soup. Add the cream when re-heating.

Arabian stuffed lamb If care is taken not to overcook the lamb it can be done the day before. The advantage is that the gravy can then be made without last-minute fuss. Re-heating roasts is tricky, though, often resulting in overcooked or not-heated-through meat. On the whole I think it best cooked on the day of the party, but plan things so that it is ready a good half-hour before lunch. Then the gravy can be made and everything kept in a warm oven until needed. The joint can be stuffed, sewn up, and buttered the day before, though it is important that the stuffing be completely cold when put into the shoulder. If you *are* cooking the shoulder the day before, lop $\frac{1}{2}$ hour off the cooking time, and allow an hour in the same temperature oven for reheating.

Fantail potatoes Peel and cut the potatoes, and leave them in cold water. Grate the cheese.

Mixed spring vegetables Prepare the vegetables and chop the herbs.

Iced bombe with black cherry sauce Make both bombe and sauce. Indeed the bombe *should* be made the day before, to ensure its freezing properly.

Le Thé a l' Anglaise chez le Prince de Conti au Temple by Ollivier

Cold buffet – egg mousse with aspic, egg mousse with anchovies, filet de boeuf en croûte, salmon mayonnaise, salade niçoise (pages 56, 82, 85 and 76)

12 · Tea Parties

Most tea parties are informal affairs for family or friends. This does not mean no work. In fact, a good tea needs considerable forward planning if it is not to end up with last-minute sandwich-making. The trolley or table can be laid well in advance, and the menu planned so that apart from making the actual tea, it is a simple assembly job.

If you do not know your guests' tastes, make a pot of China and a pot of Indian tea. To those who prefer Indian, a cup of China is disappointingly feeble; and to the China tea devotee, Indian is a barbaric beverage.

When planning the menu, always include one largish cake. It forms the table centre-piece, surrounded by dishes of scones, small cakes or tartlets.

TEA PARTY FOR 12

Cucumber sandwich fingers

Welsh scones

Lemon curd tartlets

Chocolate and orange cake

Strawberry meringue baskets

(Preparation on the day before follows recipes.)

The addition of champagne livens up the proceedings remarkably.

Cucumber sandwich fingers (makes about 24)

12 slices brown bread
Butter
Cucumber
Salt

If you are preparing the sandwiches in advance the cucumber should be salted and drained before use. (If this is not done the salt, whether in the butter or sprinkled on, has time to draw the moisture out of the cucumber, and the sandwiches become soggy.) Peel and slice the cucumber finely. Sprinkle all over with a little salt and leave in a bowl for half an hour. Then rinse the slices in water and dry them on a clean cloth. Butter the bread, make sandwiches with the drained cucumber, cut off the crusts, and cut into fingers.

Welsh scones (makes about 12)

8 oz/230 grams/1¾ cups self-raising flour
Small pinch of salt
2 oz/50 grams/4 tablespoons butter
1 oz/30 grams/1 tablespoon caster (powdered) sugar
(continued overleaf)

Sift the flour with the salt. Rub in the butter. Add the sugar and sultanas. Using first a knife and then your hand work in enough of the milk to make a soft dough. Knead lightly on a floured surface, and pat or roll out into a round about ¾ in. thick. Using a biscuit or cookie cutter stamp

133

2 oz/50 grams/4 tablespoons sultanas
or currants
About ¼ pint/⅛ litre/5 fl. oz sour milk
or buttermilk (if not available use
fresh milk)

into discs; otherwise cut into wedges. Heat a lightly greased griddle iron or thick-bottomed frying pan over gentle heat. Fry the scones on both sides until firm to the touch and browned. They will take about 7 minutes on each side. Serve hot with butter, or with butter and jam.

Lemon curd tartlets (makes about 12)

½ lb/230 grams rich shortcrust pastry
(page 88)
Lemon curd, preferably home-made
(see next recipe)

Set the oven at 400°F, gas mark 6. Roll the pastry out very thinly, and line into tartlets. Bake blind (see page 105) for 15 minutes or until just cooked. Fill with lemon curd and return to the oven for a further 10 minutes. Cool on a wire rack.

Lemon curd

3 oz/80 grams/6 tablespoons butter
2 large lemons
½ lb/230 grams/1 cup granulated sugar
3 eggs

Grate the rind of the lemons on the finest gauge on the grater, taking care to grate rind only, not pith. Squeeze the juice from the lemons. Put the rind, juice, butter, sugar and slightly beaten eggs into a saucepan and heat gently, stirring all the time until the mixture is thick. Strain into a bowl and allow to cool. This curd will keep in the refrigerator for about three weeks.

Chocolate and orange cake

For the cake
3 oz/80 grams dark sweetened chocolate
1 teaspoon vanilla
12 oz/340 grams/2 cups soft brown
sugar
Grated rind of ½ orange
½ pint/¼ litre/10 fl. oz milk
4 oz/110 grams/½ cup butter
2 eggs
8 oz/230 grams/1¾ cups plain flour
1 level teaspoon bicarbonate of soda

For the filling
½ pint/¼ litre/10 fl. oz thick cream,
whipped
Grated rind of ½ orange
Caster (powdered) sugar to taste

For the icing
4 oz/100 grams dark sweetened
chocolate
4 tablespoons milk

To make *the cake*, set the oven at 375°F, gas mark 5. Line the bottom of 3 sandwich tins (cake pans) with greaseproof (waxed) paper and brush them out with melted lard or butter. Put the chocolate, the vanilla, half the sugar and half the milk into a saucepan. Cook, stirring until quite smooth. Add the grated orange rind.
Beat the butter with the rest of the sugar until very light and creamy. Beat in the eggs, and then add the chocolate mixture and beat again. Sift in the flour and soda, mixing well. Add the rest of the milk, and stir well. Divide the mixture between the 3 cake-pans, and bake in the middle of the oven for about 30 minutes, or until the cake has a very slightly shrivelled look around the edges. Do not worry if the cake does not feel very firm—it should be moist and rather sticky. Allow to cool for 5 minutes before turning out onto a wire rack to cool. Peel off the paper.
To make *the filling* mix the orange rind into the whipped cream and sweeten to taste. Make a 3-tier cake with the cream filling between the 3 layers of cake.
To make *the icing*, put the chocolate and milk into a saucepan. Heat, stirring, until smooth and thick. Cool slightly, and pour or spread over the top of the cake.

Strawberry meringue baskets (makes about 12)

For the meringue
4 egg-whites
4 oz/100 grams/½ cup caster
   (powdered) sugar
5 oz/150 grams/1 cup icing
   (confectioners') sugar

For the filling
½ lb/250 grams strawberries
½ pint/¼ litre/10 fl. oz thick cream
1 dessertspoon kirsch
1 teaspoon caster (powdered) sugar
Extra icing sugar

To make *the meringue* put the egg-whites into a large mixing bowl and whisk them until really stiff. Add the caster sugar and beat again until very thick. Now add the icing sugar and again beat until so stiff that the mixture holds its shape, and will not flow at all. (An electric beater is excellent for this job, which can be very tiring. Standing the bowl over a saucepan of boiling water—taking care not to let the bottom of the bowl come in contact with the water—also helps to speed the process.)

Using a fluted narrow nozzle, pipe small baskets onto oiled greaseproof (waxed) paper on a baking sheet. The trick with piping is to hold the bag absolutely upright, and to keep the nozzle very close to the paper. Squeeze the bag with the top hand only, the bottom one lightly holding the nozzle. Bake in a very slow oven for two hours, or until completely dry. When done the baskets should lift easily off the paper. Allow to cool.

Whip the cream. Add the kirsch and caster sugar. Put a spoonful of cream into each meringue basket, and cover with hulled and halved strawberries. Dust lightly with icing sugar.

On the day before

Cucumber sandwich fingers can be made the day before if the instructions for draining the cucumber are followed (see recipe). Wrap in polythene and keep in a cool place.

Welsh scones are delicious straight off the griddle iron, but they can be made the day before and reheated in the oven. Keep them in an airtight container.

Lemon curd tartlets can be made days in advance, though the longer they are kept the softer the pastry gets. Ideally they should be made the day before the party.

Chocolate and orange cake will keep for 3 days in the refrigerator. Wrap or cover in polythene.

Strawberry meringue baskets The baskets can be made several days in advance and kept in an airtight container or polythene bag, but they should be filled only a few hours before eating.

TEA PARTY FOR 8

Toasted bath buns

Brandy snaps

Lemon sponge cake

Chocolate nut brownies

(Preparation on the day before follows recipes.)

Toasted bath buns (makes 12)
1 lb/450 grams/3¼ cups flour
1 teaspoon salt
½ pint/¼ litre/10 fl. oz milk
¾ oz/25 grams/1 tablespoon yeast
1 teaspoon granulated sugar
4 oz/110 grams/½ cup butter
4 oz/110 grams/¾ cup icing
  (confectioners') sugar
3 small eggs
4 oz/110 grams/¾ cup sultanas
1½ oz/45 grams/¼ cup candied peel

For the top
2 oz/50 grams/12 cubes lump sugar,
  coarsely crushed
Beaten egg

Mix the yeast and sugar in a cup. Warm the milk to blood temperature and add the yeast mixture to it. (If using dried yeast, use half the quantity given. Reconstitute it by mixing with 2 tablespoons of tepid milk or water and sprinkling with 1 teaspoon of sugar. Allow to stand for 15 minutes. When it is frothy add it to the milk.) Warm the flour and sift it with the salt into a warm dry bowl. Make a well in the centre and pour in the yeasty milk. Mix to a dough with a knife. Stand in a warm place while you beat the butter with the sugar until soft and creamy. Add the eggs, and beat well. Add the sultanas and candied peel. Work all this into the dough, and knead for about 8 minutes on a lightly floured surface. Put the dough, covered with a sheet of greased polythene or a damp cloth, in a warm place to rise: it will take 35–40 minutes. Place on a floured surface and knead slightly to 'knock down' the dough. Shape into 12 buns and put out on a lightly greased baking sheet. Cover with the greased sheet of polythene, and leave to rise again for 15–20 minutes. Brush with beaten egg and sprinkle the crushed sugar on top. Bake at 375°F, gas mark 5, for about 30 minutes or until brown and firm. Serve split, toasted, and buttered.

Brandy snaps (makes about 20)
4 oz/110 grams/¾ cup flour
4 oz/110 grams/½ cup butter
4 oz/110 grams/½ cup sugar
4 oz/110 grams/4 tablespoons golden
  syrup
Juice of half a lemon
Large pinch of ground ginger

For the filling (optional)
½ pint/¼ litre/10 fl. oz double cream
1 tablespoon brandy
Caster (powdered) sugar to taste

Melt the sugar, butter and syrup together, and remove from the heat. Sift in the flour, stirring well. Add lemon juice and ginger. Put the mixture out on a greased baking sheet in small teaspoonsful, about 6 inches apart. Bake at 375°F, gas mark 5, for 5–7 minutes: they should go golden brown but still be soft. Remove from the oven. When cool enough to handle, lever each biscuit off the baking sheet with a palette knife; and working quickly, shape it round the greased handle of a wooden spoon to form a cylinder. Once the brandy snaps are cold they will be too brittle to roll up—though they can be made pliable again if returned to the oven briefly. As each brandy snap is shaped it can be removed from the handle of the wooden spoon, and cooled on a wire tray.
Whip the cream stiffly, add the brandy, and sweeten to taste. Then, using a piping bag with a narrow nozzle, fill the brandy snaps with the cream. (They are delicious with or without cream; if they are not to be filled there is no need to roll them up, but they must be removed from the baking sheet while still warm or they will stick.)

Lemon sponge cake

For the cake

3 eggs
3 oz/80 grams/½ cup caster
  (powdered) sugar
Pinch salt
3 oz/80 grams/½ cup flour
Grated rind of two lemons
Icing (confectioners') sugar

For the filling

4 tablespoons lemon curd (see recipe,
  page 134)
4 tablespoons thick cream, whipped
  stiffly

Set the oven at 375°F, gas mark 5. Line the bottom of two sandwich tins or cake pans with rounds of greaseproof (waxed) paper. Brush them out with melted lard and dust with flour. Put the eggs and sugar together in a mixing bowl. Stand it over a saucepan of simmering water, taking care that the bottom of the basin is not in contact with the water. Using a rotary, balloon, or electric hand whisk, whisk the mixture until sufficiently thick for the impression of the whisk to stay imprinted on the mixture for a few seconds when the whisk is lifted. The mixture should be pale in colour, and mousse-like. Remove from the heat, and whisk until cold. Cooling can be hurried by standing the bowl in a tray of iced water. (If using an automatic electric mixer, warming and cooling the mixture is unnecessary.) Stir in the lemon rind. Sift the flour with the salt and fold it into the egg mixture—use a metal spoon, and lift rather than stir the mixture. Divide the mixture between the two pans, and bake for about 20 minutes or until the sides of the cake have slightly shrunk and the top is resilient and spongy to the touch. Remove from the oven and turn out onto a wire rack to cool. Peel off the rounds of greaseproof paper. When the cakes are cold, sandwich them together with a mixture of the lemon curd and whipped cream. Dust the top with icing sugar before serving.

Chocolate nut brownies

6 oz/170 grams/¾ cup butter
3 oz/80 grams sweetened dark chocolate
6 oz/170 grams/¾ cup caster
  (powdered) sugar
3 eggs
6 oz/170 grams/1 cup plain flour,
  sifted with a pinch of salt
3 oz/80 grams/¾ cup chopped walnuts

Line a 7-inch-square pan with tin foil and brush it out with melted lard. Set the oven at 350°F, gas mark 4. Melt the butter and add the chocolate. Stir over gentle heat until smooth. Beat the sugar and eggs until light and creamy. Add the chocolate mixture. Fold in the flour and the chopped walnuts. Turn the mixture into the pan and bake for ¾ hour or until the cake feels firm to the touch. Allow to cool before turning out, and then cut into small squares. (They should be tacky on the inside and crisp on the outside.)

On the day before

Toasted bath buns Make the buns and store in a tin. Split, toast, and butter them at the last minute.

Brandy snaps can be made weeks in advance but they should be absolutely cold when put into the container, which must be completely airtight. Fill them not more than two hours before the party.

Lemon sponge cake Make the cake. It can be filled the day before too, but should then be refrigerated until served.

Chocolate nut brownies keep very well for several days in an airtight container, or frozen.

13 · Outdoor Parties

Barbecues

Meat that is at once charred and raw can be avoided if you buy or build a good barbecue, light it in good time, and cook only when the coals are glowing embers with no flames.

To build your own simple barbecue, you will need about 120 bricks, two metal scraper doormats, and a piece of fine-gauge chicken wire 2 ft × 3 ft. Build the barbecue as indicated in the diagram. Wrap the chicken wire round one of the door mats, which then becomes the bottom shelf and holds the charcoal. The other mat is the upper shelf on which the food is cooked. For a more solid but non-moveable barbecue, cement the bricks together. If you buy a barbecue make sure it is not too small. It is maddening for the hungry to watch others tucking in.

Fuel Charcoal (briquettes or loose) is the best. 20 lb will easily last the evening. You will need firelighters, but do not use paraffin or methylated spirits which are dangerous.

Equipment Complete preparation is vital (see Check list page 188).

Lighting the fire Put the chicken-wire-covered grid in place. Lay the firelighters about 6 inches apart all over it. Cover them with charcoal 2 inches deep. Light the fire at least half an hour before you want to start cooking. Put the top grid in place to get sizzling hot. Paint it with oil to prevent the meat sticking. When feeding the fire, push the glowing coals from the edge to the middle, and add new ones to the sides adding only small quantities. Charcoal added to the middle will mean a half-hour wait for the flames to die down.

Planning the menu Sausages, hot dogs, and lamb chops will be the height of gastronomy for children, but the more sophisticated may like kebabs, devilled chops and fish. Have one dish that is a straight cheat—a casserole or cold dish that will stave off the hunger of guests tantalized by the smell of grilling meat. Almost anything goes at a barbecue, so the suggestions below are by no means exhaustive. But too large a choice makes the cooking complicated and the results often disappointing. Timing depends on the heat of the fire, and the thickness of the meat. Large pieces should be cooked when the fire has cooled a little.

BARBECUE SUGGESTIONS—allow $\frac{1}{2}$–$\frac{3}{4}$ lb (250–350 grams) meat per person

Chicken pieces
Brush with butter and sprinkle with rosemary.

Lamb chops, cutlets, or steaks cut from the leg
Baste with a devil sauce (see below). If the meat is soaked in the sauce for a few hours before cooking it will be really tender, with the spicy flavour right through the meat.

Chicken pieces, lamb chops or cutlets
Brush with butter and curry powder.

Pork chops, sausages, hot dogs, or steak
Spread with french mustard for the last few minutes of cooking.

Hamburgers
Mix together $1\frac{1}{2}$ lb ($\frac{3}{4}$ kilo) finely minced beef, 1 chopped raw onion, 1 small egg, a pinch of dried herbs, plenty of salt and pepper, and form into thick flat cakes. Grill on a piece of foil to prevent their falling through the wire into the fire.

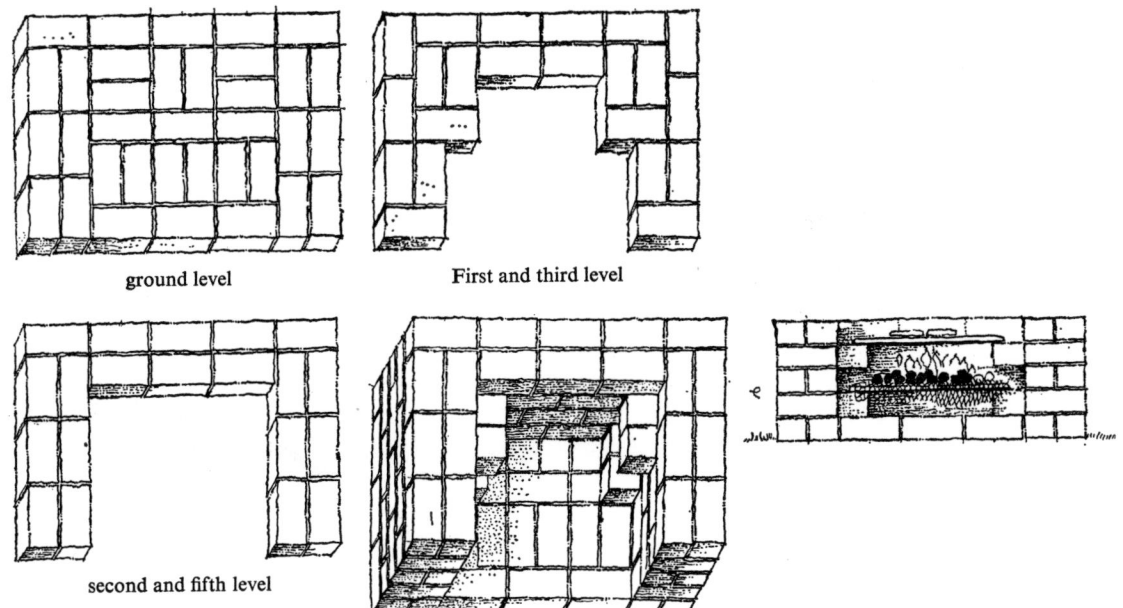

ground level

First and third level

second and fifth level

Spare ribs

Marinate (i.e. soak) skinned belly-of-pork pieces—American spare ribs—for five hours in a mixture of 1 cup runny honey, 1 cup soy sauce, 1 clove garlic (crushed), 1 dessertspoon dried basil, juice of 2 lemons, and 1 teaspoon each salt and pepper. Take out and grill them, basting with some of the marinade.

Kebabs are small pieces of meat or fish (sometimes with vegetables and flavourings) pushed onto skewers and roasted over a charcoal fire. Suggestions:—

Lambs' kidneys, fatty bacon, lambs' liver and tomatoes Skin, halve and core the kidneys, and skewer them alternately with the pieces of liver, bacon and halved tomatoes. Take care the tomatoes do not fall off with rough handling.

Lamb, shallots, green pepper and pineapple Skewer one-inch cubes of lamb (from loin or leg), baby onions or shallots, small pieces of fresh pineapple and thick strips of green pepper. Brush with slightly curry-flavoured butter.

Steak, mushrooms and onions Skewer cubes of steak with quarters or halves of the big, flat black mushrooms, and quarters of onion. Season with garlic salt.

Pork, prunes, apple and sage Skewer cubes of pork with stoned, soaked prunes and thick slices of eating apples. Brush with oil, and sprinkle with dried sage.

Chicken, chicken livers and fennel Remove the discoloured patches from the chicken livers. Skewer with small pieces of raw chicken and pieces of the vegetable fennel. Brush the kebabs with lemon juice and butter.

Scallops, prawns and ham Buy cleaned fresh or frozen scallops. Remove the hard muscle. Skewer the scallops and prawns (preferably raw) whole, the ham in cubes. Brush with plenty of lemon juice and butter; season with freshly ground black pepper.

Baked potatoes cooked in the oven, *not* in the ashes of the fire—from which they emerge half raw. Wash, prick and salt them. Wrapping them in foil results in a soggy skin; oiling them keeps the skin soft though still edible, but I prefer simply to salt them. Besides great dollops of fresh butter, there are other good things to put into a split baked potato:—

Cottage cheese and chives

Sour cream and mock caviar

Butter, grilled chopped pieces of bacon, and chopped spring onions

Curry-flavoured sour cream

Onion sauce—make a packet onion soup very thick, and add whipped cream to it.

Salad Any is suitable (see Index under 'salads').

Casserole A hearty one can be added to the feast to take the pressure off the barbecue— e.g. frankfurter, tomato and baked beans (page 76), or boeuf à la bourguignonne (page 44) made with stewing steak instead of the expensive fillet: it will need at least 1 hour longer cooking than the recipe indicates.

Note: **Devil sauce** is good either to serve with barbecued meat, to marinate it in before cooking, or for basting it during cooking:—
Simply mix together 4 tablespoons Worcester sauce, 4 tablespoons tomato ketchup, 1 level tablespoon french mustard, 1 dessertspoon anchovy essence, a good pinch each of salt, pepper and cayenne, 4 tablespoons of olive oil, and 1 onion, finely chopped.
All drinks are suitable, but one of the best is the Spanish red wine cup, Sangria (page 15). Coffee is particularly delicious outside after a barbecue, but it should be served in large mugs or breakfast cups. It is perhaps safer to make it in the kitchen—but if you do make it on the barbecue, be sure that it does not boil as this ruins the flavour.

Clambakes

Sea-shore clambakes are a particularly American tradition and seldom held in England or, as far as I know, anywhere else. But apart from a 'bake' (a steaming, really) being the perfect way to treat fresh sea-food, it is the greatest fun. However, preparations are more complicated than for a barbecue, so that if you can possibly contrive to have on hand someone who has at least *been* to a clambake, all the better.

For each person you will need:
6 soft shell clams
1 piece of chicken
½ small live lobster
1 frankfurter
1 corn-on-the-cob
Salt
Pepper
Plenty of bread and butter

Start 4½ hours before the event by digging a pit in the sand about a foot deep. The width of the pit will depend on the size of the 'bake'. A pit 3 ft × 3 ft would be ample for a bake for 20 people. Line it with smooth stones. Build a wood fire in the pit on top of the stones. Keep feeding the fire (preferably with thick pieces of hardwood) for two or three hours, then let it die down. The idea is to get the stones white hot. While they are heating, wash the clams in sea water, kill the lobsters by piercing them in the back of the head with a knife, take the outside leaves from the corn, cut the chicken into small pieces, and collect a couple of buckets of very wet rock seaweed and a bucket of sea water. When the stones are white hot rake out the embers and put a 4–5 inch layer of seaweed on the stones.
Work as fast as you can to prevent too much heat escaping. A piece of chicken-wire laid on top of the seaweed prevents the food falling through and getting lost under the seaweed, but it is not vital. Now put in the food—the chicken pieces first, then the frankfurters, then the lobsters and the corn, and finally the clams. Add another layer of seaweed, and splash a few pints of sea water over the lot. Amply cover the pit with a piece of damp canvas, weighted down with stones to prevent the steam escaping. The steaming will take about one hour, and the canvas should not be lifted during this time. After an hour lift the cover carefully. If the clams have opened the bake is done. Lift out the food, taking care not to knock any sand in. Serve with butter, pepper and salt, and crusty bread.
White Loire wines are perfect with clams, and are cool and crisp for a hot summer's night.

Check list, page 189.

An Assemblie, made in the presence of Queen Elizabeth; from Turberville's *The Noble Art of Venerie* (1575)

Fête in a Park by Watteau (Wallace Collection. Crown copyright reserved)

The Picnic by James Tissot (Tate Gallery, London)

The Pic-Nic (1842) by G. Herbert Rodwell

Beach Parties

The phrase 'beach party' can mean anything, and according to the cheap press it means a gang of youths getting up to highly suspect jinks on the sands. To me it means building a fire on the beach—not for cooking, just for fun—and having a picnic round it. It also meant to me as a child being given Marie biscuits spread with butter (and sometimes sprinkled with coloured sugar candy). I can taste the buttery crunchy biscuit now, and remember my ravenous hunger after swimming and charging about, and the hope that my brothers were not as hungry as I. However, for the purposes of this chapter, a beach party is an evening picnic—but with hot food, because no matter how balmy the evening, after a midnight swim spicy hot food is nicer than a cold chicken leg.

Check list, page 189.

BEACH PARTY FOR 8

Curried eggs with rice
Cabbage and frankfurter salad

Chocolate biscuits (cookies)

(Preparation on the day before follows recipes.)

Beer or cider would be the best drink. Stout is warming after a midnight swim, as of course is hard liquor. Hot coffee with a slug of whisky in it has miraculous powers.

Curried eggs with rice (serves 8)
16 small hard-boiled eggs, peeled
3 teacupsful boiled rice (see page 70)
1 tablespoonful sultanas
1 oz/30 grams/2 tablespoons butter
1 large onion, finely sliced
1 dessertspoon curry powder
1 oz/30 grams/1 heaped tablespoon
   flour
1 dessertspoon apricot jam
1 dessertspoon tomato paste
1 pint/¾ litre/20 fl. oz chicken stock
1 teaspoon paprika
Squeeze of lemon juice
Pepper and salt

Melt the butter. Fry the onion slowly in it until just turning colour. Add the curry powder. Fry for one minute. Stir in the flour, the jam, the tomato paste, and finally the stock. Bring to the boil, stirring. Add the paprika, the lemon juice and salt and pepper to taste. Simmer for half an hour, stirring occasionally. Add the sultanas, eggs and rice; mix all together, getting the mixture boiling hot, and pack immediately into wide-necked warmed thermos flasks.
If the dish is not for a picnic serve the rice separately.

Cabbage and frankfurter salad (serves 8)
For the salad
1 lb/¼ kilo finely shredded white
   cabbage
1 red pimento (canned or fresh), sliced
1 small green pepper, finely sliced
8 frankfurters, sliced diagonally
½ lb/250 grams sliced ham, cut into
   thin strips
½ lb/250 grams tomatoes
16 black olives, stoned
(for the dressing ingredients, see overleaf)

For *the dressing* put all the ingredients into a bowl and whisk until smooth. If this is done in an electric blender a perfect emulsion will be obtained, but even if the dressing separates it will be delicious.
Dip the tomatoes into boiling water for five seconds. Slip off their skins, and quarter them. Mix all the salad ingredients with the dressing. Pack into a plastic box with a lid.

For the dressing
3 dessertspoons salad oil
1 clove garlic, crushed
1 dessertspoon vinegar
1 tablespoon chopped fresh herbs,
   preferably including dill or tarragon
1 teaspoon paprika
¼ teaspoon each salt and black pepper
1 teaspoon made french mustard
2 tablespoons soured cream
1 dessertspoon tomato ketchup

Chocolate biscuits (cookies) (makes about 12)

4 oz/110 grams/¼ cup butter
2 oz/50 grams/2 tablespoons caster
   (powdered) sugar
4 oz/110 grams/¾ cup plain flour
2 drops vanilla essence
1 tablespoon cocoa powder
Pinch of salt

Set the oven at 375°F, gas mark 5. Cream the butter and sugar together until light and fluffy. Add the vanilla essence. Sift the flour, cocoa and salt together, and stir into the creamed mixture. Shape the mixture into small balls the size of a walnut and put them onto a greased baking sheet. With a wet fork, flatten each ball into a biscuit shape about ¼ in. thick. Bake for 10–15 minutes, or until dry to the touch. The biscuits harden as they cool.

On the day before

Curried eggs with rice Make the curry sauce the day before, and add the sultanas and eggs. Next day, before putting it into the thermos flask, add the rice and reheat thoroughly.
Cabbage and frankfurter salad Prepare the salad ingredients, and the dressing, and keep them covered in a cool place. Do not combine them until the next day.
Chocolate biscuits keep well for a week in an airtight container.

BEACH PARTY FOR 8

Thick mulligatawny

Onion flan
Potato and pea salad

Chocolate crumble cake
Irish coffee

(Preparation on the day before follows recipes.)

Sherry or vodka would be good with the soup; hock with the flan.

Thick mulligatawny (serves 8)

One 3 lb/1½ kilo chicken
Pinch of cinnamon
Salt
1 oz/30 grams/2 heaped tablespoons
   dessicated coconut soaked in milk
4 pints/3 litres water
1 green chilli
1 clove of garlic, crushed
3 oz/80 grams/3 heaped tablespoons
   ground almonds
½ teaspoon black pepper

Put the chicken with the giblets, cinnamon, salt, coconut and water into a pan. Simmer gently until the chicken is cooked—about 40 minutes. Take out the chicken and put aside to cool slightly. When cool enough to handle remove all the flesh from the carcase and mince or chop it very finely. Put the bones and skin back in the water. Boil rapidly until the water is reduced to about 2 pints. Chop the chilli finely and add it to the pan with the garlic, ground almonds and

1 oz/30 grams/2 tablespoons butter
1 onion, chopped
1 dessertspoon curry powder
1½ tablespoons flour
1 teacup cooked rice
Juice of 1 small lemon
Cayenne pepper

pepper. Bring to the boil. Strain. Melt the butter in a saucepan. Fry the chopped onion until pale brown. Add the curry powder and fry one more minute. Stir in the flour, and pour on the strained stock. Stir continuously until boiling. Add the rice, minced chicken, lemon juice and a touch of cayenne. Pour into warmed thermos flasks.

Onion flan

½ lb/250 grams rich shortcrust pastry
  (see page 88)
1 large mild onion
12 small spring onions
1 oz/30 grams/2 tablespoons butter
2 egg yolks
1 whole egg
¼ pint/⅛ litre/5 fl. oz creamy milk
3 oz/80 grams/¾ cup grated cheese
4 tablespoons cream
Salt, pepper, cayenne

Set the oven at 375°F, gas mark 5. Line a flan dish or ring with the pastry and bake blind (see page 105). Slice the large onion finely, and chop the spring onions (the white and very pale green parts only). Melt the butter and add all the onion. Cook gently until the onion colours pale brown. Remove from the heat. Mix the eggs, extra yolks, cream, milk, cheese and fried onions together. Season with salt, pepper and cayenne. Pour into the flan case and bake until the filling is slightly brown on top. Serve hot or cold.

Potato and pea salad

1½ lb/¾ kilo potatoes
1 cup shelled peas
2 hard-boiled eggs
1 medium onion, very thinly sliced
French dressing
1 teaspoon french mustard
1 carton (about 5 fl. oz/⅛ litre) sour
  cream

Cook the potatoes in their skins. Drain them, and when just cold enough to handle, skin and slice them. Add just enough french dressing to moisten. Boil and drain the peas. Slice the hard-boiled eggs. Stir the mustard into the sour cream. When the potatoes are quite cold mix everything together taking care not to break up the potatoes.

Chocolate crumble cake

¾ lb/340 grams broken biscuits
  (cookies)
3 oz/80 grams/¾ cup glacé cherries
3 oz/80 grams/¾ cup flaked almonds
3 oz/80 grams/6 tablespoons butter
1½ oz/45 grams/1½ tablespoons caster
  (powdered) sugar
2 tablespoons golden syrup
3 oz/80 grams dark chocolate

Chop the chocolate and melt it slowly with the butter, sugar and syrup, stirring all the time. Add the crushed biscuits, cherries and almonds. Grease a sheet of greaseproof (waxed) paper and the inside of an 8-inch flan ring. Press the mixture onto the paper and flatten it, using the flan ring to get a round shape. Cut into small fingers when set hard.

Irish coffee

Make good strong coffee, and sweeten it. Add Irish whisky to taste—about 2 tablespoons for each cup is good. Put the coffee in a thermos flask and take thick cream in a jar. Pour the coffee out first, and the cream on top of it. The idea is to get a layer of cream floating on the coffee. Pouring the cream over the back of a teaspoon lessens the danger of its going into instead of onto the coffee but it is delicious either way.

On the day before
Mulligatawny soup is better made the day before.
Potato and pea salad Make the salad and store in a plastic box in the refrigerator.
Chocolate crumble cake must be made in advance, and it keeps well for at least a week.

Picnics

Although picnics are said to be an English invention, in England they too often fall into the sand-in-the-sandwiches and warm-wilted-lettuce category. In France where all eating, even *alfresco*, is no trivial matter, I once saw the other extreme. There were two large cars, one loaded with guests and the other with butler, maid, food, drinks, ice, tables, chairs, tablecloths, and a flower vase for the middle of each table. Flowers were not provided, the idea being that we would gather them wild while the butler mixed the martinis.

Most picnics are not that delightfully decadent, but properly planned they can be satisfyingly civilized even if they only mean a simple snack eaten on a blanket at the bottom of the garden.

It is a good idea to take a damp cloth (in a polythene packet) for wiping sticky fingers and faces, and a large bag for rubbish. Expensive picnic sets seem to me rather unsatisfactory: there are either too many containers or not enough, and a bulky hamper may not fit into available car space. The following picnic food can be transported in jars or plastic boxes, and the salad can be eaten out of large cereal bowls (easier than plates) with a spoon or fork.

Check list, page 189.

PICNIC FOR 6

Cucumber and cream salad

Pain bagna

Apricot fool

(Preparation on the day before follows recipes.)

For drinks I recommend pure apple juice rather than fizzy pop. It is more acceptable to all ages, and less sickly and liable to explode after being shaken thoroughly in transit.

For the grown-ups a Spanish Rioja or an inexpensive Italian red wine such as Valpolicella is sufficiently hardy to stand being shaken about, and tastes all the better for being drunk in the hot sun.

Cucumber and cream salad (serves 6)
1½ lb/750 grams cucumber
¼ pint/⅛ litre/5 fl. oz thick cream
1 pint/⅛ litre/5 fl. oz sour cream
Salt, black pepper
1 dessertspoon lemon juice
1 tablespoon chopped mint
1 clove garlic, crushed (optional)

Peel and slice the cucumber finely. Salt it lightly and leave for at least ½ hour for the juice to run out. Rinse it well, washing off all the salt, and dry on a clean cloth. Whip the thick cream stiffly. Stir in the sour cream, lemon juice, mint and garlic; and season with plenty of black pepper. The cucumber will probably still be a little salty, but if it is not, salt the dressing lightly. Mix all together and chill well.

Pain bagna (serves 6)
This is a Mediterranean open sandwich, hearty but good.

2 small french loaves
1 clove garlic, crushed
1 dessertspoon lemon juice
3 tablespoons olive oil

Split the loaves lengthwise. Mix the crushed garlic with the mashed avocado, lemon juice and oil. Spread this on the bread. On top of it lay the tomato slices, strips of red and green pepper,

148

1 ripe avocado, mashed
6 tomatoes, skinned and sliced
1 large green pepper, sliced
1 large red pepper (or tinned red pimento), sliced
1 can anchovy fillets, split lengthwise
1 teaspoon chopped capers
12 black olives, stoned and chopped
Black pepper

anchovy fillets, capers and black olives. Sprinkle with black pepper. For a picnic, wrap each *pain* separately in polythene film or foil to prevent the salad falling off in transit.

Apricot fool (serves 6)
Proceed as for blackcurrant fool (page 58), substituting purée of apricots (fresh, stewed, or dried and cooked) for the blackcurrant purée. Add a dash of Grand Marnier if you like. Pack into empty cream cartons, yoghurt pots or plastic cups for the picnic. Cover with polythene secured with rubber bands.

On the day before
Cucumber and cream salad Salt and drain the cucumber, and make the dressing, but do not mix together until the morning of the picnic.
Pain bagna Prepare all the salad ingredients. Put the mashed avocado paste in a jar with a piece of waxed paper or tinfoil on top of it to prevent discolouring. Keep in the refrigerator. Keep the sliced peppers, tomatoes and anchovy fillets in a plastic box with a lid in the refrigerator. The bread should be bought on the day of the picnic. It can be bought the day before, and well wrapped and kept in a cool place, but it loses its crustiness and tends to become tough and chewy.
Apricot fool Make completely and keep covered in a cool place.

PICNIC FOR 10

Spicy tomato soup

Terrine
Salad

Coffee fudge cake

(*Preparation on the day before follows recipes.*)

For the children provide apple juice. For the adults a fairly hard wine—a St Estèphe or a Chianti—would be delicious, but remember not to take any fine wine on a car trip.

Spicy tomato soup (serves 10)
1 oz/30 grams/2 tablespoons butter
1 oz/30 grams/1 heaped tablespoon flour
1 onion, finely chopped
Salt and ground black pepper
Pinch of nutmeg, 1 clove, 1 bayleaf
1 teaspoon paprika
1 teaspoon sugar
1 large can tomatoes
1¼ pints/1 litre/2½ cups chicken stock
Squeeze of lemon
½ lb/250 grams fresh tomatoes
3 tablespoons red port

Melt the butter. Add the chopped onion and cook gently until pale yellow and transparent. Stir in the flour, then add the canned tomatoes and stock. Stir until the mixture boils. Add the bayleaf, nutmeg, a pinch of salt, about ½ teaspoon ground black pepper, the paprika, clove, sugar and squeeze of lemon. Simmer, stirring occasionally, for 30 minutes. Skin and chop the fresh tomatoes. Push the soup through a sieve and return it to the saucepan. Add the port and fresh tomatoes, reheat, and adjust the seasoning.

149

Terrine (serves 10)

A meat loaf suitable for eating with salads or on bread or toast.

¾ lb/350 grams minced beef
¾ lb/350 grams pork sausagemeat
¾ lb/350 grams minced lamb's liver
1 medium onion, finely chopped
1 small egg, beaten
Small teacupful fresh breadcrumbs
Small glass red wine
Salt and pepper
1 tablespoon chopped parsley
Small pinch thyme
½ teaspoon crushed basil
6 slices fatty bacon with rinds removed

Oil a large loaf tin lightly. Lay the bacon slices in the bottom of it, side by side. Mix everything else well together, using the fingers to get the sausage-meat well distributed. Fill the loaf tin with the mixture and cover with a piece of foil. Stand it in a roasting pan full of water and bake in a moderate oven (375°F, gas mark 5) for 2 hours, or until the loaf has shrunk away from the sides of the tin and feels firm to the touch. Leave in the tin to cool, but weight it down by standing another loaf tin, containing something heavy, on top of it. Turn out of the tin when cold and wrap in foil. Keep in a cool place.

Salad

The mixed bean salad on page 80 or the potato and pea salad on page 147 would be good with the terrine. Otherwise serve it with crusty bread and butter or thick toast.

Coffee fudge cake (serves 5)
(Make two cakes for 10 people)

For the cake
4 oz/110 grams/½ cup margarine
4 oz/110 grams/½ cup caster
   (powdered) sugar
2 eggs
4 oz/110 grams/¾ cup self-raising flour
Pinch of salt
1 dessertspoon coffee essence

For the icing
9 oz/250 grams/1 heaped cup icing
   (confectioners') sugar
3 oz/80 grams/6 tablespoons butter
3 tablespoons water
3 oz/80 grams/3 tablespoons
   granulated sugar
1 tablespoon coffee essence

Set the oven at 350°F, gas mark 4. Line the bottom of two sandwich tins (cake pans) with rounds of greaseproof (waxed) paper. Brush them out with melted lard.

To make *the cake*, beat the margarine and sugar together until light and creamy. Mix in the eggs, one at a time, beating hard. Add the coffee essence. Sift the flour with the salt and fold it into the cake mixture. Divide the mixture between the two cake pans, and bake for 25 minutes or until the top feels resilient and spongy to the touch.

To make *the fudge icing*, sift the icing sugar into a bowl. Put the butter, water and sugar into a saucepan and heat until the sugar has melted. Boil up well and pour onto the icing sugar, beating well. Add the coffee essence. Allow to cool. Beat it until light. Sandwich the cake with some of the icing, and use the rest to cover the top.

On the day before

Spicy tomato soup Make completely, allow to cool, and refrigerate.
Terrine needs about three hours to set, so it should be made the day before, or even several days before. It will keep for a week in the refrigerator.
Salad Almost all salad dressings can be made in advance, and both the two salads suggested can be prepared the day before.
Coffee fudge cake should be made the day before, iced, and stored in an airtight container. It will keep fresh for several days.

14 · Weddings, Christenings and Anniversaries

Wedding Receptions

Few mothers feel that for their daughter's wedding they can undertake the catering as well as the hundred other duties that fall to their lot. If the wedding is really large, say over 100 people, and there is not much help, then I agree it is foolish to attempt too much. But it is no more difficult to organize a small wedding than a cocktail party or buffet lunch. It is generally one or the other anyway, with a few extras like the cake, the receiving line, and odd anomalies like champagne in mid-afternoon.

The menu must be planned as for any other party (see Buffet Parties or Cocktail Parties, whichever is appropriate), but there may be additions. If the wedding is soon after lunch, it is usual to have the 'cocktail party' first, which generally means champagne and savoury canapés. In Britain, when the bridal couple have cut the cake the whole thing suddenly turns into a tea party—tea and sweet cakes (and of course fingers of wedding cake) are passed around. In America, black coffee is more likely to be offered. The cocktail party aspect of the festivities then continues until the bride and groom leave. Generally everyone else drifts off then too.

About two-and-a-half hours is the average time for this sort of wedding reception, the programme being something like the following:—

3 p.m.   Guests arrive, take about half an hour to get down the receiving line.

3.30–4.15   Party proceeds; bride and groom struggle to have quick word with everyone.

4.15   Cake is cut; speeches (if any). Tea or coffee and wedding cake served.

5 p.m.   Bride and groom quietly disappear to change into their going-away clothes, while party continues without them.

5.30 p.m.   The bride and groom are given send-off by guests, who are themselves then expected to leave.

There are countless books on wedding etiquette and procedure, and it is worth looking at one of them. It is maddening to realize too late that one has not a clue who stands next to whom in the receiving line, and to have to jostle and argue, while the guests are waiting outside in the rain in all their wedding finery.

The cocktail party menus in Chapter 1 would be fine as they are for the morning or late afternoon; or, with the addition of some sweet biscuits, at tea-time. Alternatively, here is another rather more festive mid-afternoon menu. (For lunch-time, see Wedding Breakfast, page 156).

Check list, page 187.

COCKTAIL/WEDDING RECEPTION FOR 50

As with cocktail parties, allow between eight and ten pieces per head.

Fonds d'artichauts au crabe
Smoked salmon and potted
   shrimp canapés
Curried cheese balls
Pizza rounds

Brandy snaps
Meringues
Chocolate profiteroles
Gingerbread

(Preparation on the day before follows recipes.)

Champagne is traditional, but white Burgundy or Riesling are good alternatives.

Fonds d'artichauts au crabe (makes 50)

50 artichoke bottoms (about 6 cans)
1 lb/450 grams crab meat (frozen or canned)
½ pint/¼ litre/10 fl. oz thick mayonnaise (see page 19)
1 dessertspoon lemon juice
Salt, pepper, cayenne

Drain the artichoke bottoms and lay them hollow-side-up on a tray. Drain the crab meat well, and mix with the mayonnaise, lemon juice, salt, pepper and cayenne to taste. Fill each artichoke bottom with a spoonful of crab mixture.

Smoked salmon and potted shrimp canapés (makes 100)

100 small savoury biscuits (crackers)
Butter
About 1½ lb/750 grams thinly sliced smoked salmon
2 large cartons potted shrimps
2 tablespoons chopped parsley

Butter the biscuits. Cut small strips of smoked salmon about 2½ inches long, and roll each one round two or three shrimps. Put the rolls on the biscuits, and scatter the parsley over them.

Curried cheese balls (makes about 50)

About 1¼ lb/750 grams cream cheese
2 oz/50 grams/4 tablespoons butter
1 teaspoon curry powder
Salt and pepper
About ½ lb/250 grams chopped almonds
(Cocktail sticks or paper *petit fours* cases)

Brown the nuts under the grill. Allow to cool. Melt the butter, add the curry powder and stir over moderate heat for two minutes. Mix well with the cream cheese, and season with salt and pepper. Put the mixture into the refrigerator to harden, then form into about 50 small balls, roll them in the nuts, and chill again. Spear each with a cocktail stick, or put into *petits fours* cases.

Pizza rounds (makes 100)

25 large slices white bread (about 1½ loaves)
About ½ lb/250 grams butter
25 small tomatoes
About 20 black olives
50 anchovy fillets (about 2 cans)
1 lb/450 grams cheddar cheese, thinly sliced

Slice each tomato evenly into four. Using a small round cutter or a sherry glass, cut four rounds of bread (about the size of the tomato slices) out of each slice. Melt a little of the butter, and fry the bread rounds on one side until golden. Cool. Butter the unfried side, and on it lay a slice of tomato, then a sliver of cheese, then two small pieces of anchovy fillets, and finally a piece of black olive. Grill the rounds or put them into a hot oven until the cheese melts. Serve hot or cold.

Brandy snaps

See recipe page 136. (Use 3 times the quantity for about 60 snaps. You will need about 1½ pints thick cream to fill them.)

Bacchanalian Revel by Poussin (The National Gallery, London)

An early barbecue, Brazil (from André Thevet, *La Cosmographie Universelle,* 1575)

Meringues (makes about 50 miniature or 12 large meringues)

4 egg whites
5 oz/140 grams/1 cup icing
  (confectioners') sugar
4 oz/110 grams/½ cup caster
  (powdered) sugar

Filling
1 pint/¾ litre/20 fl. oz thick cream,
  whipped

Set the oven at 250°F, gas mark ½. Beat the whites until very stiff; add the icing sugar and beat again. Add the caster sugar and continue beating until the meringue will hold its shape without flowing at all. This process can be greatly speeded up with an electric mixer, or by standing the bowl over a saucepan of simmering water while whisking, but take care not to let the bottom of the bowl touch the water.

Put two sheets of greaseproof (waxed) paper on baking sheets, and brush them with oil. Put the meringue mixture out in teaspoonsful (or pipe small rosettes with a forcing bag). Bake in the oven until the meringues are dry right through and will lift easily off the paper. When cool sandwich them together in pairs with whipped cream. *Note.* To make less dry, more toffee-like, meringues use 8 oz caster sugar but no icing sugar. Substitute 4 oz of it for the 5 oz icing sugar. *Fold* rather than beat in the second 4 oz and cook the meringues at 280°F, gas mark 1. After being filled, this type of meringue goes soggy quicker than the drier kind.

Chocolate profiteroles

Follow the instructions for profiteroles on page 23, but fill them with whipped cream (about 1 pint) instead of the cheese mixture. Melt 6 oz chocolate with 1 cup of water, and boil to a thick cream, stirring. Dip the tops of the profiteroles in the chocolate, and allow to cool.

Gingerbread (makes 1 loaf)
(One gingerbread will cut into about 20 small slices. Make three of them for this party.)
N.B. Good gingerbread can be bought commercially.

4 oz/110 grams/½ cup preserved ginger
4 oz/110 grams/½ cup butter
4 oz/110 grams/½ cup treacle
4 oz/110 grams/a good ¼ cup soft
  brown sugar
½ teaspoon bicarbonate of soda
4 tablespoons milk
8 oz/230 grams/1¾ cups plain flour
1 teaspoon ground ginger
Pinch of salt
1 egg

Line the bottom of a shallow rectangular cake pan with a sheet of greaseproof (waxed) paper, and brush out the pan with melted lard. Set the oven at 325°F, gas mark 3.

Chop the preserved ginger finely. Melt the butter, treacle and sugar together without boiling. When the sugar has dissolved add the chopped ginger and allow to cool. Mix the bicarbonate of soda with a tablespoon of the milk. Sift the flour into a bowl with the salt and the ground ginger, and make a well in the centre. Add the milk and the slightly beaten egg to the treacle mixture. Slowly beat it into the flour, pouring a little at a time into the well, and drawing the flour in from the sides as you mix. When all the flour is incorporated in the treacle mixture, stir in the bicarbonate of soda. Turn the mixture into the prepared cake pan and bake for about 1 hour. The gingerbread should feel moist and slightly tacky but firm. Let it cool before turning it out. It will keep for about 2 weeks in an airtight container, or it freezes perfectly.

On the day before

Fonds d'artichauts au crabe Make the filling and keep covered in a bowl in the refrigerator. Drain the artichoke bottoms; they can be filled six or seven hours before the party, and kept covered with polythene.

Smoked salmon and potted shrimp canapés Prepare the smoked salmon and potted shrimp rolls; lay them in a plastic box, well covered to prevent them drying out, and keep refrigerated. The biscuits (crackers) should not be buttered more than 4 hours before the party.

Curried cheese balls can be made the day before, but the nuts will soften. It is best to make the balls in advance, chill them well, and have the nuts ready browned. Roll the balls in the nuts at the last convenient moment.

Pizza rounds can be prepared the day before, but if they are to be eaten hot the final grilling or cooking in the oven should not be done more than an hour or two before the party. They can be kept in a cool oven, or re-heated as needed. If they are to be eaten cold complete them the day before.

Brandy snaps Make them, and when cold put into an airtight container or plastic bag. Fill with cream not more than 2 hours before the party.

Meringues Make them, and store in an airtight container or plastic bag. Fill with whipped cream not more than 6 hours in advance. If the meringues are at all toffee-ish, they should not be filled more than an hour before serving.

Chocolate profiteroles can be completed the day before and kept well covered and refrigerated until needed. The pastry will be very soft, however. If a firmer pastry is wanted the profiteroles should be kept frozen or refrigerated, well covered, and only filled with cream and dipped in chocolate a few hours before the party.

Gingerbread is best made 2 or 3 days before eating, as it becomes moister and tackier in an airtight container.

Wedding Breakfasts

If the guests are sitting down to lunch, it is usual for everyone except those at the 'high table' (occupied by the immediate family, bridesmaids, best man, bride and groom) to seat themselves informally. The high table seating should look like this:

156

Any of the large dinner party menus in Chapter 3 would be suitable, or the rather more extravagant menu described below.

The wedding cake is traditionally placed on the high table in front of the bride and groom, but if it obscures them from view it is better on a separate table; this also makes taking photographs easier. If there are to be speeches, they are made after lunch, but before coffee. The bride and groom then cut the cake before circulating among their guests while coffee is served.

If there are sufficient staff, all the guests are served at their tables, but if the helpers are hard pressed it is quite permissible to expect people other than those at the high table to fetch their food from a buffet. Plain cold chicken for some of the children might be needed.

Check list, page 187.

WEDDING BREAKFAST FOR 50

Melon and prawn cup

Cold stuffed boned duck with mushrooms and ham

Green salad with avocado pear dressing

Cauliflower, cucumber and potato salad

Orange ice cream with hot strawberry sauce

Wedding cake

(Preparation on the days before follows recipes.)

Champagne, or Sekt (German champagne-type wine) would be suitable throughout, including the toasts.

Melon and prawn cocktail cup (serves 8)
(Do 6 times the recipe for 50 people)

1 medium Honeydew melon
1 lb/450 grams cooked peeled prawns
1 green pepper, finely chopped
½ pint/¼ litre/10 fl. oz thick mayonnaise
4 tablespoons cream
1 tablespoon tomato ketchup
1 dessertspoon lemon juice
2 drops tabasco, or a pinch of cayenne
3 tarragon leaves, finely chopped
1 large whole cooked prawn per person

Cut the melon flesh into cubes, and divide between eight goblets. Put the peeled prawns on top of the melon. Mix together the mayonnaise, cream, ketchup, tabasco, lemon juice and chopped tarragon. Taste, and add salt and pepper if necessary. Put a large spoonful of the sauce into each glass. Sprinkle the chopped green pepper on the top. Remove the legs and roe (if any) from the whole prawns, and tuck one into the side of each glass.

Cold stuffed boned duck with mushrooms and ham (serves 8)
(Cook six ducks for 50 people)

One 5–6 lb/2½–3 kilo duck, boned
1 bunch watercress
½ large white loaf of bread, made into crumbs
Four ¼ in. thick slices ham, cut into small cubes
(continued overleaf)

To make *the stuffing*, melt the butter, add the chopped onion and fry gently until it is soft and transparent. Add mushrooms and crushed garlic and cook for 2 more minutes. Take the pan off the heat and add its contents to the breadcrumbs in a bowl. Combine with the diced ham, the egg

157

1 medium onion, finely chopped
1½ oz/45 grams/3 tablespoons butter
¼ lb/100 grams mushrooms, sliced
1 egg
1 extra egg yolk
Salt and pepper
1 small clove garlic, crushed (optional)

and the yolk, and plenty of salt and pepper. Mix well. If the duck has not been boned for you, follow the instructions for doing it yourself in the recipe for stuffed boned duck with olives, page 50. Scrape off any meat still on the bones, and add it to the stuffing. Stuff the duck. Put it into a roasting pan with a loaf tin wedged against the side of the duck to prevent it flattening and losing its shape. Roast for 1½ hours at 400°F, gas mark 6, or until the bird is brown and crisp all over. Drain off the fat, and dish the bird on a platter. Garnish with a bunch of washed watercress.

Green salad with avocado pear dressing

Follow the recipe for green salad on page 71 but add 1 small ripe avocado, well mashed, to the french dressing (3 avocados and 1 pint french dressing would be enough for 50 people.)

Cauliflower, potato and cucumber salad (serves 8)
(Do 6 times the quantity for 50 people)

1 large cauliflower
1 cucumber, peeled and sliced
1 lb/450 grams potatoes
¼ pint/⅛ litre/5 fl. oz french dressing
1 teaspoon french mustard
1 tablespoon chopped fresh chives
4 tablespoons thick cream

Cook the potatoes in boiling salted water until tender. Drain, peel and slice them. Toss them while still hot in half the french dressing. Leaving the cauliflower whole, boil it in salted water until just cooked. Drain it carefully. Put the potatoes in a dish or shallow salad bowl. Put the cauliflower on top. Surround it with the cucumber slices. Mix the rest of the french dressing with the mustard and the cream, and spoon it over the cauliflower and the cucumber. Sprinkle the chives on the cucumber.

Vanilla ice cream with hot strawberry sauce (serves 8)
(Do 6 times the quantity for 50 people)

2 whole eggs
2 extra egg yolks
2 oz/50 grams/2 tablespoons sugar
½ pint/¼ litre/10 fl. oz milk
¼ teaspoon vanilla essence
½ pint/¼ litre/10 fl. oz thick cream

Set the refrigerator at coldest. Beat the eggs and yolks together until smooth. Bring the milk, sugar and vanilla essence together to boiling-point, stirring. Pour immediately onto the eggs, stirring. Return the mixture to the milk saucepan and cook, stirring, over very gentle heat, until the custard is thick enough to coat the back of the spoon (take care not to boil it, lest the custard curdle). Strain into a bowl. Cool completely. Whip the cream until thick but not stiff and fold into the custard. Pour the mixture into a freezing tray and freeze for ¾ hour—or until solid round the edges and still slushy in the middle. Tip the mixture into a cold bowl and whisk until smooth. Re-freeze. Serve with hot strawberry sauce.

Hot strawberry sauce

1 lb/450 grams fresh or frozen
  strawberries
1 can raspberries
1 tablespoon sugar
2 tablespoons kirsch

Put the raspberries, their juice, the strawberries and the sugar into a saucepan and heat to boiling point. Add the kirsch and serve hot with ice cream.

Wedding cake

In Britain, wedding cakes are traditionally rich fruit cake covered with royal icing. They are generally ordered (well in advance) from large stores, caterers, or bakers; but they can be made at home, and it is easy to get a degree of professionalism into the icing if you have plenty of time and explicit instructions. Decorations can be bought in bridal shops or confectioners, or can be made at home—given patience and a good book on the subject. The cake illustrated on page 163 is really simple to do and was in fact decorated by an amateur in about two hours, with ribbons and fresh flowers supplying the ornament rather than fancy icing. It could be varied by separating the tiers with pillars (bought from most bakers and large stores) or by making it a two-, three- or five-tier affair.

Follow the instructions for Christmas Cake on page 179, but making however many cakes you need. Each tier should be about 2 inches smaller than the one beneath it. The tins we used were 6 ins, 7½ ins, 10½ ins and 12 ins in diameter. The quantities given in the recipe fill an 8-inch tin. Five times the quantities filled our four cake tins, but it is better to make the mixture in two or three batches—otherwise the bulk becomes unweildy. The large cake will take about 3–3½ hours to cook, the middle ones 2–2¼ hours, and the smallest 1½ hours. The large cakes may need to be covered with thick brown paper after an hour of cooking to prevent the tops getting too hard or burnt. Follow the instructions for covering the cakes in marzipan and for making the royal icing.

When you have covered the cakes with marzipan, make up the royal icing and proceed as follows: put a layer of smooth icing on all the cakes, using a palette knife dipped in very hot water to get an even finish. Do not worry if the icing is not as smooth as it should be—most of it will be covered by the cakes above, ribbons, and decorations. Strictly you should apply two thin layers of icing, but we only did one.

Set the largest cake on a cake-board 2 inches wider than the cake, and set the others one on top of the other, the smallest at the top. If you have an icing turntable to put all this on, icing will be easier; but if not, put it on a cake stand, large bowl, or cake tin so that you can turn the cake round without touching it, by moving the stand or bowl beneath. Using a medium size star-shaped nozzle, pipe a line of shell shapes round the bottom of each cake. (Practise on the table top until you have the hang of it.) Holding the forcing bag at the top in your right hand and steadying it with your left hand, squeeze some icing out, keeping the nozzle close to the surface. Allow the supply of icing to trail off as you move the nozzle slightly to the right, then move it back again, slightly over the end of the shell shape you have just piped, and repeat the process. See drawing.

Note: Do not eat any icing in its wet state—you will almost certainly feel sick.

When the icing is dry, pin wide white ribbons round each tier, and narrow pale-coloured ones over the white. Pin lacy white ribbon round the top of each cake, sticking slightly above the edges—see plate on page 163.

With the help of a small disc of florists' polystyrene 'moss' for a base, arrange a few small fresh flowers and leaves for the top decoration. Pin trailing ribbons (the shiny Christmas-wrapping kind is excellent) into the 'moss' and fix a white ribbon round the base. Damp the polystyrene and put the arrangement on the top cake tier (a disc of cardboard or small coffee saucer will prevent the moisture getting through to the icing). Add odd flowers or leaves haphazardly to the other tiers, and tie a bow onto the middle of the bottom tier. See plate on page 163.

American wedding cake

In America wedding cakes are often made with a 'white cake' mixture. This has the advantage of being lighter, and better liked by children, than the heavy fruit cakes more common in Britain. The disadvantage is that the cake must be made only a few days before the wedding.

This mixture will comfortably fill a 9-inch round cake tin (pan) about 2½ inches deep. Four times the quantity will make a wedding cake comparable in size to the one illustrated on page 163.

1 lb/500 grams/3½ cups plain flour
4 level teaspoons baking powder
½ teaspoon salt
14 oz/400 grams/2 cups caster (powdered) sugar
7 oz/200 grams/1 cup butter
½ pint/2 decilitres/1 cup milk
1 teaspoon vanilla essence
8 egg whites

Lightly butter the cake pan, and set the oven at 375°F, gas mark 5. Sift the flour with the baking powder and the salt. Beat the sugar and butter together until very light and creamy. Stir the flour and the milk into the creamed mixture alternately, a few spoonsful at a time. Add the vanilla essence and beat until quite smooth. Whip the egg whites until they will hold their shape but do not look dry. Fold them into the mixture. Turn the mixture into the cake pan, making sure that there are no large air pockets. Bake for about 30 minutes, or until the cake is firm to the touch, slightly springy, and has shrunk from the sides of the pan. Allow the cake to cool for 10 minutes before turning it out onto a rack.

Ice the cake as described on page 159, with or without a thin layer of almond paste under the royal icing (page 180).

On the days before

Melon and prawn cup If the prawns are frozen, take them from the freezer the day before the party to allow them to thaw. The melon can be prepared the day before, and kept refrigerated, but it should be well covered, because the smell of melon gets into milk or butter very easily. Make the sauce a day or two in advance and keep in a cool place, though not in the refrigerator. Chop the green pepper the day before, keeping it well covered. The melon and prawn cups can be assembled several hours before the party, though it is wise to cover each cup or glass with a square of polythene to prevent the mayonnaise forming a skin.

Cold stuffed boned duck with mushrooms and ham should be completed the day before the party. Keep in a cool place.

Green salad with avocado pear dressing Make the dressing, omitting the avocado (this should be mashed and added only a few hours before the salad is to be served). Ideally the salad should be bought and prepared on the morning of the party, but if this is not possible, pick over the salad the evening before, and put the washed leaves in a polythene bag in the refrigerator.

Cauliflower, potato and cucumber salad Prepare and cook the cauliflower and the potatoes, but do not add the cucumber or the dressing until a few hours before the party.

Vanilla ice cream with hot strawberry sauce Make or buy the ice cream a few days in advance, and keep well frozen. If the fruit for the sauce is frozen, take it from the freezer the day before the party, but do not heat it until the ice cream is about to be served.

Wedding cake of the rich fruit kind should be started at least three weeks before the wedding (two months would be better) and completed with a week to spare.

The American wedding cake should not be made more than 5 days in advance. Ice it the day after baking. The heavy royal icing will protect the cake from the air and from going stale. If the cake is not to be iced immediately, it can be stored for a few days in an airtight container or well wrapped in polythene.

Of course, if plenty of freezer space is available, the cake can be made well in advance and frozen until a few days before the wedding. It must be thawed completely before icing.

Christening Parties

Christening parties, like wedding receptions, vary according to the time of day the ceremony is held. The party can be a tea, lunch or cocktail party or a combination (see Wedding Receptions, page 151). The great difference is that christenings are very much more relaxed and informal, and the cake is generally a one-tier affair, fairly simple, though pretty. If the parents' wedding cake was the rich fruit kind described on page 159, the top tier may have been kept for the first child's christening. In that event it will need re-icing, and a little brandy or rum will moisten it if it has become dry.

Check list, page 184.

Serve champagne or any good sparkling wine.

Anniversary Parties

Coming-of-age, wedding anniversaries and similar occasions can be celebrated with any form of party, usually with the addition of speeches. The best time for these is when the party is sufficiently advanced for the guests to be feeling well disposed towards the speaker, and the speaker relaxed and confident.

A coming-of-age, because it is a birthday too, generally has a cake (if necessary in lieu of the pudding). An iced bombe (page 129) is less burdensome than rich fruit cake. The young guest of honour may be presented with the 'key of the door' made of cardboard (or solid gold if preferred) as a token of his freedom from parental restriction. As he has certainly had the house-key and probably his parents' car-keys too for several years, the gesture is not without quaintness.

I once catered for a wedding anniversary that took the 'golden' theme about as far as it can go. It must be admitted that our client was extremely rich. We hired gold cutlery, and china with a heavy gold border. We bought gold foil to put under a gold lace tablecloth; chocolates wrapped in gold; amber-coloured glasses. We gilded the leafy flower decorations with gold paint. And the hostess wore a gold lamé dress, gold shoes and gold ribbons in her hair. The menu, as far as possible, was gold-coloured too (see below). This may sound too much of a good thing, but it was exceptionally pretty and the guests were enchanted.

This menu needs a cook in the kitchen.

Check list page 190.

GOLDEN WEDDING DINNER FOR 8

Hot cheese soufflé

Canard à l'orange
Glazed onions
Orange salad with butterbeans,
  butternut and red peppers

Goldenberry flan

(*Preparation on the day before follows recipes.*)

Serve a Volnay with the cheese soufflé, and follow with a bigger and grander Burgundy such as Romanée Conti or Echézeaux. Serve a German dessert wine—a Trockenbecrenauslèse or a sweet white Bordeaux, preferably the great Château d'Yquem.

Hot cheese soufflé (serves 4 or 5)
(Make twice the quantity for eight people and cook it in two dishes.)

3 oz/80 grams/6 tablespoons butter
2 oz/50 grams/2 heaped tablespoons
  flour
½ pint/¼ litre/10 fl. oz milk
4 eggs, separated
½ teaspoon made English mustard
Pinch cayenne pepper
Salt and pepper
2 oz/50 grams/½ cup strong grated
  cheddar or gruyère cheese
Cheese sauce (optional)—see next
  recipe.

Set the oven at 400°F, gas mark 6. Melt a knob of the butter and brush out a 6-inch soufflé dish with it. Melt the rest in a saucepan and stir in the flour. Add the milk and cook, stirring vigorously, for 1 minute. The mixture will get very thick and leave the sides of the pan. Take it off the heat. Stir in the cheese, egg yolks, mustard, cayenne, pepper and salt. Whisk the egg whites until stiff, but not dry-looking, and mix a spoonful into the mixture. Then fold in the rest and pour into the soufflé dish, which should be about two-thirds full. With a knife cut through the mixture several times to ensure that there are no over-large pockets of air. Bake for 35–40 minutes and serve straight away. Do not test to see if the soufflé is done for at least 30 minutes. Then open the oven just wide enough to get your hands in. Stick a warmed thin skewer or knitting needle into the middle of the soufflé from the side. If it comes out clean the soufflé is done. However, many people —myself included—*like* their soufflés slightly runny in the middle. Once you have made one soufflé you will know exactly how long it needs in your oven, and you will not need to bother with testing the next time. If the soufflé cannot be served the minute it is cooked, turn the oven off and leave it in there. It will not sink for 10 minutes, but it may become a little dry. A cheese sauce (see below) served with it would counteract any dryness.

Traditional English wedding cake (page 159)

16th-century wedding feast; detail from *The Life and Death of Sir Henry Unton, c.* 1596 (National Portrait Gallery, London)

And now let M.ʳ Lambkin speak for himself.
"Ladies and Gentlemen, unaccustomed as I am... (Bravo)...return...
(Bravo) on the part of Miss... (oh! oh! ha! ha!), I beg pardon, I mean M.ʳˢ
Lambkin (Bravo) and myself for the great...hum...ha...hum.... and
kindness, (Bravo) In return hum...ha...pleasure to drink all your healths
(Bravo),–Wishing you all the happiness this world can afford (Bravo)
I shall conclude in the words of our immortal bard–"may the single
be married and the(hear! Hear! hear! Bravo) married happy."
Bravo! Bravo!! Bravo!!!

From *The Bachelor's Own Book*, 1844, by George Cruickshank

hos eo adunatos pax æpietas sociauit Quos coniuuatos patris hostia sanctificauit.

Job and his sons and daughters
Detail from the Bayeux Tapestry

HIC FECERVNT PRANDIVM ET HIC EPISCOPVS CIBV ET POTV BENEDICIT ODO

Cheese sauce

1 oz/30 grams/2 tablespoons butter
1 oz/30 grams/1 heaped tablespoon
  flour
Pinch of dry English mustard
1 pint milk/¾ litre/20 fl. oz milk
Few slices onion
1 bayleaf
Handful of parsley
Salt and pepper
2 oz/50 grams/½ cup strong cheddar
  or gruyère

Melt the butter in a saucepan. Mix the mustard with the flour and stir into the butter. Cook over gentle heat for one minute, then add the milk gradually, stirring briskly all the time. Add the onion, bayleaf, and parsley. Still stirring, bring to the boil, then leave to simmer for 10 minutes. Grate the cheese. Strain the sauce into a fresh saucepan and stir in the cheese. Season with salt and pepper, and reheat until the cheese is melted.

Canard à l'orange (serves 8)

Two 5–6 lb/2½–3 kilo ducks
4 oranges
1 tablespoon sugar
2 tablespoons wine vinegar
Ground black pepper, salt
2 tablespoons Grand Marnier
1 level dessertspoon arrowroot
1 onion, sliced
1 carrot, sliced
Bouquet garni (a sprig each of parsley
  and thyme, a stick of celery, and a
  bayleaf, tied together with string)
12 peppercorns
Bunch watercress

Set the oven at 400°F, gas mark 6. Prick the ducks all over and season them inside and out with pepper and salt. Put them into the oven, lying upside down, and roast for ½ hour. Turn them over and continue roasting until cooked (another ¾ hour or so). Meanwhile make some stock: put the sliced onion, carrot, bouquet garni and peppercorns into a saucepan with the giblets (except the liver) and the neck of the duck, cover with water, and bring to the boil. Simmer all the time the duck is roasting, then strain and reserve. Grate the rind of 3 of the oranges finely, and squeeze their juice. Put the sugar and vinegar together into a saucepan, and cook slowly until the sugar has caramelized. Immediately pour on the orange juice, taking care not to lean over the pot (it hisses and sizzles dangerously and steam comes billowing out). Add ¾ pint of the strained duck stock, and salt and pepper to taste. Pour in the Grand Marnier. In a cup, slake (mix) the arrowroot with two tablespoons cold water or stock, then add enough of the hot sauce almost to fill the cup, stirring as you do so. Pour this mixture into the sauce, stir well, and bring to the boil. If it is too thin, do *not* use more arrowroot, but reduce and thicken it by turning up the heat and boiling fast until the sauce is of the desired consistency. If the sauce is too thick add more stock. When the ducks are cooked (test by sticking a skewer into a thigh—if the juice comes out pink, they need further cooking) take them out and joint them. Put the pieces onto a warmed platter and return to the oven—switched off—to keep warm. Pour off all the fat from the roasting pan, but add any juices left in the bottom to the sauce. Skim the sauce if there is any fat floating on it.
Cut the remaining orange in half, and slice it with the skin on. Surround the duck with the orange slices and garnish with bouquets of watercress.

Glazed onions
See page 126.

Orange salad with butterbeans, butternut and red peppers (serves 8)

4 large oranges
2 small or one large can butterbeans
1 medium-sized fresh butternut
  (Calabash squash)
2 red peppers
French dressing
1 tablespoon chopped onion
1 tablespoon chopped parsley

Cook the butternut whole in plenty of salted water until tender right through. Drain and allow to cool. When quite cold, peel it and slice thinly. Peel the oranges, removing skin and pith, and slice across. Remove the seeds from the peppers and slice thinly.

Arrange the orange rings round the edge of a shallow salad bowl. Gently mix the butternut, butterbeans and most of the peppers with just enough french dressing to moisten without soaking. Lay in the salad bowl. Put the rest of the strips of pepper on top. Mix the chopped onion and parsley with another two tablespoons of french dressing and spoon over the top.

Goldenberry flan (serves 6)
(If Cape gooseberries are not available, this could be made with golden plums)

¾ lb/340 grams rich short crust pastry
  (see page 88)
2 cans Cape gooseberries
  (goldenberries)
1 teaspoon arrowroot
2 tablespoons smooth apricot jam

Line a large flan ring or pie plate with the pastry and bake blind (see page 105). Drain the fruit, reserving the juice, and put the fruit into the flan. In a teacup mix the arrowroot with enough of the juice to make it smooth. Put ½ pint of the juice into a saucepan with the arrowroot mixture and bring to the boil, stirring all the time. Add the jam, and boil to a thick syrupy consistency. When it is tepid, but not stone cold, pour into the flan—all over the fruit—and leave to get quite cold. The glaze (the syrup and jam mixture) should set when cold, but be just warm enough to run when poured on the fruit. (This flan is quite perfect when made with fresh ripe Cape gooseberries. Fill the cooked case with the raw berries, and pour over 3 oz melted sieved apricot jam.)

On the day before
Hot cheese soufflé Prepare the base (the yolk mixture) but do not whip the whites. Butter the soufflé dish.
Canard à l'orange Prepare the sauce, and the garnish of orange slices and watercress. Put them into plastic bags in the refrigerator or into covered plastic boxes.
Glazed onions Cook completely. Reheat in a little more butter next day.
Orange salad with butterbeans, butternut and red peppers Prepare the ingredients, but do not combine them earlier than about 6 hours before the party.
Goldenberry flan Bake the flan case. Do not fill it more than six hours before eating if you want the pastry to stay crisp. It can be filled further in advance, but the pastry will then be rather soft.

15 · Annual Feasts

Hallowe'en Parties

The witching night of 31 October provides a good party theme for teenagers particularly, because there is endless scope for making the setting spooky. They can have a great time making cut-outs of witches for the walls, and hallowe'en masks. Black crêpe paper for the tablecloth, black candles, and soup served from a cauldron, are a few other ideas.

Small children like to put hallowe'en masks over their heads to frighten themselves; but once they tire of this, the masks can be put over the candles or night lights, giving unearthly flickering grins.

For making the masks, use honeydew melons, watermelons or pumpkins. If the melons are the long sort, cut them in half across the middle, to make two masks from each. If pumpkins or round melons are used, cut one end off. The flesh is then scooped out without damaging the shell. With melons this should be done well in advance to allow the inside of the skin to dry. Eyes and a hideous mouth (with a few jagged teeth, if the sculptor is handy enough) are then cut out.

The following menu assumes that three such masks have been made, one from a pumpkin (hence the pumpkin pie) and two from one large or two small watermelons (hence the iced watermelon).

Check list page 184.

HALLOWE'EN PARTY FOR 20

Moussaka

Green salad

Garlic bread

Pumpkin pie

Iced watermelon

(Preparation on the day before follows recipes.)

If the party is for teenagers, a 'witches' brew' of mulled cider (cider heated with a few cloves and a touch of cinnamon in it) could be replaced cunningly by a non-alcoholic brew later on (see Teetotaller's Tipple, page 15). For adults, Retsina —Greek resinated wine—is ideal with Moussaka, but many people do not like it, so serve an inexpensive Burgundy as well.

Moussaka (serves 10)
(Make 2 for 20 people)

2½ lb/1 kilo lean mutton, minced
2 large onions, finely chopped
1 clove garlic, crushed
6 tomatoes
¼ pint/¼ litre/10 fl. oz. white wine
(continued overleaf)

Heat a little olive oil in a large saucepan and brown the onion slowly in it. Add the meat and garlic; then cook, stirring, for 5 minutes. Dip the tomatoes in boiling water for 5 seconds, skin them, chop them and add to the meat. Add wine,

Salt and black pepper
½ pint/¼ litre/10 fl. oz. water
Handful of parsley, finely chopped
½ teaspoon ground nutmeg
8 aubergines (eggplants)
1 oz/30 grams/1 heaped tablespoon
  dried breadcrumbs
6 oz/180 grams/1½ cups grated dry
  cheddar cheese
2 large potatoes, thinly sliced
1 oz/30 grams/2 tablespoons butter
1 oz/30 grams/1 heaped tablespoon
  flour
1 bayleaf
1 pint/¾ litre/20 fl. oz milk
2 egg yolks
2 tablespoons cream
Olive oil

water, salt, pepper, parsley and nutmeg, and cook over a gentle heat, stirring often, until most of the liquid has evaporated. This will take at least an hour. Cut the aubergines in thin slices, salt them lightly and leave for about ½ hour for some of their juice to drain out. Rinse them and dry well on a cloth. Heat a little more oil in a frying pan and fry each slice of aubergine on both sides until well-browned but not burnt. Put them in the bottom of a large casserole. Sprinkle on the breadcrumbs. Now tip in half the meat mixture. Put half the sliced potatoes in next, seasoning with salt and pepper, then the rest of the meat, and then the rest of the potatoes. Melt the butter in a saucepan. Stir in the flour, add the bayleaf, then the milk and stir constantly while bringing slowly to the boil. Season with salt and pepper and leave simmering while you mix the egg yolks with the cream in a bowl. Pour the sauce onto the yolks and cream, stirring all the time, and add half the cheese. Pour over the dish and sprinkle the rest of the cheese on top. Put the dish into a slow oven (325°F, gas mark 3) until the potatoes are tender. Test after one hour with a skewer. The top should by then be browned too, but it may be necessary to finish the browning under the grill.

Green salad
See page 71.

Garlic bread
See page 96.

Pumpkin pie (serves 6)
(For 20 people make 3 pies)

½ lb/250 grams rich short-crust pastry
  (see page 88)
½ lb/250 grams pumpkin flesh
3 oz/80 grams/½ cup soft brown sugar
1 teaspoon ground cinnamon
Large pinch ground ginger
A dessertspoon lemon juice
2 eggs
¼ pint/⅛ litre/5 fl. oz milk
2 tablespoons cream

Set the oven at 350°F, gas mark 4. Roll out the pastry and line a 7-inch flan ring or pie-plate with it. Bake blind (see page 105). Peel the pumpkin, throw away the seeds, and chop it roughly. Simmer in salted water until soft, drain well, and mash thoroughly. Add the cinnamon, ginger, sugar and lemon juice. Separate the eggs, and beat the yolks slightly. Heat the milk and pour onto the yolks. Add the cream and mix into the pumpkin mixture. Whisk the egg whites, fold them in, and pour into the flan case. Bake until the filling has set (about 25 minutes). (A layer of white sugar sprinkled on the top and browned under the grill gives the top a crunchy texture.)

Iced watermelon (serves 10)

1 medium-sized watermelon
Juice of one orange and one lemon
Caster (powdered) sugar

Cut the melon flesh into large chunks. Do not bother to remove the seeds. Sprinkle with lemon juice, orange juice, and sugar. Chill well before serving.

On the day before

Moussaka Make completely. It will re-heat perfectly in the oven.
Green salad Make the dressing. If you have bought the salad it can be washed, dried and put in a plastic bag in the refrigerator—but it is best bought on the day of the party.
Garlic bread Prepare the bread and leave it well wrapped in foil in the refrigerator. It will then be ready for the oven, but remember to open the foil so that the top can become crisp.
Pumpkin pie Make completely. It should be served slightly warm, but can easily be reheated in the oven.
Iced watermelon Chill the melon whole in the refrigerator. Squeeze the lemon and orange but do not cut the melon until the day of the party.

Thanksgiving Day

In America, Thanksgiving Day is traditionally celebrated with a dinner including roast turkey with cranberry sauce, and pumpkin pie. The Christmas turkey recipe given on page 172 could be used, and a recipe for pumpkin pie is given in the Hallowe'en menu on page 170.

Christmas Dinner & Tea

Even in blazing Africa my childhood Christmas dinner consisted of roast turkey, plum pudding, mince pies—*et al.*

In a freezing English winter, this is still a mad menu, unbalanced, heavy, not good for you. But the Victorians coped with Oxtail Soup, Boiled Turbot, Roast Beef and Scotch Woodcock *as well*, so perhaps we have trifled enough with tradition.

Yet though the food varies little, Christmas procedures differ from family to family: each makes its own tradition by doing the same thing year after year, giving children something solid and memorable to be sentimental about in time to come.

In my family, Christmas started on Christmas Eve when we were given nuts and raisins, and port out of purple Napoleonic glasses, while my father read us *Scrooge*. We went to church at midnight, and came home to open our presents. This curious routine was dictated by my mother's objection to being woken at 4 a.m. by excited children exhibiting their loot. We went exhausted to sleep at 3 a.m. or so, and slept late. Relatives and friends arrived in time for 'the Christmas Tree'—an apple tree with cotton wool snow—on the lawn: more presents (little ones this time) and my father sweating in his Father Christmas kit. Lunch was light, held in the garden. Then everyone slept or played until tea when we attacked the Christmas cake. (One year, when I made it, I left out the glycerine and we broke the carving knife and hammer trying to crack the icing.) Christmas dinner was held at night and we ate until no-one could move. And I remember it all so well because from one year to another not one detail changed.

The day on which all good British housewives started their Christmas baking used to be known as Stir-up Sunday—from the Collect for the Sunday next before Advent:

'Stir-up, we beseech thee, O Lord, the wills of thy faithful people, that they, plenteously bringing forth the fruits of good works, may of thee be plenteously rewarded ...'. Certainly if Christmas baking is to be enjoyed it must be done well before the full rush of Christmas descends.

The traditional English Christmas Dinner menu set out below is followed by a plan of preparations during the days before, and a work programme for Christmas Day itself. (Christmas Tea is dealt with on page 179.)

Check list page 190.

CHRISTMAS DINNER FOR 12

Roast turkey
Cranberry sauce
Bread sauce
Glazed (sugar-baked) ham
Brussel sprouts and chestnuts
Roast potatoes

Plum pudding and brandy butter
Mince pies

Preparation on the days before and Christmas morning programme follow recipes.

Big powerful wines are called for to go with this heavy menu. A Vosne Romanée or a Corton would be ideal. If white wine is wanted, Liebfraumilch Spätlese is big enough in bouquet and flavour. A light dry wine would be lost.

Roast stuffed turkey (serves 12)

One 14 lb/7 kilo turkey, weighed when plucked and drawn
2 oz/50 grams/4 tablespoons butter
The turkey giblets
1 onion, sliced
1 carrot, sliced
Good pinch of dried herbs
1 bayleaf
Salt, pepper

For the chestnut stuffing
¾ lb/350 grams chestnuts
(or ½ lb/250 grams unsweetened tinned chestnut purée)
1 pint/¾ litre/20 fl. oz turkey or chicken stock
4 slices fatty bacon, diced
4 oz/110 grams/1 cup white breadcrumbs
Pinch nutmeg
½ teaspoon sugar
Grated rind of ½ lemon
Salt, black pepper

For the sausagemeat stuffing
1½ lb/¾ kilo pork sausagemeat
Good pinch of dried sage
The turkey liver
1 onion, chopped
Salt and pepper
2 tablespoons bacon fat or butter

To make the *chestnut stuffing*, first skin the chestnuts. This is easier said than done, so allow plenty of time. The best method is to make a split in the skin with a knife, and then briefly deep-fry the chestnuts in a chip-pan—the skins then come off quite easily. Alternatively, the chestnuts can be boiled for twenty minutes to loosen the skins— more tedious and less effective, but also less messy. When skinned, boil the chestnuts in the stock until tender. Drain them, reserving the liquid. Mash roughly with a fork. Fry the bacon bits and add to the chestnuts. Add the crumbs, nutmeg, sugar, lemon rind, salt and pepper. Stir in enough stock to bind the stuffing together. Stuff the crop of the bird with it, tuck the flap of skin under the turkey and skewer it in place.

For the *sausagemeat stuffing* fry the chopped onion gently in the bacon fat or butter until soft. Discard the discoloured part from the turkey liver, and chop the liver roughly. Add it to the onion in the pan and fry until the liver is cooked but still pink inside. Remove from the heat and add the sage, salt and pepper. Work all this into the sausagemeat, and use it to stuff the body of the bird.

Truss the bird, or at least tie the legs close to the body. Put the turkey into a large roasting pan, and spread the butter all over it. Put the neck and giblets (except the liver which you have used in the stuffing) round the bird, with the onion, carrot, pinch of herbs, bayleaf, salt and pepper. Pour in enough water to come to within 1 inch of the top of the roasting pan. Do not overfill it as the fat running from the bird may make it overflow. Cover the turkey *loosely* with tin foil and cook for about 3½ hours at 350°F, gas mark 4. Baste the bird after 1 hour, and again towards the end of the cooking, removing the foil at the same time to allow the breast to brown. Test whether or not the turkey is cooked by sticking a skewer into the thigh: the juice that runs out should be colourless, not pink. Lift the turkey onto a warm dish, and put back into the oven—turned down very low—to keep warm.

To make *the gravy*, strain the juices from the pan into a shallow saucepan. Skim off as much fat as you can. Absorbent paper laid across the top of the liquid will absorb most of the fat. Sprinkle a tablespoon of flour onto the liquid, and using a wire or rotary whisk, whisk the gravy while you bring it to the boil. Taste it, adding more salt and pepper if needed.

Cranberry sauce

½ lb/250 grams cranberries
6 oz/175 grams/¾ cup sugar
¼ pint/⅛ litre/5 fl. oz water
1 tablespoon sherry or brandy

Add the sugar to the water in a saucepan and bring to the boil, stirring. When the sugar is quite dissolved, add the cranberries and simmer for 10 minutes. Add the sherry.

Bread sauce

1 onion
2 cloves
1 pint/¾ litre/20 fl. oz.
1 oz/30 grams/2 tablespoons butter
4 oz/110 grams/1 cup fresh white
  breadcrumbs
Salt and white pepper

Peel the onion, and stick the cloves into it. Put it in a pan with the milk and breadcrumbs, salt and pepper. Leave to stand for at least an hour. Just before serving, bring to the boil, simmer for a few minutes, remove the onion and add the butter.

Glazed (sugar-baked) ham See recipe on page 82.
This can be served hot or cold. With the turkey, vegetables, sauces, plum pudding and mince pies to keep warm, it will probably be easier to serve the ham cold.

Brussels sprouts and chestnuts (serves 12)

4 lb/2 kilos very small brussels
  sprouts
1 lb/½ kilo fresh chestnuts
3 oz/80 grams/6 tablespoons butter
Juice of ½ lemon
Salt, black pepper, ground nutmeg

Wash and trim the sprouts, paring the stalk and removing the outside leaves if necessary. Make a slit in the skin of each chestnut, and fry in deep fat for a few minutes or boil in water for about 20 minutes to facilitate removing the skins. When just cool enough to handle, take off the skins and boil the chestnuts in salted water or stock until just tender. Drain well. Melt the butter in a frying pan, and slowly fry the chestnuts (which will break up a little) until brown. Bring a large pan of salted water to the boil, and tip in the sprouts. Boil fairly fast until the sprouts are just cooked, but not soggy: the flavour changes disastrously if boiled too long. Drain them well. Mix the sprouts and chestnuts together gently; add the butter from the frying pan, and the lemon juice. Season with salt, pepper and nutmeg.

Roast potatoes (serves 12)
5 lb/2½ kilos potatoes
Dripping, lard, or margarine

Peel the potatoes, and if they are large, cut them into 2-inch pieces. Bring them to the boil in plenty of salted water. Boil for 5 minutes. Drain them, and while still hot, scratch all over with a fork to roughen and slightly crumble the surface of each potato. This produces potatoes with delicious crunchy outsides, that can be kept warm for up to 2 hours without coming to any harm. (Potatoes roasted without this preliminary boiling and scratching tend to become tough and hard if not eaten straight away.) Melt the dripping in a roasting pan, and add the potatoes, turning them so that they are coated with fat. Potatoes can be roasted at almost any temperature, usually taking an hour in a hot oven, or 1½ hours in a medium one. They should be basted and turned over once or twice during cooking, and they are done when a skewer glides easily into them. Potatoes roasted in the same pan as the joint have the best flavour, but this is not always possible if the joint—or turkey—is very large, or if liquid has been added to the pan.

Plum pudding (makes one large or two smaller puddings (serves 12–16)
8 oz/230 grams suet
8 oz/230 grams/1¼ cups soft brown
  sugar
4 oz/110 grams/¾ cup flour
4 oz/110 grams/1 cup breadcrumbs
8 oz/230 grams/1½ cups each of
  raisins, sultanas and currants
4 oz/110 grams/¾ cup mixed peel
2 oz/50 grams/½ cup shredded almonds
1 teaspoon grated nutmeg or a large
  pinch of ground nutmeg
1 small teaspoon mixed spice
1 small teaspoon ground cinnamon
4 standard eggs
1 tablespoon marmalade
Juice and grated rind of one lemon
1 small apple, grated
¼ pint/⅛ litre/5 fl. oz milk
1 sherry glass of brandy

Put all the dry ingredients into a large bowl and mix well. Add the milk, eggs and marmalade and beat well. Add grated apple, brandy, lemon juice and rind. Put into well-buttered pudding basins (bowls), not more than two-thirds full, pushing the mixture down well to prevent airholes.
Cover with 2 or 3 layers of buttered greaseproof (waxed) paper across the top and tie down under the rim of the bowl. Cover the paper with a scalded and wrung-out cloth. Tie string round the bowl, over the cloth. Now tie the four corners of the cloth loosely on top of the bowl. Stand the bowl in a large saucepan of water, being sure that the water does not reach the greaseproof and cloth covering. Then cover tightly. (The saucepan lid *must* fit.) Boil for 6–8 hours (6 hours if using two small bowls, 8 if one large), topping up the water with more from a kettle as necessary.

A Wedding Breakfast by Richard Doyle

Bringing in the Boar's Head by J. Gilbert, Radio Times Hulton Picture Library

Lift the pudding out by the cloth, and allow to cool. Untie the knot and let the cloth hang round the pudding to dry. Do not remove the coverings; when they are dry, store the pudding in a cool airy place (*not* in a container) until Christmas Day, when it should be reheated by boiling again for another 2 hours. Turn the pudding onto the dish. Small silver coins or charms can be pushed into the pudding just before serving. In England, a sprig of holly on top of the pudding is traditional. If you want to flame it, warm the brandy or rum in a small saucepan before lighting and pouring it over.

Brandy butter (or hard sauce)

6 oz/170 grams/¾ cup caster (powdered) sugar
3 oz/80 grams/6 tablespoons butter
6 tablespoons brandy

Beat the butter and sugar together until really light and almost frothy. Beat in the brandy and put in the refrigerator to harden.

Mince pies (makes 12)

The secret of good mince pies is a large proportion of fruit to pastry. Use deep tartlet pans, and roll the pastry out very thinly. They are best served warm, but are quite acceptable cold. Mincemeat can be bought in jars; but if you have the time, making home-made mincemeat can be very satisfying. It keeps for about three weeks in the refrigerator.

1 lb/½ kilo mincemeat (see recipe below)
1 lb/½ kilo rich shortcrust pastry (page 88)

Set the oven at 350°F, gas mark 4. Flour a tray of deep tartlet pans. Roll out the pastry very thinly, and using a cutter rather bigger than the diameter of the tartlet moulds, cut out 12 rounds of pastry. Line these into the tartlet pan. Put a large spoonful of mincemeat into each. Roll out the rest of the pastry again, and, using a smaller cutter, cut rounds of pastry for lids. Press the lids into place, wetting the edges to assist sealing. Prick each lid with a fork, and brush with milk. Sprinkle with a little caster (powdered) sugar and bake for 20–30 minutes or until the pastry is pale brown. Dust with icing (confectioners') sugar. Serve warm.

Mincemeat

8 oz/250 grams/1½ cups sultanas
8 oz/250 grams/1½ cups seedless raisins
8 oz/250 grams/1½ cups currants
4 oz/110 grams/¾ cup mixed peel
4 oz/110 grams/¾ cup glacé cherries, chopped
3 fresh apples, peeled and chopped
3 large bananas, chopped
4 oz/110 grams/1 cup flaked almonds
(*continued overleaf*)

Melt the butter, and mix it into all the other ingredients.

177

Grated rind and juice of one lemon
6 oz/180 grams/1 cup brown sugar
Pinch salt
Pinch each of ground cloves, all spice,
    ground cinnamon, ground nutmeg
4 oz/110 grams/½ cup butter
1 wine glass of brandy, sherry, rum,
    or a mixture of any of these

On the days before

The plum pudding should—indeed ought—to be made *weeks* in advance. *The mince pies, brandy butter and cranberry sauce* should all be made about a week before Christmas. Keep the cranberry sauce and brandy butter refrigerated, and the mince pies in an airtight container.

Roast stuffed turkey The stuffing can be made the day before, the bird stuffed, spread with butter and put ready in its roasting pan. The giblets, onion, etc. can be put round the bird, but the water should not be added until just before roasting. Keep the turkey in a cool place overnight. The *bread sauce* should be prepared but not heated.

Glazed ham should be boiled 1–2 days in advance, and the sugar glazing done on Christmas Eve.

Brussels sprouts and chestnuts Wash and trim the sprouts the day before and keep them in a plastic bag in a cool place overnight. Skin and fry the chestnuts.

Roast potatoes The day before the party, part-boil the potatoes and scratch them with a fork. Roast potatoes are not good reheated so the roasting must be done on the day.

Christmas morning programme

Traditions at Christmas differ, so that this programme may not suit everyone, but similar plans can easily be worked out. This one is for Christmas morning, if the dinner is to be eaten at about 1 p.m. There is bound to be *some* fluster at the serving stage. But with a little Christmas spirit, and maybe some help from the rest of the family, all should be well.

9 a.m.   Put the turkey in the oven. Have a simple breakfast, or just coffee and fruit.

9.30 a.m.   Wash up the breakfast things and start to lay the lunch table.

10 a.m.   Put the pudding on to steam. Finish laying the table, adding decorations, etc. Put the ham on the sideboard, and also the cranberry sauce, any fruit and nuts, brandy butter, and anything that need not be heated.

11 a.m.   Put the potatoes in to roast. Baste the turkey. Top up the pudding water. Put the plates into the warming drawer or onto the hotplate.

12 noon.   Put on the bread sauce and the chestnuts. Put on the water for the sprouts, and when boiling add them. Put the bread sauce in a serving dish. Keep warm.

12.20 p.m.   Test the turkey. Turn back the foil to brown the bird if necessary. Prepare the sprouts for serving, adding the chestnuts. Turn the potatoes.

12.45 p.m.   Place the turkey on a carving dish and put it back in the switched-off oven. Make the gravy. Turn the pudding down to simmer. Take out the potatoes and put them into a serving dish.

1 p.m.   Serve the turkey, and while someone else is carving it, turn out the pudding and put it in the oven to keep warm. Put the mincepies in to warm too, and pour the brandy for flaming the pudding into a little saucepan so that it can be easily heated at the last minute. Have ready the sprig of holly and coins and/or charms for the pudding.

CHRISTMAS TEA FOR 12

Anchovy toast
Coffee éclairs
Christmas cake
Yule log

(Preparation on the days before follows recipes.)

Anchovy toast

9 large slices white bread
Butter
Anchovy paste

Toast the bread, butter it, and spread with the anchovy paste. Cut off the crusts, and cut each slice into fingers. Serve while still warm.

Coffee éclairs

Choux paste (see recipe for profiteroles, page 23). Éclairs are made from the same paste as profiteroles, differing only in shape.
Crème pâtissière (page 118) flavoured with coffee essence to taste.

For the icing
8 oz/250 grams/1½ cups icing (confectioners') sugar
2 tablespoons very strong black coffee, or water plus a few drops coffee essence

Using a forcing bag with a ½-inch plain nozzle, pipe 2-inch lengths of choux paste mixture onto a baking sheet and bake as you would profiteroles. When the éclairs are cool, split them and fill them with the coffee-flavoured crème pâtissière.

Mix the icing ingredients together and beat with a wooden spoon until smooth. The mixture should be just runny enough to pour but not so liquid that it runs off the éclairs. Spoon a strip of icing onto the top of each éclair and allow to dry.

Christmas cake

This cake is for an 8-inch cake pan, 3 ins deep.

6 oz/170 grams/¾ cup butter
6 oz/170 grams/1 cup light brown sugar
4 standard eggs
8 oz/230 grams/1¾ cups plain flour sifted with a pinch of salt
½ teaspoon mixed spice
1 tablespoon black treacle
8 oz/230 grams/1½ cups washed and dried currants (you can buy them ready cleaned)
1 lb/½ kilo/3 cups sultanas
12 oz/340 grams/2½ cups raisins
2 oz/50 grams/⅓ cup chopped candied peel
8 oz/230 grams/1 cup glacé cherries, cut in half
4 oz/110 grams/1 cup chopped almonds
3 tablespoons brandy or stout (dark beer)
1 small grated apple

Cream the butter and sugar; beat the eggs in one by one, then fold in the flour, and spice. Stir in the remaining ingredients with the grated apple last. Beat very well.

Put the mixture into a greased and lined pan. The greaseproof (waxed) paper lining to the pan should be three layers thick, and it is a good idea to tie a few layers of brown paper or newspaper round the outside of the tin too, to prevent the edge burning.

Put into a moderate oven (350°F, gas mark 4) for an hour, then turn the oven down to 325°F, gas mark 3, and bake for a further 1½ hours. Cover the top of the pan with thick brown paper for the first hour. The cake is cooked when a skewer will emerge dry after being stuck into the middle of the cake. Cool the cake before turning it out. Remove the paper. When the cake is quite cold, wrap it up again in greaseproof (waxed) paper and put into an airtight container.

If the cake is to be iced it should be covered in marzipan at least 2 weeks before Christmas. See the following recipe.

Almond paste (or marzipan)
(If you are not making your own, buy the best. It is expensive but worth it.)

1 lb/450 grams ground almonds
8 oz/230 grams/1 cup caster
 (powdered) sugar
8 oz/230 grams/1 cup icing
 (confectioners') sugar
2 whole eggs
2 egg yolks
6 drops vanilla essence
2 teaspoons lemon juice
Apricot jam

Sieve the sugars together into a bowl and mix with the ground almonds. Mix together the egg yolks, whole eggs, lemon juice and vanilla essence. Add to the sugar mixture and beat briefly with a wooden spoon. Kneed with the hands just enough to give smoothness. (Over-working will draw the oil out of the almonds, giving too greasy a paste.)

Melt and sieve the jam. Paint the cake, upside down, all over with it. On a sugared board, roll or press half the marzipan into a round the diameter of the cake. It should not be more than $\frac{1}{4}$ inch thick. With the help of a fish slice, lift the marzipan onto the cake and trim to shape. Using the rest of the marzipan cover the sides of the cake with strips cut to fit. Press firmly into position.

Leave the cake out of the container for 2 days for the almond paste to dry a little. Then put on the first layer of royal icing.

Royal icing
1 lb/450 grams/2 cups icing
 (confectioners') sugar
2 egg whites
1 teaspoon lemon juice
1 teaspoon glycerine (this prevents the
 icing setting hard as concrete)

Beat the whites lightly, add the sugar and continue beating until the mixture is very white, stiff and smooth. Add the lemon juice and glycerine. Put the cake on a cake-board, and stand it on an icing turntable if you have one. Otherwise use a cake-stand or upside-down bowl.

Spread the icing thinly all over the cake, using a knife dipped in very hot water to get it smooth. Two layers of icing is usual, but not vital. Let the first layer dry before adding the second. Final decoration should be done the next day. One of the simplest and prettiest ways is to put a few sprigs of holly (with artificial berries if need be) right in the middle of the cake, and fix a wide red ribbon round it. Cover the join in the ribbon with another sprig of holly, secured with a pin.

Yule log
1 chocolate sponge roll (see recipe on
 page 111) filled with whipped cream
1 lb/$\frac{1}{2}$ kilo/2 cups icing (confectioners')
 sugar
8 oz/250 grams/1 cup butter
3 oz/80 grams/3 oz dark chocolate
$\frac{1}{2}$ lb/250 grams marzipan
Colourings (red, green, blue)
Extra icing sugar

Beat the butter until soft and creamy, and gradually beat in the 1 lb icing sugar. Melt the chocolate and add it to the butter icing. Put the chocolate sponge roll onto a plate and completely coat it with the chocolate butter icing, marking it with a fork to look like a log. (Gnarled wood knots can be made by putting a small lump of cake or marzipan on the log, and covering it with chocolate butter icing, making swirls round it with a fork.)

Make two or three toadstools out of the marzipan, and a gnome with a sombrero—see drawing. Paint stripes or spots on the toadstools, and paint the gnome's trousers, buttons, and hat in different colours. Arrange the toadstools and gnome round the log, and at the last minute dust a very small amount of icing over the log to look like snow.

If marzipan is not liked, the log can be simply decorated with holly or other dark leaves.

On the days before

Coffee éclairs can be made and iced the day before, but the pastry will be a little soft. If a firmer pastry is wanted the éclairs should be made, well wrapped and kept frozen or in the refrigerator; ice and fill a few hours before tea.

The Christmas cake would be best made at least three weeks before Christmas, and the marzipan put on about a week before. Icing and decoration can be done well in advance too—say four days.

Yule log Make the cake two days in advance. Fill, ice and decorate it on the day before serving. Keep refrigerated once it has the cream filling.

New Year's Eve Parties

The problem is thwarting the riotous drunk. The most sober people faced with a party from 8 p.m. till after midnight, and another whole year ahead, tend to take to the bottle. So I would advise starting the party fairly late, say 10 p.m. This may mean that everyone arrives glowing from someone else's cocktails, but it cannot be helped. Feed everyone fairly substantially and hope for the best. A record of Auld Lang Syne (if you have a player) is a good investment, as it discourages your guests from singing over and over again the one line they know. Make sure that your most precious treasures are not on the coffee table, because the clasping of hands and ritual swaying arc not conducive to their safety.

See the menus under other headings, depending on the kind of party—buffet, dinner, etc.—you want.

Café brulé (recipe below) is a delicious gimmick to herald New Year with. Turn out the lights and serve the flaming coffee in the dark.

Café brulé

2 pints/1½ litres fresh strong black
   coffee
½ pint/¼ litre Eau de Vie de Marc or
   other inexpensive brandy
Sugar to taste
2 oranges
20 cloves

Pare the rind from the oranges in very long strips—like peeling round and round an apple. Stick the cloves into the strips of orange rind and put them in a bowl with the brandy. Leave covered, for several hours or overnight. When the coffee is made and hot, pour it into a warmed punch bowl and add the two oranges with sugar to taste. Have ready a pair of kitchen tongs for holding the orange rind. Warm the brandy slightly, light it and switch out the lights. With the tongs lift the flaming orange rind from the bowl. It should look very dramatic. When the

flames die down tip the brandy—and the rind—
into the coffee, and serve.

This is not as good as Irish Coffee (page 147) or coffee with a spoonful of Athol Brose (page 51) in it, but it is certainly *du théâtre*.

Twelfth Night Parties

Twelfth Night parties seem a rarity these days but I think the occasion provides the best possible excuse for banishing the feeling of anti-climax after Christmas and New Year. Twelfth Night parties can be like any other—dinner, buffet or, in the Southern hemisphere, barbecue or beach party. The essential difference is choosing the Bean King or Bean Queen. This means cutting a cake, any kind of cake, in which a dried bean is buried: whoever gets the bean, reigns, I suppose, for a year—though with what monarchal powers I know not. The food should not be rich, and at all costs should not be turkey.

TWELFTH NIGHT PARTY FOR 20

Charentais or Ogen melon with port

Simple fish pie
Salad of avocado, apple and lettuce

Twelfth Night cake

(*Preparation on the day before follows recipes.*)

There will be port in the melon so do not serve anything with it, and follow with a hock to go with the fish pie.

Charentais or Ogen melon with port (serves 10)
(Double the quantities for 20)

5 large Charentais or Ogen melons
5 tablespoons port

Chill the melons well, cut them in half, scoop out the seeds and put a tablespoon of port into each melon half. Ginger wine in melon is good, too.

Simple fish pie (serves 10)
(Make two pies for 20)

4 lb/1½–2 kilos fillet of haddock, whiting, cod, or a mixture of any of them
10 hard-boiled eggs
2 tablespoons chopped parsley
1 pint/¾ litre/20 fl. oz milk
1 bayleaf
1 onion, sliced
12 peppercorns
1 oz/30 grams/2 tablespoons butter
1½ oz/45 grams/2 tablespoons flour
3 tablespoons cream
Salt and pepper
About 1½ lb/750 grams creamed potatoes (see page 63)

Lay the fish fillets in a roasting pan. Heat the milk with the sliced onion, the peppercorns, bay-leaf and a pinch of salt. Pour over the fish, and cook in a moderate oven (350°F, gas mark 4) until the fish is firm and creamy-looking (about 25 minutes). Strain off the milk, reserving it for the sauce. Flake the fish into a pie dish. Halve the hard-boiled eggs and add them to the fish. Sprinkle over the chopped parsley. Heat the butter in a saucepan, stir in the flour and cook for half a minute. Add the milk and stir briskly while you bring it slowly to the boil. When it boils taste it and add salt and pepper as needed. Stir in the cream and pour over the fish. Spread a layer of creamed potatoes on the top and mark with a fork in a criss-cross pattern. Dot a little butter over the surface and brown in a hot oven (450°F, gas mark 8) for about 10 minutes.

Salad of avocado, apple and lettuce (serves 10)

3 large ripe avocado pears
3 eating apples
1 big cos lettuce, or 2 small round
  lettuces
¼ pint/⅛ litre/5 fl. oz french dressing
  (see page 71)

Peel, core and slice the apples thinly. Put them straight into the french dressing. Peel and slice the avocados and turn them carefully with the apples in the french dressing until they are completely coated. Use only the best lettuce leaves and pull them into small pieces. (Breaking lettuce in the fingers is better than cutting it up, which bruises and mangles the leaves. Never wring a head of lettuce off its stalk or break leaves by twisting them in handfuls.) Put the lettuce at the bottom and round the sides of a salad bowl, and the avocado and apple mixture in the middle.

If the apples are the shiny red kind do not peel them, for their bright colour improves the look of the salad.

Twelfth Night cake (serves 6)

(Triple the quantities for 20 people, and bake in an 11-inch cake tin, or in a large roasting pan.)
Twelfth Night cakes have a bean or silver charm hidden in them. Whoever gets the bean in his slice is Bean King or Queen for a year. The cake can be baked in an angel-cake pan, or in ordinary shallow sandwich tins (cake pans).

4 egg-whites
¼ teaspoon cream of tartar
5 oz/140 grams/½ cup caster
  (powdered) sugar
2 oz/50 grams/⅓ cup plain flour
Pinch of salt
2 drops of almond essence
Grated rind of one orange
1 dried haricot bean

For the filling
¼ lb/110 grams/½ cup very good cream
  cheese
1 tablespoon sugar
1 tablespoon creamy milk
2 tablespoons orange juice

For the icing
½ lb/250 grams/1 cup icing
  (confectioners') sugar
Juice of half an orange
Orange colouring (one tiny drop each
  of red and yellow)

To make *the cake* set the oven at 275°F, gas mark 1. Whisk the egg-whites until the mixture will just stand up in peaks but not very stiff ones. Add the cream of tartar and whisk again until stiff (when the mixture should stand up in rigid peaks). Add 4 oz of the sugar; whisk until stiff again. Stir in the almond essence and add the dried haricot bean. Mix the remaining ounce of sugar with the flour and grated orange rind and fold it in very lightly. Grease the cake pan(s) with melted lard or oil and fill with the mixture. Using a knife, cut through the mixture several times to break up any over-large air pockets. Bake for ½ an hour, then increase the heat to 325°F, gas mark 3, and cook for another 15 minutes. Allow the cake to get cool before turning it out.

Beat the filling ingredients together until soft and creamy. Split the cake, if it has been cooked in one piece, and sandwich with the filling.

Sieve the icing sugar into a bowl and add two tablespoons orange juice and enough colouring to tint it very palely. Stand the bowl in a basin or deep tin of hot water to get the icing soft and runny. Spoon it over the cake. Leave to set.

On the day before

Charentais or Ogen melon with port Put the melons, uncut, into the refrigerator to chill.
Simple fish pie Make it (but do not brown the top) and keep it in a cool place. Reheat in a moderate oven (375°F, gas mark 5) until the top is browned (about ½ hour).
Salad of avocado, apple and lettuce Make the dressing.
Twelfth Night cake Complete the cake, and put into the refrigerator.

General Check List for Most Parties

A check list such as the following, compiled in advance and kept under constant review, is the best way to prevent that Oh-my-God-I-forgot-to-post-the-invitations trauma. For almost all parties some food, drink, china, silver, linen and glass are necessary, though of course for most parties very few of the items I have listed will be needed. For specific types of parties, the lists on pages 187 to 190 should be useful in addition to the general one below.

Drinks

Where to get it

Wine Cups

Fruit Cups

Non-Alcoholic Cups

Aperitifs (Lillet, Dubonnet, Pernod, Campari, Vermouth red and white, Pimm's No. 1)

Wine shop or supplier (All drinks may be bought on a sale or return basis. Unopened bottles are not charged for. Most suppliers will lend glasses free of charge but expect them returned clean and will charge for any breakages.)

Spirits (gin, brandy, Scotch and rye whisky, vodka, rum)

Fortified Wines (sherry—sweet, medium or dry, port)

Liqueurs (Drambuie, Cointreau, Benedictine, Crème de Menthe, Curaçao, Grand Marnier, Kümmel, Tia Maria)

Beers (ales, stout, lager)

Wines (red, white, rosé, sparkling)

Fruit Juices (orange, pineapple, tomato, grapefruit)

Mineral Waters (soda, tonic, Malvern, Perrier, Vichy)

Soft Drinks (Coca-cola, ginger beer, ginger ale, lemonade, bitter lemon)

Bar equipment

Lemons, a board and knife, icebucket and tongs, napkins, tea towels, water jug, bottle opener, corkscrew, cocktail shaker, punch bowl and ladle. Ice for drinks and to fill the ice bath to chill the wine.

Hire company or hire department of large store

Ice cube company or machine, or fishmonger (in Britain)

China

Plates—soup, dinner, side, dessert, fish (generally the same size as the dessert)

Soup cups and saucers

Tea cups and saucers

Coffee cups and saucers

Hire company, hire department of large store or catering company. (Hired china can be returned dirty, but obviously food should be scraped off plates, and bowls etc. emptied.)

Cream and milk jugs (pitchers)

Sugar bowls

Teapots, coffee pots

Extra dinner plates for passing round large cakes, bread and butter, or fruit

Butter dishes, ash trays

Silver

Knives (dinner, dessert, bread, fruit, fish)
Forks (dinner, dessert, fruit, fish)
Carving knives and forks
Spoons (tea, coffee, table, dessert, soup)
Serving spoons and forks, fish slice, cake slice, cheese knife
Cakestands
Teapots, coffee pots
Cream and milk jugs (pitchers)
Salvers
Wine coolers
Sugar bowls, sifters, tongs
Flower vases
Cruet sets (salt cellars, pepper pots, mustard jars)
Candelabra and candlesticks
Soup tureens, ladles
Sauceboats, ladles
Oval dishes for meat and entrées
Vegetable dishes
Bowls—individual and large
Butter dishes
Ashtrays

Where to get it

Can be hired, as china. (If so, should be returned clean though it need not be dried or polished.)

Glass

All-purpose stem 'Club' goblets, 6 oz for cocktails and spirits, or wine
'Paris' goblets for wine, 6 oz, 8 oz, or 12 oz
'Worthington' glasses for beer, or ½ pint beer mugs
'Old Fashioned' glasses for whisky
Tumblers for soft drinks
Port
Sherry
Champagne: tulip-shape (better for preserving the sparkle and spills less), or saucer-shape
Hock
Brandy 'thistles' or balloons
Water jugs
Decanters
Large bowls for salad
Sundae glasses
Prawn cocktail glasses (a 6 oz 'Paris' goblet is fine)
Butter dishes
Dessert bowls, individual and large
Ashtrays

All-purpose glasses, sherry glasses and tumblers can often be supplied free of charge by the wine supplier, but other glass items can be hired from hire companies, the hire department of large stores or from catering companies

Linen
Tablecloths for bar, buffet, dining and work tables
Napkins for guests; also for wrapping wine bottles and as traycloths
Tea towels, glass cloths
Hand towels
Staff uniforms

Where to get it
From hire companies, hire department of large stores or catering companies

Usually supplied by the staff themselves

Paper, Plastic etc.
Baskets—bread, fruit etc.
Cheeseboard
Trays
Plastic spoons
Plastic forks
Paper napkins—soft, crinkly, coloured, white, patterned
Tablecloths—paper, plastic
Paper cups (should be plasticized for hot liquids)
Paper plates
Paper dessert dishes
Lavatory paper
Face tissues
Kitchen paper towels
Paper hand towels
Drinking straws

From drug stores, department stores, stationers and similar

Miscellaneous
Invitations
Staff (waiters, waitresses, coat-check ladies, butlers, barmen)
Fees and tips for the staff (20% of the fee is usual)
Supper for the staff (not necessarily the same as the guests' but should be substantial)
Transport for the staff (if they do not have cars, and the party continues after public transport has stopped, they will have to be driven home or given money for a taxi)
Taxi and hire car telephone numbers
Flowers—arrangements for tables, pedestals or fireplaces

Stationer or printer
Staff agencies or catering firms

Local florist

Check List for Large Parties (eg. Dances, Balls, Buffets, Garden Parties & Weddings)

For drinks, china etc. see General Check List, and Check List for Weddings, see below.

Other equipment

Where to get it

Tables (round or long for dining, long for buffet, bar and serving stations) — Hire company or hire department of large department store or catering company
Coat-rails and hangers
Thermal tea urns
Gas rings and cylinders
Hotplates and hot-cupboards
Tubs of water for rinsing hands and equipment
Seating (gilt chairs or benches)
Cleaning materials—dusters, detergents, etc.

Tent equipment

Marquee tent and awning — Tenting contractor or catering company
Service (kitchen) tent
Matting/flooring for dancing, raised dais for speeches or band
Heating for tent — Tenting contractor, catering company or plumber
Water point, tap or hose for service tent
Lighting for tent, garden lights, flood-lighting — Tenting contractor, catering company or electrician

Music

Bands, groups, singers, guitarist — Theatrical agencies
Discothèque — Discothèque company

Entertainment

Films and projector — Hire company or film distributor
Fortune tellers, jugglers, magicians — Theatrical agencies
Games equipment, e.g. croquet sets, badminton sets, coconut shies — Hire company and some sports shops

Signposts

Directing guests to the party, car park etc. — Automobile Associations, police or handyman

Check List for Weddings

(In addition to the following list, see both the General Check List on page 184—for crockery, silver, linen, glass, tables, etc.—and the list for large parties above.)

Where to get it

Hired house—hall or rooms if reception not held at home. It is wise to pay well in advance, and confirm booking in writing. — Local libraries keep lists of places for hire. An advertisement in the local paper should produce a few alternatives.

Flowers—for the bride and bridesmaids' bouquets, the buttonholes for the men in the wedding party, and the flowers (if any) for the top of the cake. Also for the church and reception rooms.

Local florist

The Wedding cake—

Caterer, local baker, department store, or home-made

Pillars — Bridal shop or baker

Ribbons — Stationer or department store

Decoration

Cake board

Cake stand and knife — Catering or hire company or supplier of cake

Small boxes for posting squares of cake — Stationer or printer

Printed paper napkins—with the names of bride and groom and the date on them.

Bakers, printers, some stationers, department stores

Confetti—many churches and halls will not allow confetti-throwing. Rose petals or rice are not objected to so strongly.

Stationers

Transport—to the church for the bride and her father, and from the church for the whole wedding party.

Car hire firm

Parking facilities

Speak to the police, borrow a neighbour's field, or put a note on the invitation that parking will be impossible

Toastmaster or Master of Ceremonies

From a staff agency or catering company

Check List for Barbecues

(See General Check List, page 184, for drinks, china, silver etc. Plates and forks, however tatty, are a good idea, because then salads, potatoes and sauces can be added to the menu)

Where to get it

The barbecue (see page 138 for how to make your own) — Hardware shop, hire shop

Firelighters

Matches

Fuel

Cooking utensils—long forks, tongs, spoon, knife, chopping board, pastry brushes for basting

Old thick gloves for the chef

Aluminium foil

Tea towels, dishcloths, paper napkins

Rubbish bin for the debris

Bucket of water to rinse hands in

Bellows or roll of newspaper for fanning
   the fire
Tarpaulin or blanket for sitting on, or old
   cushions
Two large tables—one for the meat and
   cooking utensils, one for plates, salads,
   drinks, glasses etc.

Check List for Beach Parties and Picnics

(See General Check List, page 184, for drinks, paper plates etc. See also Check List for Barbecues, page 188, if you are going to make a camp-fire.)

Rubbish sack for the debris
Tea towels, dishcloths, paper napkins
Damp face cloth or sponge in plastic bag
   for wiping sticky fingers
Blanket/groundsheet for sitting on

Check List for Clambakes

(See General Check List, page 184, for drinks, china, silver, etc.)

Spade(s)
Piece of chicken wire
Round rocks that have not been baked
   before
Soaked rock seaweed
Buckets
Long-handled cooking tools, or thick
   gloves for handling hot food
Firelighters
Hardwood and tinder
Matches
Square of damp canvas for covering bake
Paper napkins or cloths
Towels for sitting on
Bag(s) for rubbish
Aluminium foil

Check List for Children's Parties

(See General Check List, page 184, for drinks, crockery, cutlery, etc.)

Birthday cake
Candles for the birthday cake
Matches for lighting them
Presents for everyone
The rules for party games
Prizes for the winners

Equipment for party games (bucket and apples for bob-an-apple; parcel, paper and string for musical parcel, etc.)	*Where to get it*
Entertainment—juggler, Punch and Judy, magician	Theatrical agents
Television	
Movies	Film hire company
Telephone numbers of guests' parents in case of mishap	
First-aid box for cuts and bruises	
Doctor's telephone number	
Balloons, decorations, streamers, funny hats, etc.	Novelty shop, stationer

Check List for Anniversary Parties

(See General Check List, page 184, for drinks, china, silver, etc.)

Birthday, Golden Wedding, or etc. cake
21st Birthday 'Key'
Candles for the cake
Matches to light them

Check List for Christmas Parties

(See General Check List, page 184, for drinks, china, silver etc.)

Christmas decorations for rooms, tree, front door, and table	*Where to get it*
Christmas crackers	
Silver charms or coins for the pudding	
Holly decoration for the pudding	
Matches to set the pudding alight	
Gifts for the guests	
Paper frills for the ham-bone and turkey legs	Stationer, butcher (or make yourself, see page 10)
Really sharp carving knives	
Indigestion tablets!	

ndex *Page numbers in italics refer to illustrations on those pages*

er theatre suppers 93–6:
r 8 93–4
r 10 95–6
mond:
lmond paste 180
rapefruit, prawn and almond
up 59
ixed bean salad with almonds
0
erican wedding cake 160
chovy:
chovy toast 179
g mousse with anchovies
6, *132*
nabel's cheesecake 49
niversary parties 161–8, 190
ole:
tticed apple flan 55
pples baked in cider 92
lad of avocado, apple and
ttuce 183
iced marmalade apples with
rème chantilly 121
ffee apples 115, *103*
atercress and apple salad 90
ricot:
pricot fool 149
pricot slice 60
bian stuffed lamb 128
ichoke:
nds d'artichauts au crabe
52
aragus rolls 18
ic 11
ol brose 51
cado pear:
ocado dip 30
ocado pear dressing 158
lad of avocado, apple and
ttuce 183
on:
con and egg flan 105
icken liver and bacon
voury 39
icken livers wrapped in
con 20
ewell tart 119
ing blind 105
ana and coconut side dish
con 20
r curry 59
s, wholemeal 106
equipment 184
ecues 138–40, 188
buns, toasted 136
h parties 145–7, 189
:
nkfurter, tomato and baked
an casserole 76
xed bean salad with almonds
xed buttered beans 38
nge salad with butterbeans,
tternut and red peppers 168
a and flageolet salad 54
:
rried beef 59
t de boeuf à la
urguignonne 44
t de boeuf en croûte 82, *132*
due Bourguignonne 73
mburgers 138
k kebabs 139
oot and onion salad with
rseradish cream 90
re manié 35
day cakes 109, 110
its:
colate biscuits 146
rtbread fingers 115
k cherry sauce 129
k velvet 15
currant fool 58
s with sour cream and
viar 37
dy butter (or hard sauce)
7
dy snaps 136
d sauce 41, 173
crumbs, fried 41
kfast, hearty, for 60 98–100
kfast, simple, for 200 98–100
fast parties (Brunch)
–22
ning meat and vegetables,
portance of 8

Brussels sprouts and chestnuts
173
Buck's Fizz 98
Buffet parties 75–92, 187:
for 20, simple inexpensive 76–8
for 30, slightly grander 78–88
for 40, quickly prepared 89–90
for 20, quickly prepared 91–2
Bulk cooking 8
Butter, to clarify 95
Buttered leaf spinach 57
Buttered rice 70

Cabbage:
Cabbage and frankfurter salad
145
Cole slaw with raisins 90
Red cabbage 42
Café brulé 181
Cakes:
Chocolate crumble cake 147
Chocolate hedgehog birthday
cake 109
Chocolate nut brownies 137
Chocolate and orange cake 134
Chocolate roulade with cream
64
Chocolate Swiss roll 111
Christmas cake 179
Coffee fudge cake 150
Coffee rum tipsy cake 77
Gingerbread 155
Lemon sponge cake 137
Locomotive birthday cake 110
Twelfth Night cake 183
Walnut and lemon meringue
cake 54, *45*
Wedding cake, traditional
English 159, *163*
Wedding cake, American 160
Yule log 180
Camembert fritters 36
Canapés *25*:
Asparagus rolls 18
Caviar eggs 18
Celery filled with cream cheese
21
Chicken livers wrapped in
bacon 20
Cocktail sausages 20
Curried prawn bouchées 20
French bread with pâté and
cress 22
Pâté on baked bread 21
Prawn Ritz 19
Pumpernickel with salami 24
Smoked salmon and potted
shrimp canapés 152
Smoked salmon triangles 18
Smoked salmon wheels 21
Stuffed dates 19
Canard à l'orange 167
Canneloni with spinach and
mushroom filling 79
Caramel sauce 78
Carré of lamb 37
Carrot:
Glazed carrots 42
Carrottes Vichy 42
Casseroles:
Frankfurter, tomato and baked
bean casserole 76
Pigeon casserole with celery
and walnuts 57
Cauliflower:
Cauliflower and ham salad 69
Cauliflower, potato and
cucumber salad 158
Caviar:
Blinis with sour cream and
caviar 37
Caviar cream 31
Caviar eggs 18
Consommé caviar 49
Celery:
Celery filled with cream cheese
21
Crab and celery cup 78
Pigeon casserole with celery
and walnuts 57
Champagne 14
Champagne cocktails 15
Champagne cup, strawberry 15
Charentais melon with port 182
Checkerboard of sandwiches 108
Cheese:

To store cheese 12
Annabel's cheesecake 49
Celery filled with cream cheese
21
Cheese for cocktail lunch/
supper party 24
Cheese pictures 108
Cheese and pineapple on
sticks 108
Cheese profiteroles 23
Cheese sauce 41
Cheese and wine parties 29–31,
28
Cream cheeses 13
Cucumber filled with blue
cheese 23
Curried cheese balls 152
English cheeses 12
French cheeses 12–13
Hot cheese soufflé 162
Italian cheeses 13
Soft eggs with cheese 121
Swiss cheese fondue 74
Cheesecake 49
Chestnut:
Brussels sprouts and chestnuts
173
Chestnut stuffing 172
Game chip baskets filled with
chestnuts 42
Chicken:
Barbecued chicken 138
Chicken Elizabeth 79
Chicken kebabs 139
Chicken liver and bacon
savoury 39
Chicken liver pâté 95
Chicken livers wrapped in
bacon 20
Coq au vin 69, *65*
Lemon chicken 126
Poulet François I 52
Chicory:
Chicory and endive salad 94
Watercress and chicory salad 77
Children's parties 107–15, 189,
102:
for 12 5-yr-olds 108–10
for 12 10-yr-olds 110–15
China 184
Chocolate:
Chocolate biscuits 146
Chocolate crumble cake 147
Chocolate hedgehog birthday
cake 109
Chocolate mousse 81
Chocolate nut brownies 137
Chocolate and orange cake 134
Chocolate profiteroles 71, 155
Chocolate roulade with cream
64
Chocolate sauce 72
Chocolate Swiss roll 111
Choux pastry 23
Christening parties 161
Christmas cake 179
Christmas parties 171–81, 190:
dinner for 12 172–8
tea for 12 179–81
Chutney and cucumber side dish
for curry 60
Clambakes 140, 189
Clarified butter 95
Cocktail parties 17–24: see
also Canapés
for 30 18–19
for 60 19–20
cocktail lunch/supper party for
40 22–4
Coffee:
To make in large quantities 9
Café brulé 181
Coffee éclairs 179
Coffee fudge cake 150
Coffee rum tipsy cake 77
Irish coffee 147
Cole slaw with raisins 90
Consommé caviar 49
Cooling foods 8
Coq au vin 69, *65*
Coronation chicken (Chicken
Elizabeth) 79
Courgette:
Courgettes with tomatoes 44
Stuffed courgettes 77
Courtbouillon 85

Crab:
Crab and celery cup 78
Crab sauce 41
Fonds d'artichauts au crabe
152
Cranberry sauce 173
Cream cheeses 13
Creamed potatoes 63
Creamy vegetable soup 98
Crème chantilly 121
Crème pâtissière 118
Cress as garnish 11
Croissants 99
Croûtons 11
Crudités 11
Cucumber:
Cauliflower, potato and
cucumber salad 158
Cucumber and cream salad 148
Cucumber filled with blue
cheese 23
Cucumber salad 53
Cucumber sandwich fingers 133
Curried dishes:
Curried beef 59
Curried cheese balls 152
Curried eggs with rice 145
Curried mayonnaise 73
Curried prawn bouchées 20
Side dishes for curry 59
Stuffed curried eggs 22

Dances and balls 97–106, 187
Date:
Stuffed dates 19
Yoghurt, honey and dates 127
Déglaçage 44
Desserts *see* Puddings and
desserts
Devil sauce 140
Dinner parties 32–60:
for 8 34–43
for 6 43–54
for 6 (inexpensive) 54–60
Dinner parties, large 61–72:
for 30 62–4, 69
for 50 (economical) 69–72
Dinner parties, unusual 72–4
Dips and sauces for fondue 73
Dips and spreads 30–1
Dressings:
Avocado pear dressing 158
Chive and sour cream dressing
77
French dressing 71
Horseradish cream 90
Mustard dressing 87
Drinks 16, 184. *See also* Wine
Duck, duckling:
Canard à l'orange 167
Cold duck à l'orange 85
Cold stuffed boned duck with
mushrooms and ham 157
Leith's duckling 62, *48*
Stuffed boned duck with
orange and green olives 50

Éclairs 179
Egg:
Bacon and egg flan 105
Caviar eggs 18
Curried eggs with rice 145
Egg mousse with anchovies 56,
132
Egg mousse with aspic 56, *132*
Framed eggs with tomatoes and
mushrooms 122
Miniature egg-and-chive
sandwiches 22
Soft eggs with cheese 121
Stuffed curried eggs 22
Tongue and egg rolls 91
Elizabeth sauce 79
Endive:
Chicory and endive salad 94
Entertainments 187

Family Sunday lunch 127–9
Fantail potatoes 128
Fennel baked in the oven 35
Filet de boeuf à la
Bourguignonne 44
Filet de boeuf en croûte 82, *132*
Filets de sole Dugléré 125
Fish. *See also* Haddock, Salmon
etc.

Hot thick fish soup or stew 95
Kedgeree 99
Simple fish pie 182
Flans *see* Tarts etc.
Fonds d'artichauts au crabe 152
Fondue Bourguignonne 73
Fondue, Swiss cheese 74
Frankfurter, tomato and baked
bean casserole 76
French bread with pâté and
cress 22
French dressing 71
Fritters:
Camembert fritters 36
Fruit. *See also* Apple, Apricot
etc.
Fresh fruit for cocktail lunch/
supper party 24
Fruit salad 88
Fruit tartlets 118
Green fruit salad 36
Muesli with fruit and yoghurt
120
Fudge icing 150

Game chip baskets filled with
chestnuts 42
Game chips 41
Garden parties 117–19, 187
Garlic bread 96
Garlic cream 73
Garnishing 9–11
Gaspacho, iced 51
Ginger syllabub 94
Gingerbread 155
Gingerbread men 108
Glass 185
Glazed carrots 42
Glazed ham 82
Glazed onions 126
Golden wedding dinner 162,
167–8
Goldenberry flan 168
Grape:
Jellied grape and mint ring 53
Rum baba with raspberries and
grapes 124
Grapefruit, prawn and almond
cup 59
Green salad 71

Haddock:
Haddock soufflé 40
Kedgeree 99
Hallowe'en party 169–70
Ham:
To make a ham frill 10
Cauliflower and ham salad 69
Cold stuffed boned duck with
mushrooms and ham 157
Sugar-baked (glazed) ham 82
Sweet and sour ham rolls 91
Hamburgers 138
Horseradish cream 90
Hot dogs 115

Iced bombe with black cherry
sauce 129
Iced gaspacho 51
Iced watermelon 171
Icing:
Chocolate icing 134
Fudge icing 150
Royal icing 180
Irish coffee 147

Jellied grape and mint ring 53
Jelly boats 109

Kebabs 139
Kebabs, miniature 112
Kedgeree 99
Kidney:
Sauté of kidneys Turbigo 55

Ladies lunch for 6 125–7
Lamb and mutton:
Arabian stuffed lamb 128
Barbecued lamb 138
Carré of lamb 37
Lamb kebabs 139
Moussaka 169
Roast crown of lamb 84
Tranche d'agneau à la catalane
124
Latticed apple flan 55

Leith's duckling 62, *48*
Lemon:
 Lemon chicken 126
 Lemon curd 134
 Lemon curd tartlets 134
 Lemon sponge cake 137
 Lemons as garnish 11
 Sardine and lemon sandwiches 118
 Walnut and lemon meringue cake 54, *45*
Linen 186
Lobster sauce 41
Locomotive birthday cake 110
Lunch parties 123–30:
 Businessmen's, for 6 123–5
 Ladies, for 6 125–7
 Family Sunday for 8 127–30

Mackerel:
 Soused mackerel with mustard sauce 123
Mange-tout peas in onion sauce 50
Marzipan 180
Mayonnaise 19
Mayonnaise, curried 73
Meat. *See also* Beef, Lamb etc.
 Cold meat platters 90
 Hot meat loaf 94
 Terrine 150
Melon:
 Charentais or Ogen melon with port 182
 Iced watermelon 171
 Jelly boats 109
 Melon and prawn cocktail cup 157
Menu, to choose a balanced 8
Meringues 155
Mince pies 177
Mincemeat 177
Moussaka 169
Mousse:
 Chocolate mousse 81
 Egg mousse with anchovies 56, *132*
 Egg mousse with aspic 56, *132*
 Smoked trout mousse with smoked salmon 62
Muesli with fruit and yoghurt 120
Mulled cider 169
Mulligatawny, thick 146
Mushroom:
 Cannelloni with spinach and mushroom filling 79
 Cold stuffed boned duck with mushrooms and ham 157
 Framed eggs with tomatoes and mushrooms 122
 Mushroom soup 93
Music 187
Mussel soup 127
Mustard dressing 87
Mustard sauce 123

New Year's Eve parties 181

Oatcakes 122
Ogen melon with port 182
Olives as garnish 11
Onion:
 Beetroot and onion salad with horseradish cream 90
 Glazed onions 126
 Onion flan 147
 Onion sauce 50
 Sausages and onion in tomato sauce 105
 Tomato, onion and pimento salad 87
Open sandwiches and rolls 112
Orange:
 Canard à l'orange 167
 Chocolate and orange cake 134
 Cold duck à l'orange 85
 Orange salad with butterbeans, butternut and red peppers 168
 Orange and tomato juice 120
 Orange and watercress salad 64
 Stuffed boned duck with orange and green olives 50
Osso buco 53
Outdoor parties 138–50:
 Barbecues 138–40, 188
 Clambakes 140, 189
 Beach parties 145–7, 189
 Picnics 148–50, 189

Pain bagna 148
Paper frills 10
Paper napkins, plates etc. 186
Parsley, use of 10

Partridge:
 Roast partridge 41
Passion fruit syllabub 38
Pastry:
 To bake blind 105
 Choux pastry 23
 Puff pastry 83
 Rich shortcrust pastry 88
Pâté:
 Chicken liver pâté 95
 French bread with pâté and cress 22
 Pâté on baked bread 21
 Taramasalata 30
 Wine and pâté party 30
Pea:
 To cook peas 55
 Mange-tout peas in onion sauce 50
 Petits pois à la française 35
 Potato and pea salad 147
Peach:
 Lady Elizabeth Anson's spiced peach brulée 96
 Whole white peaches in brandy 91
Pepper:
 Green pepper, apple and raisin chutney 60
 Orange salad with butterbeans, butternut and red peppers 168
 Tomato, onion and pimento salad 87
Petits pois à la française 35
Picnics 148–50, 189
Pies:
 Mince pies 177
 Pork pie 86
 Pumpkin pie 170
 Simple fish pie 182
Pigeon casserole with celery and walnuts 57
Pineapple:
 Cheese and pineapple on sticks 108
 Pineapple with kirsch 43
Pizza rounds 152
Planning a party 7
Plastic spoons, forks etc. 186
Plum pudding 174
Polythene wrap 8
Poppadums 60
Pork:
 Barbecued pork 138, 139
 Pork kebabs 139
 Pork pie 86
Potato:
 Baked potatoes 139
 Cauliflower, potato and cucumber salad 158
 Creamed potatoes 63
 Fantail potatoes 128
 Game chip baskets filled with chestnuts 42
 Game chips 41
 Hot baked potatoes with sour cream, walnuts and chives 90
 Hot boiled potatoes with French dressing 92
 Hot new potatoes with chive and sour cream dressing 77
 New potato salad with mustard dressing and olives 87
 Potato and pea salad 147
 Potatoes boulangère 58
 Roast potatoes 174
 Potted shrimps on water biscuits 24
Poulet François I 52
Prawn:
 Curried prawn bouchées 20
 Grapefruit, prawn and almond cup 59
 Melon and prawn cocktail cup 157
 Prawn Ritz 19
Presentation 9–11
Profiteroles 23, 71, 155
Puddings and desserts. *See also* Pies *and* Tarts, tartlets and flans
 Annabel's cheesecake 49
 Apples baked in cider 92
 Apricot fool 149
 Apricot slice 60
 Athol brose 51
 Blackcurrant fool 58
 Chocolate mousse 81
 Chocolate profiteroles 71, 155
 Chocolate roulade with cream 64
 Coffee rum tipsy cake 77
 Fruit salad 88

Ginger syllabub 94
Green fruit salad 36
Iced bombe with black cherry sauce 129
Jelly boats 109
Lady Elizabeth Anson's spiced peach brulée 96
Passion fruit syllabub 38
Pineapple with kirsch 43
Plum pudding 174
Raspberry vacherin 80
Rum baba with raspberries and grapes 124
Spiced marmalade apples with crème chantilly 121
Strawberries and cream 119
Strawberry meringue baskets 135
Tangerines in caramel sauce 78, *68*
Trifle 87
Vanilla ice cream with hot strawberry sauce 158
Walnut and lemon meringue cake 54
Whole white peaches in brandy 91
Yoghurt, honey and dates 127
Puff pastry 83
Pumpernickel with salami 24
Pumpkin pie 170

Quiche lorraine 105

Radishes as garnish 11
Raspberry:
 Raspberry vacherin 80
 Rum baba with raspberries and grapes 124
Red cabbage 42
Red wines 14
Reheating foods 8
Rice:
 Buttered rice 70
 Curried eggs with rice 145
 Fried rice 59
 Kedgeree 99
 Rice salad 80
 Royal icing 180
 Rum baba with raspberries and grapes 124

Salads:
 Beetroot and onion salad with horseradish cream 90
 Cabbage and frankfurter salad 145
 Cauliflower and ham salad 69
 Cauliflower, potato and cucumber salad 158
 Chichory and endive salad 94
 Cole slaw with raisins 90
 Cucumber and cream salad 148
 Cucumber salad 53
 Fruit salad 88
 Green fruit salad 36
 Green salad 71
 Mixed bean salad with almonds 80
 New potato salad with mustard dressing and olives 87
 Orange salad with butterbeans, butternut and red peppers 168
 Orange and watercress salad 64
 Potato and pea salad 147
 Rice salad 80
 Salad of avocado, apple and lettuce 183
 Salade Niçoise 76, *132*
 Tomato, onion and pimento salad 87
 Tuna and flageolet salad 54
 Watercress and apple salad 90
 Watercress and chicory salad 77
Salami 90
Salami with pumpernickel 24
Salami on rye 118
Salmon. *See also* Smoked salmon
 Kedgeree 99
 Salmon mayonnaise 85
Sandwiches:
 Checkerboard of sandwiches 108
 Cucumber sandwich fingers 133
 Miniature egg and chive sandwiches 22
 Open sandwiches and rolls 112
 Open smoked salmon sandwiches 22
 Pain bagna 148
 Sardine and lemon sandwiches 118

Sangria 15
Sardine and lemon sandwiches 118
Sauces:
 Black cherry sauce 129
 Brandy butter or hard sauce 177
 Bread sauce 41, 173
 Caramel sauce 78
 Cheese sauce 167
 Chocolate sauce 72
 Crab sauce 41
 Cranberry sauce 173
 Devil sauce 140
 Elizabeth sauce 79
 Hot strawberry sauce 159
 Lobster sauce 41
 Mustard sauce 123
 Onion sauce 50
Sausage:
 Barbecued sausages 138
 Cabbage and frankfurter salad 145
 Cocktail sausages 20
 Frankfurter, tomato and baked bean casserole 76
 Hot dogs 115
 Miniature kebabs 112
 Sausages and onions in tomato sauce 105
 Sausages on sticks 108
 Sausagemeat stuffing 172
 Sauté of kidneys Turbigo 55
Scallop:
 Scallops, prawn and ham kebabs 139
 Seafood coquille 35
Scones:
 Welsh scones 133
Seafood coquille 35
Seating for dinner parties 33
Serving at dinner parties 33
Shortcrust pastry, rich 88
Short cuts 9
Shortbread fingers 115
Shrimp:
 Potted shrimp on water biscuits 24
 Smoked salmon and potted shrimp canapés 152
Silver 185
Smoked salmon:
 Open smoked salmon sandwiches 22
 Smoked salmon and potted shrimp canapés 152
 Smoked salmon triangles 18
 Smoked salmon wheels 21
 Smoked trout mousse with smoked salmon 62
Sole:
 Filets de sole Dugléré 125
Soufflé:
 Haddock soufflé 40
 Hot cheese soufflé 162
Soup:
 Consommé caviar 49
 Creamy vegetable soup 98
 Hot thick fish soup or stew 95
 Iced gaspacho 51
 Mushroom soup 93
 Mussel soup 127
 Spicey tomato soup 149
 Thick mulligatawny 146
Soused mackerel with mustard sauce 123
Spare ribs 139
Spiced marmalade apples with crème chantilly 121
Spinach:
 Buttered leaf spinach 57
 Cannelloni with spinach and mushroom filling 79
Staff for larger parties 61, 186; coping without 61
Strawberry:
 Hot strawberry sauce 159
 Strawberries and cream 119
 Strawberry champagne cup 15
 Strawberry meringue baskets 135
Stuffed boned duck with orange and green olives 50
Stuffed courgettes 77
Stuffed curried eggs 22
Stuffed dates 19
Stuffing:
 Chestnut stuffing 172
 Sausagemeat stuffing 172
 Stuffing for duck 50
Sugar-baked (glazed) ham 82
Sweet and sour ham rolls 91

Swiss cheese fondue 74
Syllabubs 38, 94

Table-setting 32; for a children's party 107
Tangerines in caramel sauce ?
 68
Taramasalata 30
Tarts, tartlets and flans:
 Bacon and egg flan 105
 Bakewell tart 119
 Fruit tartlets 118
 Goldenberry flan 168
 Latticed apple flan 55
 Lemon curd tartlets 134
 Onion flan 147
 Treacle tart 88
Tea parties 133–7:
 for 12 133–5
 for 8 135–7
Teenagers' parties 116
Teetotaller's tipple 15
Tent equipment 187
Terrine 150
Thanksgiving Day 171
Toffee apples 115, *103*
Tomato:
 Baked tomatoes 38
 Courgettes with tomatoes 44
 Framed eggs with tomatoes and mushrooms 122
 Frankfurter, tomato and bak... bean casserole 76
 Orange and tomato juice 12...
 Sausages and onion in toma... sauce 105
 Spicy tomato soup 149
 Tomato dip 73
 Tomato, onion and pimento salad 87
 Tomato and onion side dish curry 60
Tongue:
 Boiled tongue 85
 Tongue and egg rolls 91
Tranche d'agneau à la catal... 124
Treacle tart 88
Trifle 87
Trout:
 Smoked trout mousse with smoked salmon 62
Tuna and flageolet salad 54
Turkey:
 Roast stuffed turkey 172
Twelfth Night cake 183
Twelfth Night party 182–3

Vanilla ice cream with hot strawberry sauce 158
Veal:
 Osso buco 53
Vegetable. *See also* Artichok... Asparagus etc.
 Creamy vegetable soup 98
 Mixed spring vegetables 12...
 Vegetable mornay 124

Walnut:
 Hot baked potato with sou... cream, walnuts and chives
 Pigeon casserole with celery and walnuts 57
 Walnut and lemon meringu... cake 54, *45*
Watercress:
 Orange and watercress sala...
 Watercress and apple salad
 Watercress and chicory sala...
 Watercress as garnish 11
Watermelon, iced 171
Wedding cake 159, *163*
Wedding cake, American 16
Wedding receptions 151–61, 187–8
Welsh scones 133
White wines 14–15
Wholemeal baps 106
Wine 13–16:
 To store wine 13
 Cheese and wine parties 29
 Red wines 14
 White wines 14–15
 Wine cups and cocktails 1...
 Wine and pâté party 30

Yoghurt:
 Muesli with fruit and yog...
 120
 Yoghurt, honey and dates
Yule log 180

Zucchini *see* Courgette